Tuisco Greiner

How to Make the Garden pPay

Tuisco Greiner

How to Make the Garden pPay

ISBN/EAN: 9783337242299

Printed in Europe, USA, Canada, Australia, Japan

Cover: Foto ©Lupo / pixelio.de

More available books at **www.hansebooks.com**

How to Make the Garden Pay

By
T. Greiner

Second, Revised and Enlarged Edition

Published by
WM. HENRY MAULE
Philadelphia
1894

Entered according to Act of Congress in the year 1890, by
WM. HENRY MAULE,
in the office of the Librarian of Congress at Washington.

Prefatory Remarks

(To the First Edition)

By the Publisher.

A work on gardening, up to the times and fully explaining all modern methods, has long been needed. Several years ago I started the rough outline of a treatise on this subject, but owing to my time being so largely taken up with my varied business interests, I found it impossible to finish it; and, to tell the truth, I did not feel competent to handle the subject as it deserved. At this stage of the proceedings my friend, Mr. T. Greiner, offered to take a hand, and for a year or more he has been busy writing the following pages, which I take pleasure in presenting to the public as the very best and most practical work ever written for the benefit of the American vegetable gardener.

I am confident it will prove the stepping-stone to successful gardening for many thousands who are now unacquainted with this, the noblest calling on earth; while I know it will give many profitable common-sense ideas to those who are even now high up in the profession.

In this revised edition I have little to add to the above remarks, further than that the unqualified endorsement and success of this work has far exceeded both Mr. Greiner's and my own highest expectations. Its cordial reception has encouraged us to make the second edition up to and abreast of these progressive times, and I can ask of my friends nothing more than this new revised edition of "How to Make the Garden Pay" shall receive as kind a reception as has been accorded the first edition of this work.

Yours very truly,

WM. HENRY MAULE.

January 15, 1895.

INDEX.

A

Anise	180
Ants	111
Aphis	111
Aquaculture	108
Artichoke, Globe	180
Artichoke, Jerusalem	181
Asparagus	182
Asparagus Beetle	112
Asparagus Buncher	185
Asparagus Knife	186
Asparagus Marketing	185
Asparagus Planting	184
Asparagus, Varieties	186
Asterias, Butterfly	119

B

Balm	186
Barrow Sprayer	121, 137
Basil, Sweet	187
Bean Anthracnose	138
Bean Blight, or Spot	138
Beans, Bush	187
Beans, Pole	190
Beans	187
Beans, Varieties of Bush	188
Beans, Varieties of Pole	192
Bean, Weevil	113
Beet Leaf Spot	139
Beet, Mangel and Sugar	196
Beet Rust	138
Beet, Varieties	195
Beets	194
Bichloride of Mercury	136
Birds as Helpers	132
Blister Beetles	127
Boll Worm	115
Borage	200
Boreal Ladybird	128
Borecole, or Kale	245
Bordeaux Mixture	135
Broccoli	200
Brussels Sprouts	201
Buhach	114

C

Cabbage	201
Cabbage, Diseases	139
Cabbage, Late	203
Cabbage, Plusia	113
Cabbage, Varieties	206
Cabbage, Wintering	202
Cabbage Worm	113
Cardoon	209
Caraway	210
Carrots	210
Catnip	213
Cauliflower	213
Celeriac	228
Celery	215
Celery, Blanching	219
Celery Bleachers	221
Celery Blights	139
Celery, Growing South	224
Celery, New Culture	216
Celery Planting	218
Celery Soft Rot	140
Celery, Storing	221, 223
Celery, Varieties	226
Celery Worm	115
Chervil, Turnip-rooted	228
Chicory	229
Chives	229
Club Root	139
Cold Frames	57
Cold Vegetable Houses	76, 77, 78
Cold Vegetable Houses, Crops in	79
Colewort	229
Collard	229
Colorado Potato Beetle	120
Composting Manure	37

Coriander	230
Corn Salad	230
Corn, Sweet	230
Corn, Sweet Varieties	233
Corn Smut	145
Corn Worm	115
Cotton Seed Meal	44
Cress	234
Cucumber	235
Cucumber Beetle	115
Cucumber Blight	140
Cucumber Mildew	141
Cucumber, Varieties	237
Cut Worms	116

D

Damping Off	144
Dandelion	238
Diabrotica, Twelve-spotted	128
Dibbers	49
Dill	238
Diseases of Plants	134
Drainage	95
Drainage by Board Troughs	98
Drainage for Boiler Pit	88
Drainage, Surface	99
Draining Tools	96
Drill and Wheel Hoe	54
Drought, Means of Protection	166

E

Egg Plant	239
Electric Light Influence	317
Electro-Horticulture	317
Endive	240

F

Farmers' Kitchen Garden	20
Fennel	241
Fertilizer Application	41
Fertilizers for Garden	39
Fetticus	230
Fire Hot-beds	71-73
Firming Board	66
Firming the Roots	163
Flats	68
Flats, Soil for	69
Flea Beetle	117
Flooding, Sub-earth	103

Forcing Houses	82
Forcing Pit, Model	83
Forcing Vegetables in Cold Frames	60-62
Frames, Use of	59
Frost, Precautions Against	168
Fungicides	135

G

Gardening for Local Markets	29
Garlic	241
Germination, Principles of	148
Gourds	242
Grading Vegetables, etc.	33
Greenhouses	82
Grasshoppers	128
Grub, White	118
Gypsine	131

H

Hand Weeders	158
Harlequin Cabbage Bug	125
Harrows	48
Heating Forcing Pits	84
Hen Manure	43, 44
Hillside Forcing House	90
Hired Help	171
Home Gardening	12
Home Garden, Profits of	13
Horehound	243
Horse Hoes	55
Horse Radish	243
Hose, Home-made	102
Hot-beds	64
Hyssop	245

I

Insect Enemies	110
Insect Powder	114
Insects, Friendly	133
Irrigated Field, Plan of	103
Irrigating Celery by Tile	104
Irrigation	100
Irrigation, Surface	101

K

Kale, or Borecole	245
Kerosene, Attachment to Sprayer	131

Kerosene Emulsion	112
Kerosene for Insects	130
Kitchen Garden Plan	21, 23, 25
Knapsack Sprayer	137
Kohl-Rabi	246

L

Lavender	247
Leek	247
Lettuce	249
Lettuce in Electric Light	318
Lettuce, Mildew	141
Lettuce, Varieties	250
Lima Beans	190
Lima Beans, Trellis	191
List of Seeds for Home Garden	26
Liver of Sulphur	136
Location of Southern Truck Farm	28

M

Manure, Composting	37
Manure for Hot-beds	64
Manures for Gardening	35
Marjoram, Sweet	251
Markers	49
Market Gardening	17
Marketing	32
Martynia	252
May Beetle	118
Melon Leaf Spot	144
Melon, Musk	252
Melon, Water	255
Mice	129
Mint	259
Moles	129
Monthly Memoranda	173
Mushroom	259
Mushroom, A Summer	260
Mustard	261

N

Nasturtium	261
Nitrate of Soda	43
Nitrates, Effect of	45
Novelties	153

O

Okra	262
Onion	262
Onions for Bunching	264

Onion, Growing Sets	263
Onion Fly	118
Onion Smut	142
Onion Spot	142
Onion, The New Culture	268
Onion, Varieties	270
Onions for Market	264
Oyster Plant	294

P

Parsley	271
Parsley Worm	119
Parsnips	272
Peanuts	273
Peas	274
Pea Weevil	120
Pennyroyal	279
Pepper	277
Peppergrass	234
Peppermint	279
Pit for Storing Roots	200
Plan of Home Garden	21, 23, 25
Planet Jr. Garden Drill	52
Plant Box in Window	93
Plant Lice	111
Planting in Hard Soil	149
Plants for Home Garden	92
Plants, Starting Early	66
Plowing, Sample of Faulty	47
Popcorn	234
Potash Seldom Needed	45
Potassium Sulphide	136
Potato Beetle	120
Potato Blights	142
Potato Scab	143
Potato Stalk Borer	128
Potato Stalk Weevil	127
Potato, Sweet	287
Potato, Varieties	286
Potatoes, Rotation	281
Potatoes, White	280
Powder Bellows	114
Preliminary Remarks by the Author	9
Prevention of Disease	137
Protecting Plants, Devices for	169
Puddling	163
Pumpkin	289
Putty Bulb	58

R

Radish	289
Radish Fly and Maggot	122
Rats	129
Reptiles as Friends	132
Rhubarb	293
Rhubarb Curculio	128
Rosemary	293
Rotation of Cropping	155
Rue	294

S

Sage	294
Salsify	294
Savory, Summer	295
Savory, Winter	295
Sea Kale	295
Scorzonera	295
Seed Drills	51
Seed Sowing	147
Seeds, Vitality of	151
Shallot	296
Shutters for Frames	67
Skunks as Insect Eaters	133
Snails	123
Soil Tester	107
Sorrel	296
Sparrow, English	132
Spinach	296
Spinach Anthracnose	144
Spinach, Mildew	144
Spindling Plants	165
Spraying for Diseases	135
Spraying Pumps	137
Squash	298
Squash Bug, Black	124
Squash Vine Borer	123
Squash, Varieties	299
Stable Manure, Value of	36
Storing Roots	200
Strawberry Insects and Diseases	314
Strawberry Growing	307
Strawberry Planting	311, 315
Strawberry Plants	309
Strawberry, Varieties	316
Strawberries, Forcing	315
Strawberries, Gathering	313
Strawberries, Manure for	309
Strawberries in Home Garden	313
Strawberries, Winter Protection for	313
Straw Mats	68
Subirrigated Bench	106
Subirrigation by Flower Pots	107
Subirrigation, Cole's	108
Subirrigation for Greenhouse	105
Sulphate of Ammonia	43
Sweet Potato Diseases	145

T

Thinning	160
Thyme	300
Tile in Drains	97
Toad as Insect Eater	132
Tobacco as Insecticide	112
Tobacco Worm	127
Tomatoes	301
Tomato Diseases	145
Tomato Worm	126
Tomato, Varieties	302
Transplanting	161
Transplanting Devices	165
Turnips	304
Turnips, Varieties	306
Tweezers for Killing Bugs	124

U

Underdrainage, Advantages of	98

V

Vegetable House	30
Vitality of Seeds	151

W

Watering Cold Frames	62
Water Cress	234
Weeds, How to Fight	157
Wheel Hoes	53
Wintering Cabbage	202, 204
Wire Worm	124

Z

Zebra Caterpillar	125

PRELIMINARY REMARKS

BY THE AUTHOR.

HE considerations which guided me in writing up the first edition of this work, five years ago, are still potent to-day. Gardening, in the minds of many people, is still a dreadful combination in its requirements of skill and unceasing drudgery. There are yet persons, especially farmers, who doubt their ability to acquire the one without giving more time and thought than they can afford to devote to the garden, and fear the other. But our efforts in the direction of clearing up this only too common error, of convincing people in rural districts, and in the suburbs of cities, that gardening in reality is a very strong combination of pleasure, health and profit, and of pointing out the ways and means how to relieve the task of all semblance of drudgery, have not been without their desired effect. We are continuously making converts to our faith. The good home garden is not any more the rarity and curiosity that it once was. It is getting to be a very common institution.

Wonderful, indeed, is the progress which we have made during the past five years not only in the practice of gardening, but also in garden practices. Methods of cultivation have materially changed and are changing every day, decidedly in the direction and with the tendency of cheapening the cost of production, lessening hand labor, and making gardening more profitable and more pleasant. A new onion culture, a new celery culture, a new potato culture and other innovations have come to the front.

On the other hand, the market gardener of to-day finds himself beset with difficulties of which he little dreamed years ago. Insect foes and plant diseases have multiplied in an alarming degree, calling for increased vigilance, enlarged knowledge, and new modes of treatment and protection. At the same time the prices of garden products have materially fallen, and made old-style, clumsy and therefore expensive methods of production unremunerative.

In short, every gardener in these days must keep well informed about every forward move made in horticulture. He will need a guide giving minute instructions in every department of vegetable gardening—a guide which he can confidently consult in every emergency, and which will teach him, the servant of the soil, how to make himself

Master of the Situation.

The book, as it now lies before the reader, is intended to be a guide, safe and true in every respect.

I have no reason to complain of the reception that was accorded to the first edition by the American public. It has been very favorably commented on, and my kind critics have overlooked or excused many of its shortcomings. I myself have perhaps been a more severe critic of my own work than the great mass of my readers who have been so universally and often undeservedly kind to me and my efforts.

I could not blind my own eyes to the fact, however, that serious shortcomings did exist. Then there had been these changes in methods, so great, so violent, that the first edition, only these few years after publication, had already become out of date, and had to be radically amended in many respects. In short, a thorough revision was imperatively demanded, and the results of this revision are now before the reader.

Let me say that I am proud of this work. There is no book on the same subject now in the world that can compare with it in completeness and freshness.

Finally, I wish to advise the reader to try the newer ways that I point out; for gardening, like life, is what you yourself make of it—a paradise of pleasure or a veritable sheol of drudgery. You have the decision in your own hands: You may leisurely accompany your visitors through the well-kept grounds that are beaming with thrifty, sparkling vegetation, as your own countenance is beaming with pleasure and satisfaction, and that is as free from weeds as your face is from care; or you may crawl through the beds on hands and knees, piling up stacks of weeds, with a face sour and distorted in hatred of yourself and the life you are leading. My instructions, if faithfully followed, will insure you the former conditions, and save you from the curse of the latter.

It still remains to be said that the work was composed and revised on the suggestion of Mr. Wm. Henry Maule, of Philadelphia, who has undertaken its publication, and if the reader receives any benefit from its perusal, he is indebted to him as well as to the author.

T. GREINER.

Autumn, 1894.

Part I.

Gardening in General.

CHAPTER I.

HOME GARDENING.

GARDENING FOR PLEASURE, HEALTH, PROFIT AND MORALITY.

"Man shall not live by bread alone."

HOW I pity the people who from choice or necessity are confirmed eaters of hog, and the murderous monotony of whose scrofulous diet is not broken or offset by the gratifying changes which the home garden affords. How I pity the sad-eyed house-wife with the daily questions on her mind "What shall I cook for breakfast, what for dinner, and what for supper?" with nothing but the pork barrel, the flour chest and the potato bin from which to draw material. How I pity the mother whose children are crying for fruit and vegetables, and who is compelled to hand them—worse than a stone—a piece of salt meat. And above all, how I pity the children—the blessed children with their natural craving for the luscious fruits and the crisp vegetables of the garden, ever yearning for them as the deer is for salt, or the famished traveler in the desert for water—but their desire never to be satisfied, unless they steal the articles that their nature urgently demands from the gardens of more fortunate neighbors.

With the opportunities that the vast territory of the States, with its thirty acres of land, six of them arable, to each inhabitant, affords to its people, there is no need of many families depriving themselves of garden privileges, and there is not the slightest excuse for people in the rural districts to do without them.

The physician, the lawyer, the preacher, the book-keeper, the bank clerk—in short all people whose life occupation confines them to study or office for a large part of the day, and who for this reason are in danger of waxing tender and sensitive like hot-house plants—will find the gratification of the greatest need of their lives in a little garden of their own, namely, contact with nature, unadulterated air, relaxation and recreation, pleasure, health and ruggedness, not to speak of the more substantial and more immediate results: freshly-plucked berries (not the stale fruit of the market stands, in the first or more advanced stages of decay—in other words, half-rotten), crisp lettuce and radishes (not the wilted stuff of the dealer), peas and beans, with the morning dew still on them, and melons in all their perfection, freshness and lusciousness. With people of this class the question of profit may have little weight; but the home-garden affords a combination of pleasure and health which nobody, and be he a millionaire, can well afford to overlook or ignore. The greatest luxuries of the garden cannot be bought with mere money.

For the hard-working mechanic, on the other hand, who passes so many hours daily in the dust-laden, gas-impregnated atmosphere of the shop, the point of profit enters more largely into this question, with that of recreation in open air, and pleasurable contact with nature still prominent. The garden need only be small, for much manual exercise in not often desirable, although as it comes in a different way from that of the shop, resting the muscles already tired, and giving exercise to those not called in operation by the regular shop work (thus serving to produce the natural balance of the life forces and muscles in the same way as garden work served to establish the equilibrium between the mental and physical functions of the office man), the work of the garden may only come as a pleasant change to the mechanic, and not at all appear tiresome. His good spouse, less occupied with household duties than the farmer's wife, will also find a needed change from indoor life and kitchen routine in the fragrant atmosphere of the home garden, and the manual labor for both should not be feared, for an abundant supply of superior vegetables can be produced on a small piece of ground, if proper tools and methods are used.

With the farmer the question of raising vegetables is chiefly one of profit, although other points are not unimportant. Many farmers who till plenty of good land concentrate all their efforts upon the production of wheat, corn, oats, wool, cattle or other so-called "money crops," and pay little or no attention to the home garden.. So we have the astonishing and deplorable fact that a majority of American farmers have no garden worthy to be called a "family garden," unless so named because it is entirely given into the care of the already over-worked farmer's wife and other members of the family, especially of the half-grown boys, if they in true appreciation of the good things to be had in compensation, consent to spend an extra working hour now and then in hoeing and pulling weeds. Outraged nature, unappeased hunger for vegetable food often makes them submit without grumbling to the lesser outrage of imposing an extra amount of work on their young shoulders.

Fried Pork, fried potatoes, poor bread from poorly ground flour, lardy pies, and rich cakes—these, with hardly a variation, are the chief articles of food for thousands of farmer families.

Can you draw health from a pork barrel? No more than you can gather grapes from a thorn bush.

Many a farmer having sown a half acre or so of Black-Eye Marrowfat or Canadian Field peas, from which his family may have an abundant supply of green peas for a whole week, and given them the privilege to help themselves to all the roasting ears they may desire from the corn field (half a mile away) for another whole week, is self-satisfied with his generosity, and boasts that his full duty is done. According to statistics taken in Illinois in 1888, only seventeen per cent. of the farmers had the luxury of a strawberry patch. Think of this. Only one boy in every six knew what it was to pluck the luscious fruit from the vine, and eat to his heart's content! Without the stimulating, cooling and cheering effect of fruit and vegetable diet, what wonder that the blood of so many becomes sluggish and laden with impurities; what wonder the stomach revolts at the excess of grease, and becomes nauseated from want of change; what wonder the race degenerates, dyspepsia, scrofula, and similar afflictions are becoming alarmingly frequent and general, while the concocters and venders of patent quack medicines are making fortunes! What wonder the sons leave the farm, and rush to the city, and the daughters have no desire to sell themselves into new bondage and deprivations by marrying farmers! Boy nature (and girl nature either) will not long submit to the daily farm routine of

"All work and no play
All pork and no pay."

Even the dullest kind of a Jack will remonstrate against and resent this treatment. I have been a boy once, and I have learned the irresistible attraction that luscious strawberries, raspberries, gooseberries, currants, plums, pears, nuts, etc., have for young people—and old ones too, for that matter. Nature only claims her rights, and will not be outraged with impunity. I have learned the charms hidden in crisp lettuce, radishes, green peas, and the like, in spring when the human internal machinery is clogged with a winter's excess of animal food.

There is nothing in this wide world, that with just and fair treatment otherwise will keep the farmer's boys and girls content with rural life, and make them appreciate the great natural advantages of their situation as does a good home garden and a bountiful supply of good fruits, and nothing that will bring the bloom and happy smile on the good wife's face as the assistance she will receive from the same source in solving the problem how to provide the three daily meals to the satisfaction of all.

I have already alluded to the moral side of the question. The half-starved, lean-faced street gamin standing in front of the baker's show window, and longingly contemplating the loaves, pies, cakes and other dainties displayed in tempting array before his eyes, is not an uncommon sight, and it has often filled my inmost soul with pity. Imagine the youngster with an intense longing for fruit and vegetables peeking through the picket fence which divides his brute father's possessions from the garden of his neighbor whose fortunate children he can watch as they are gathering strawberries, or pulling crisp radishes in joy and glee. There is the luscious and coveted fruit almost within his reach, and temptingly displayed. Will you wonder if the boy, the first chance he gets to do so unobserved, removes a picket, and crawls into what to him is paradise beyond, and helps himself to what really is his due? If the father refuses to grow these things in his garden, and has "no money to spare for such luxuries," the boy will have no scruples to take surreptitiously what is so temptingly put before him. Average human nature is not built that way, to be strong enough against such odds. You cannot extract purity from glittering temptation, or morality from undue restriction, no more than health from the pork barrel. The man who willfully and needlessly deprives his family of the privileges of a good vegetable garden fails in one of his foremost duties. He cannot possibly be a good husband, nor a good father, *and he certainly is not a good Christian!*

Neither does he deserve to be called a good manager; for the question of profit also enters in this combination. Self-interest is a strong motive power. Here I wish I were able to convince every farmer in this glorious country of the great truth that an *acre of vegetable or fruit garden, properly taken care of, will be the most profitable acre on the farm.* While at present prices many of our farm products grown as "average crops" do not return the full equivalent for manure and labor expended on them, much effort and energy seems to be simply wasted, and might be turned to much better account for the production of the garden stuff which is now so sorely missed in the household, or might be sold at remunerative rates.

The amount of "green stuff" that can be grown on a single acre, well tilled, in a single summer, is simply incredible—wagon loads upon wagon loads; and there need not be a single meal from early spring until winter that is not made more cheerful, more palatable, more wholesome, and altogether more enjoyable by the presence of some good dishes from the garden, not to say anything about the canned tomatoes, sweet corn, berries and the crisp stalks of celery, etc., during the winter months. I and my family live largely on the products of garden and poultry yard during the entire summer, and we enjoy pretty good health generally. No meat bills to pay, no nausea caused by greasy food, no dyspepsia! Think of sixty meals with big plates of strawberries, and sixty more with raspberries and blackberries! Think of the wholesome dishes of asparagus, of the young onions, radishes, the various salads, the green peas and beans, the pickles and cucumbers, the tomatoes, squashes, melons, etc.! And all this practically without expense, at least, without cash outlay. There is plenty of good manure in the barn-yard; horses stand in the stable more or less unused during the gardening season, and the needed labor can also be had in an emergency. At the same time few farmers will have difficulty to sell or trade off the surplus to advantage. The village blacksmith may take part if not all of his pay in good vegetables. The wagon maker, the carpenter, the storekeeper, the physician, the banker—all of them need vegetables, and often are glad to take what good things you have to offer in exchange for money, goods, or services. If the working forces on the farm are insufficient, it will often be advisable to reduce the area of wheat or oats, and grow an acre of garden stuff instead; for the same work devoted to the garden will pay you 500 per cent. profit above that realized from grain culture.

CHAPTER II.

MARKET GARDENING AND TRUCK FARMING.

GARDENING FOR PROFIT ONLY.

"To produce is one thing, to sell another."

ONEY—and money alone—is the object of the market gardener; and the considerations of pleasure, health and morality are necessarily subordinate to that of profit. Business, not pleasure—that is gardening for the man who tries to support himself and family by growing vegetables for market. To be successful it often requires a rare combination of skill and experience, with a thorough understanding of the wants of his available market, and considerable tact, if not shrewdness, in the sale of articles produced. It is no business for the careless, the lazy, or the stupid.

Neither is it a royal road to fortune, and I feel it my duty to dispel the cherished delusions of people who wish to engage in market gardening as an easy and sure way of making a comfortable living. Before me is a letter received some time ago from a "preacher of the gospel," 35 years of age, who having been compelled to resign his position on account of throat affliction, has hit upon the idea of growing garden stuff for market.

"Is it possible," he asks, "to make a living on three acres of ground, 115 miles from Philadelphia? Soil good, and in town, near railroad station. I am happiest when I am hard at work, and oh! I love to work in the soil! This alone gives me renewed vigor, and a degree of health. Yet I am not willing to become a market boy, and I cannot peddle out what I raise off the soil."

Here, evidently, we have met with a wrong conception of market gardening; but it is a somewhat common one. I know of localities where three acres of good ground well-managed would afford quite a respectable living to a small family, with a market right at the door, and grocers in the near town willing to take almost any good garden produce brought them at fair prices. Advantage might often be taken of a local demand for certain productions, as berries, onions, celery, etc., and such articles grown on a larger scale, for sale to retailers, thus avoiding the "peddling" feature. But kid-glove and silk-hat gardening will under no consideration fit into successful market gardening or truck farming; "barter and trade" is one of the essentials of the business anywhere, and the grower must be in readiness, if an emergency arises, to take hold and become merchant or peddler. This feature is an indispensable part of the business in most cases.

Gardening for money requires unceasing attention, close and thorough management, considerable hard labor, and often more or less exposure to the vicissitudes and inclemencies of the seasons. Nevertheless it is true that the majority of the profession make altogether too much work of it, especially by neglecting to make use of the newer improved implements of tillage. The hand hoe is yet left to play a by far too prominent part in garden culture, and the advantages of the wheel-hoe are not yet recognized and made use of as they deserve.

There was a time when even the rudest methods combined with hard work insured to the market gardener near large cities a good income. But competition has grown with the demand, and with cheapened and increased production prices have gradually declined until now they are far below what only a few years ago growers would have considered mere cost of production. It is not so many years since the main crop of strawberries sold at 25 cents per quart; and when the price first dropped down to 20 cents, the cry went forth that "Strawberry growing does not pay." Then thousands of growers abandoned the business in disgust. At present, strawberries are grown at 6 and 8 cents per quart in many localities, and people are satisfied with the profits. So with vegetables. We have learned to produce much cheaper than formerly, and we can afford to produce and sell at figures which did not cover first cost ten or twenty years ago, and yet realize a fair profit. Hence people who continue to grow garden crops in the old laborious and unsatisfactory ways, and with old-style implements, who produce inferior vegetables and fruits at old-time cost, cannot successfully meet the competition of their progressive brethren. This is simply a question of the "survival of the fittest;" and the fittest is the man who by taking advantage of the latest labor-saving methods and devices manages to raise the best produce at the smallest cost, thus preserving or even widening the narrow margin of profit which at the present time characterizes all legitimate branches of business. The spade must give way to the plow; the rake, and often cultivator also, to the harrow; hand and fingers in sowing seeds to the drill; the hand hoe to the wheel-hoe, etc. These changes are imperative and unavoidable, if the business is to be made profitable. The grower who has learned to produce most cheaply and can offer the earliest or best articles in his line, is the one who succeeds; and efforts to excel must be made continuously to prevent getting left in this race. This requires the exercise of thought, study—in short of brains as well as of muscle. Excellence will have its reward; but he who neglects a single point, who allows himself to be excelled by others, is not likely to receive a prize.

Special vegetable crops are often grown on a large scale in localities especially adapted to their cultivation, or having special market facilities for such crops. So we have the celery fields of Kalamazoo, Mich., the onion patches of Wethersfield, Conn., and Danvers, Mass., and other places, the cauliflower gardens of Long Island, the tomato fields of New Jersey, the melon patches of Virginia, etc. To produce is often much easier than to sell the product at a profit, and it is not safe to engage in a business of this kind on an extensive scale, or invest much money in it, unless a local demand is assured for the produced articles. Wagon and carloads of good vegetables are yearly thrown away for want of chance to sell them in time at an acceptable price. Where the enterprise is carried on in colonies, however, there is always a local market; for the centre of production is also the centre of demand.

CHAPTER III.

FARMERS' KITCHEN GARDEN.

SELECTION OF LOCALITY AND ARRANGEMENT OF BEDS.

"Well begun—half done."

THE home garden in a majority of cases is a fixed affair, and no choice is left as to the selection of site. While the condition of soil, its fertility, convenient lay and proper slope, are questions of no mean import, they are almost always secondary to the point of nearness to the house. The garden may be filled with good things of the season, but if half a mile from the house, compelling the over-worked and hurried house-wife to tramp such a distance every time she wants a supply of vegetables fresh from the garden, the cheering presence of young onions, radishes, lettuce, tomatoes, egg plants, and other vegetables will be missed by the family at many a meal that might have been more palatable and more wholesome by the vegetable addition and by the change otherwise. What good are the choicest things in our possession if we cannot make ready use of them?

The condition of many a home garden seems sufficient excuse for hiding it from sight. The best location for the garden is in a prominent place where it will crowd itself upon constant observation from the house. If well kept, it is one of the greatest ornaments to the premises, and a source of everlasting admiration; if neglected and left to grow up in weeds, it will be a shame to the owner, an ever present accuser—a sort of conscience—and loudly calling for attention. A good garden is a sort of summer resort, to which the owner can take his visitors, and show them about with excusable pride; an inducement for an after-dinner or after-supper walk, affording opportunities for a few touches of improvement, for pulling up some stray weeds, or for the destruction of injurious insects, when thus encountered, for watching with pleasurable interest the growth and development of the things that are "new and curious." Nearness to the house means nearness to your thoughts and affections; better care and closer attention; more enjoyable and diversified meals; increased pleasure, health and happiness for the whole family. Nearness to the house also increases the chances for convenient

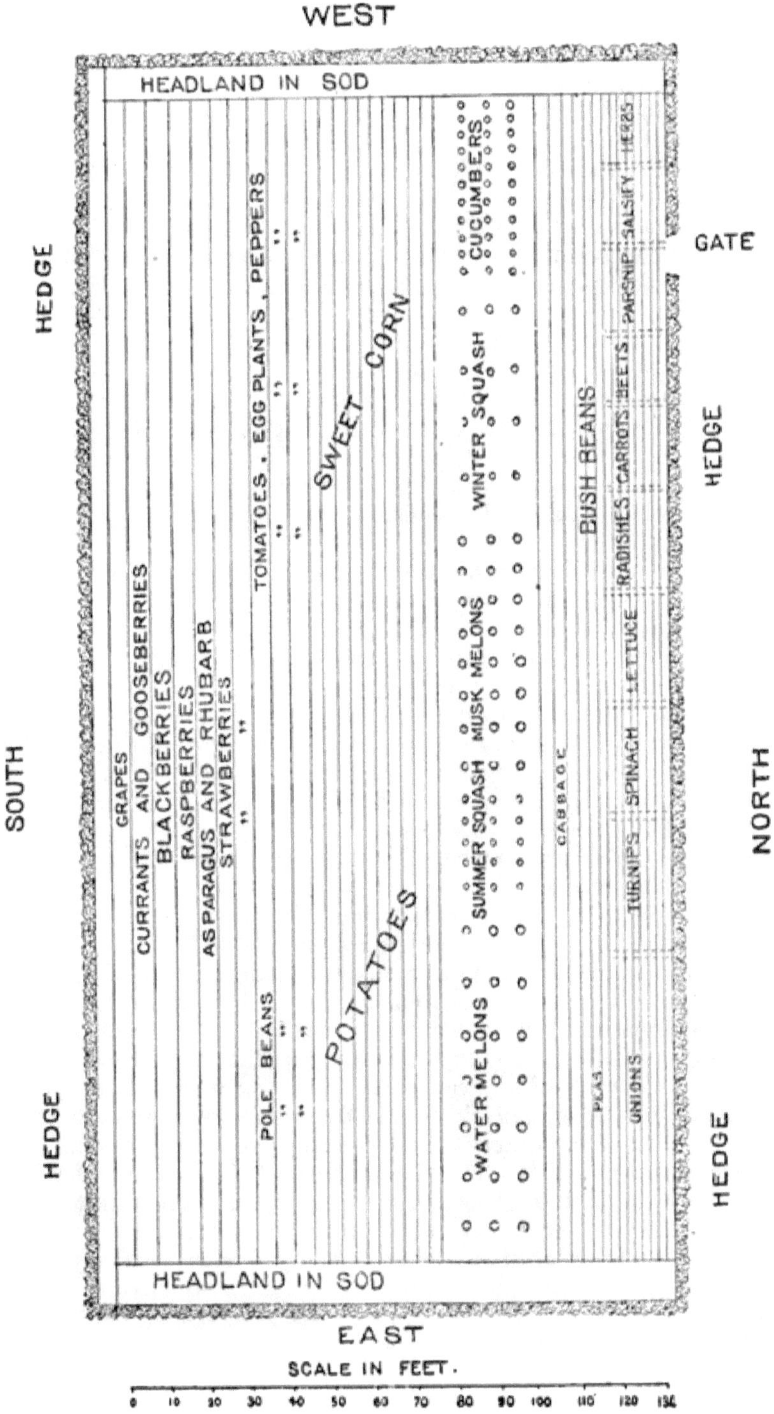

Farmer's Kitchen Garden.—21

WEST

HEADLAND IN SOD

- GRAPES
- CURRANTS AND GOOSEBERRIES
- BLACKBERRIES
- RASPBERRIES
- ASPARAGUS AND RHUBARB
- STRAWBERRIES
- POLE BEANS
- TOMATOES, EGG PLANTS, PEPPERS
- SWEET CORN
- POTATOES
- WATER MELONS
- SUMMER SQUASH
- MUSK MELONS
- WINTER SQUASH
- CUCUMBERS
- CABBAGE
- PEAS
- ONIONS
- TURNIPS
- SPINACH
- LETTUCE
- BUSH BEANS
- RADISHES
- CARROTS
- BEETS
- PARSNIP
- SALSIFY
- HERBS

HEADLAND IN SOD

EAST

SCALE IN FEET.

0 10 20 30 40 50 60 70 80 90 100 110 120 130

SOUTH — HEDGE (left)
NORTH — HEDGE (right), GATE
HEDGE (top and bottom)

and prompt utilization of house slops, washing suds, etc., in the garden, where they will add to the productiveness of the soil, and may aid in doing away with the stagnant pools, rank sink drains and offensive odors found near the kitchen door of many people, and endangering their health and lives.

Concerning composition, state of fertility and slope of the ground, there is in many cases little latitude for choice. People have often to take such as they find, and try to make the best of it. A rich, warm sandy loam, naturally drained, should always be given the preference, and if slightly sloping to the south, south-east or east, all the better. If deficient in drainage, thorough drainage must be provided; if too heavy and cold, applications of sand, coal ashes, sandy loam and plenty of stable manure will make it lighter and warmer; if too sandy, the addition of clay will improve it. Peat and other vegetable matter in a state of decay will often correct either extreme, and good compost will ameliorate any soil, both in point of fertility and mechanical texture. It tends to make clay soil porous and sandy soil retentive.

The old-style gardens, as a rule, are not up to our modern ideas as to size. Having in a measure discarded the use of spade, and particularly that of rake and hand hoe, and substituted horse-power and machinery for hand labor and hand implements, we need room to work in with convenience and pleasure. The farmer has no excuse to stick to his little corner lot. Throw down the old fences, and enclose an acre or even two, in a field long and narrow if possible; then arrange it somewhat as shown on opposite page. The whole field should be free from trees, stumps, boulders and other obstructions, and enclosed by a tight hedge or substantial fence. Neither pigs, hens nor dogs are wanted in a garden.

Commencing on one of the long sides we might have a row of grapes, selecting varieties that are known to do well in that locality, and training them to a suitable trellis or over an arbor; next a row of gooseberries and currants; then a row or more each of red and black raspberries and blackberries, and one of asparagus, with a dozen or more rhubarb plants at one end, and next a few rows of strawberries. Now we come to the real (vegetable) garden, and this may be arranged as indicated in diagram, or in any other order according to the fancy or convenience of the gardener. The arrangement of the vegetable garden proper in this fashion gives abundance of opportunity for rotation, and the various vegetables may be shifted about as circumstances demand, and the location of each changed from year to year. The adoption of this plan gives us long rows which are easily and cheaply kept under perfect tillage by horse and cultivator, adjusting width of the latter to suit width of row. The narrow

Farmer's Kitchen Garden.—23

rows at north side alone are to be cultivated by hand, using one of the modern wheel-hoes, a work also greatly facilitated by the length and small number of rows, as it is the turning that requires valuable time and effort.

For a number of years I have practised a plan differing from the preceding, and I find it superior in many respects. The fruit patch is entirely separate from the vegetable garden, and will need no description here. The diagram on opposite page shows the arrangement and general plan of garden.

One of its chief advantages is the easy access it affords to all the different kinds of vegetables, especially to the close-planted, and most frequently visited ones, lettuce, onions, radishes, carrots, beets, etc., and its only disadvantage the necessity of turning with horse and cultivator in the field and not at the fence near the highway. This is not a serious matter, however, as a strip eight feet wide is left next the path at the foot of the narrow rows, and including it, without planting except with a single row of squashes or other running vines at the end of the long rows. This arrangement gives every opportunity for turning without damage to growing crops, and the empty space will be occupied by running vines by the time that cultivation by horse power has to cease. Nor is there any want of chance for rotation, and the order of both the small stuff and the crops in the larger section can be changed to suit the requirements of the case from year to year.

When, as it often happens with me, beans, or early cabbages, peppers, egg-plants, etc., are planted in the upper part, in rows two and a-half feet apart, with radishes between each two rows, the cultivator can here be run right through the whole length of the garden after the radishes have all been gathered. At the end of rows, facing the path, short numbered stakes may be driven in the ground; and if these are not over eight inches high, the double wheel-hoe can be run right over them without being interfered with in doing its work properly. When sowing seed or setting plants, the varieties and numbers are carefully noted down, especially in testing new sorts. The opportunity which this affords to compare the behavior of varieties, and to speak of them intelligently, greatly enhances the pleasure of making and taking care of a garden.

Where there is no lack of land, it may be well to make the garden of double size, so that each one-half (divided lengthwise) may be renewed and rendered clean from time to time by seeding to clover and mowing once or twice before it is cropped again with vegetables. Or one-half may be planted to potatoes, corn, or tomatoes, or other field crops, and the two halves used alternately for garden purposes. The great advantage of a thorough system of rotation can hardly be pointed out too often.

Farmer's Kitchen Garden—25

```
  80    70    60    50    40    30    20    10    0
   PEAS, Late
        Early
        Medium    Followed by Cucumbers or Late Celery
        Late
    Spinach   Celery Plants
   Barletta Onion   Onion Sets
    Onions
    Early Cabbage          Radish
    Kohlrabi, Caulif       Radish
    Lettuce                Radish
                           Radish
    Carrot Beet
    Bean
      " Wax
         Bush Lima
    Parsnip              Salsify
    Peppers, Eggplant

    Tomatoes


   Winter Squash    Summer         Melons
   Early Potatoes   Squash


        Late Cabbage and Cauliflower


   Early Sweet Corn Followed by Late Celery, Late String Beans


        Later Sweet Corn


        Sweet Potato
        Early Celery
   STRAWBERRIES, Followed by Turnips, Spinach, Late Cabbage, etc.



   Sage, Parsley, Winter Onion, Leek, Garlic, Winter Savory, Thyme
         Asparagus
         Rhubarb
         Currants and Gooseberries
         Raspberries

         Grape Vines
```

PLAN OF ONE-QUARTER ACRE GARDEN.

26—How to Make the Garden Pay.

If the aim is simply to provide an abundance of vegetables and small fruits for an average-sized family, a quarter-acre garden, closely planted and well cropped, would be large enough. Usually we like to have the rows the long way, but local conditions differ and every plan must be fitted into its particular surroundings.

On preceding page I give plan of a one-quarter home garden with rows running the short way. Perennial growths, like grape vines, currants, gooseberries, rhubarb, asparagus, herbs, etc., are planted at the further end. The wide-planted vegetables, to be also cultivated by horse power, come next, while the close-planted stuff, which is to be cultivated by hand machines, is planted nearest the entrance, *i. e.*, nearest the kitchen.

A list of the seeds required to plant this quarter-acre, and keep it planted and cropped as persistently as it should be, is about as follows:

QUANTITY.	ARTICLE.	TIME OF SOWING. For New Jersey, Southern Penna., etc.*
1 qt.	Extra Early Smooth Peas,	Mar. 1-15
1 qt.	Early Dwarf Wrinkled Peas,	Mar. 8-25
2 qts.	Later Wrinkled Peas,	Mar. 8-25
¼ lb.	Spinach,	Mar., Aug., Sept., Oct.
1 pkt.	Celery, for plants,	Mar. 1-8
2 ozs.	Barletta Onion, for pickling,	Mar. 1-25
2 ozs.	Yellow Dutch Onion, for sets,	Mar. 1-15
	Small quantity to be started in box in window,	Feb. 1-15
2 qts.	Onion sets,	Mar. 1-15
1 pkt.	Prizetaker Onion, started in box,	Feb. 1-15
1 oz.	Danver's Onion,	Mar. 1-15
1 pkt.	Cabbage, Prize Wakefield, in box,	Feb. 1
2 pkts.	Cabbage, Late,	June 1
1 oz.	Early Beet, Eclipse,	Mar. 15-25
1 oz.	Blood Turnip Beet,	April, May, June
1 pkt.	Carrot, Early Scarlet Horn,	Mar. 15-25
1 pkt.	Carrot, Chantenay,	April 1-May
1 pkt.	Carrot, Danver's,	April 1-June
1 pkt.	Pepper, Ruby King, in house,	Feb. 1
1 pkt.	Egg Plant, New York Purple, in house,	Feb. 1
1 pkt.	Tomatoes, Earliest, in house,	Feb. 1
1 pkt.	Tomatoes, Main Crop, in house,	Feb. 1
¼ lb.	Radish, Earliest Turnip,	Mar., April, May
2 ozs.	Radish, Long Rooted,	June 1-15, etc.
1 pkt.	Radish, Winter,	Aug.-Sept.
3 pkts.	Lettuce,	Mar., May, June
1 pkt.	Cauliflower, Earliest,	Mar. 1-June
1 oz.	Sugar Beet, Imperial Sugar,	April 1-15
1 pkt.	Cress, Extra Curled,	April 1
1 pkt.	Kohl Rabi, Large White,	April 1-15 and May

*From one to two weeks later further north.

QUANTITY.	ARTICLE.	TIME OF SOWING.
1 pt.	Beans, Green String,	May 1-15
1 pt.	Beans, Wax String,	June, July
1 pt.	Beans, Henderson's Bush Lima,	May 15
1 pt.	Sweet Corn, Extra Early Cory,	May 1
1 pt.	Sweet Corn, Medium,	May 8
1 pt.	Sweet Corn, Late,	May 8, June, July 1
2 ozs.	Cucumbers, Long Green or Early White Spine,	May to June
1 oz.	Musk Melon, Emerald Gem,	May 15
1 pkt.	Water Melon,	May 15
1 pkt.	Squash, Summer Crookneck,	May 15
1 pkt.	Squash, Hubbard,	May 15
1 pkt.	Parsley, Double Curled,	Mar. 15
1 pkt.	Sage,	June
1 oz.	Ruta Baga,	July-Aug.
1 oz.	Turnip, Red Top Strap Leaved,	July-Aug.
½ bus.	Early Potatoes,	April 15
100	Sweet Potato Plants,	May 15 to June 1
240	Strawberry Plants,	April 1-15
50	Asparagus Roots, 2 years old,	April 1
20	Rhubarb Roots,	April 1
12	Currant Bushes,	April 1
8	Gooseberry Bushes,	April 1
40	Raspberries, Red and Black,	April 1
10	Grape Vines,	April 1

This list may be varied more or less, according to taste or notion. Most gardeners will like to plant some novelties, and many have special favorites among the vegetables. It is but fair that all whims, in this line, should be humored.

Let us add one more word of advice in regard to the purchase of seeds. I find it most economical, and surely most convenient, to purchase at least a double quantity of seed of all my staple varieties which can be depended upon to retain their vitality for a number of years, especially cabbage, cauliflower, beet, carrot, turnip, pepper, tomato, cucumber, melon, squash, radish, lettuce, etc. I can buy such seeds cheaper in quantity than by the packet or ounce.

These seeds are always on hand when wanted, and of some of them we desire to sow little patches quite frequently during the summer. What is left one year comes handy next year, and after the first year we know exactly what kind of vegetables we will get from the once-tested seed.

CHAPTER IV.

REQUIREMENTS OF SUCCESS IN MARKET GARDENING.

SELECTION OF SOIL AND LOCATION.

"Look before you leap."

WHILE the home gardener must take the circumstances as he finds them, and try to make the most of opportunities ready-made for him, the prospective gardener "for profit only" cannot safely do so. He must select the most favorable conditions, or run the risk of seeing his proud business structure tumble down, and his high anticipations wrecked at the very start. It will not do for him to select a location most favorable to the production of perfect vegetables, if such location has no market for them. Of the two considerations, that of market opportunity stands first. Before locating anywhere with the intent of growing garden vegetables for money, the near markets need the closest study. The difficulty often encountered of putting stuff already produced on a paying market, and to turn it into cash, is the chief cause of failure with many otherwise good gardeners. Vast quantities of choice vegetables are left to spoil every season simply for want of a local demand for them. The great cities, as a rule, are well supplied with the products of the garden by growers near by, and the competition there is large, often ruinous, at least to the extravagant hopes of the shipper; hence the dependence on distant city markets to be reached through the instrumentality of express companies and railroads as carriers, is not often justified except in case of the early southern products, and of such vegetables as tomatoes, onions, sweet potatoes, melons and others that are grown in the farm garden (truck farm) on an extensive scale.

The growers of vegetables for market may be divided into three classes, as follows, viz.:

First.—The southern truck farmer who grows early stuff for northern markets. His location must be selected with especial regard to his railroad connections with the principal city markets, nearness to station, and the conditions favorable to earliness and perfect development of vegetables, such as rich and warm soil, southern exposure, etc.

Second.—The market gardener near the large cities who raises garden stuff in day-time, and draws his products to the city, and city stable manure back to the farm, during the night, leading a life of unceasing toil, in perpetual fight with competition, but receiving good pay for skillful management.

Third.—The local gardener whose aim it is to fill a comparatively small demand in his immediate neighborhood. Sometimes he gives his goods to grocers in near towns to sell on commission; or sells to them to retail to their customers; or he loads up his wagon and peddles his crops directly to the consumer. He has the advantage of cheap land, cheap help, and few expenses generally, and if he is a good salesman as well as a good gardener, he may do well.

Localities near summer resorts and watering places afford special chances. Many of the gardeners near such places, as for instance along the beach in New Jersey, in the vicinity of Long Branch, have what might be called a " soft snap " so far as marketing is concerned. The demand for choice vegetables here is reasonably large at any time, but reaches enormous proportions when city people have taken up their abode amongst them, and prices often rise to excessive figures just at a time when the season is naturally most favorable to the production of these articles. The established gardens in these sections have their regular customers, and little trouble in disposing of good produce. The truckers or peddlers who run their vegetable wagons during the bathing season, supplying their regular customers (the cottagers, boarding houses and hotels), make their daily calls at the gardens, and load their wagons, paying high prices for produce for which in turn they charge excessive, often outrageous rates to the wealthy, city-bred consumer. Here money is plenty, easily earned, and easily spent. Some of these people run gardens and truck wagons in combination; they supply the consumer directly, charging for their own produce the high retail price of the truckers; and their profit for two months often keeps them in easy circumstances for the whole year. Others sell both to the regular truckers and to the grocers in the near towns; but there is seldom much difficulty encountered by the good salesman to sell what once is produced. Here, as might be expected, land is high, often $500 to $1,000 per acre; but considering the market advantages it is much cheaper at that figure than the $10 an acre clay lands of Virginia colonies, or the $30 an acre white sand plains of Central or South Jersey.

As nearness to the house or kitchen (in this case the centre of demand) is one of the first considerations in the location of the home garden, so is nearness to a market with good steady demand the chief point of importance for every market gardener. It makes considerable difference whether produce has to be hauled to market, and manure back to the farm, one mile or ten. Often a sudden scarcity of a certain article in the market, caused by delayed shipments, or by other chances, can at once be taken advantage of by the near grower who is enabled to rush the demanded article to market at short notice, and to benefit by the higher prices, while the gardener living at a greater distance cannot do as well. This advantage alone will outweigh even a considerable difference in price or rent of land.

The next consideration, and one of scarcely less importance, is the suitability of the land. The soil should be a warm, sandy loam, level or slightly sloping to the south or south-east, free from obstruction, trees, etc., and in a good state of cultivation.

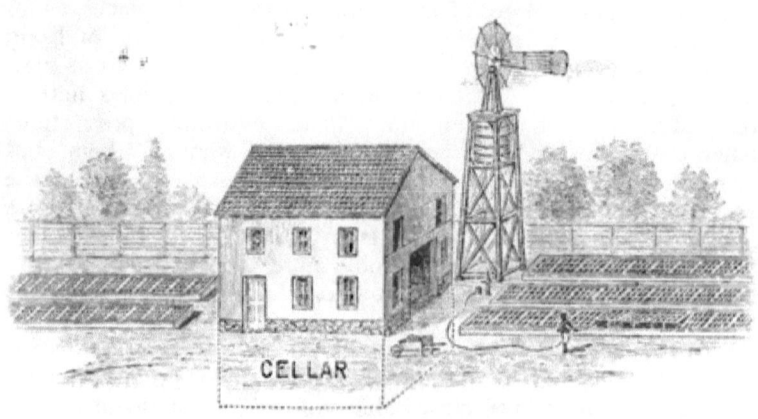

Vegetable House, Windmill and Hotbeds.

Want of fertility can be remedied in time, and is not as grave a defect as faulty composition of soil would be. Nor should the soil be excessively weedy, although this defect can also be remedied by perseverance and painstaking, and at some expense. Natural drainage is desirable, but if not perfect, should be made so by thorough underdraining. A piece of drained muck-land is generally a valuable addition to the upland property.

Plenty of water is one of the chief needs of the market gardener, and the careful calculator will have an eye on the chance of supply when selecting his location. A running stream, an artesian well, or a pond in close proximity to the beds and buildings, so situated that it can be readily utilized for the various purposes of watering, irrigating, washing vegetables, etc., is likely to be worth hundreds of dollars to the owner. If such a convenience is not in existence, the next best thing is a good large cistern near the vegetable house. This latter may be a cheaply constructed affair, of any desired or needed size, with frost-proof cellar for storing vegetables, a washing department above, with tank; also a storage room for tools, seeds and other equipments. A good well is a necessary convenience, and will supply water when the cistern fails.

The degree of success in gardening depends largely on the abundance and steadiness of the water supply; for the liquid element is needed in vast quantities, and must be furnished at just the time when the crops require it. Hand sprinklers and force pumps are yet the common means of distributing water over the often large area of the beds in many market gardens, but through the employment of a modern windmill, tanks and rubber hose in their capacities as forcing power, storage room, and carrier, respectively, this originally tedious job can be made comparatively pleasant and inexpensive.

This chapter, in my estimation, would not be complete without an earnest word of warning to the new beginner. I only follow the plain path of duty when I point out the dangers of engaging in this (as in any other) business on a larger scale than experience and available capital will warrant. Profits are easily figured out on paper, and often allure the novice into a feeling of unjustified confidence and security. Debts are contracted, to be paid with the prospective profits; but such profits do not often materialize. It is safe to commence on five acres of good land paid for, and with implements and conveniences also paid for. It is very risky to start in on twenty acres, mortgaged for half their value, and to work with tools obtained on credit. The former plan admits of a gradual increase of the business on a safe foundation, and as increasing experience and means warrant. The latter plan leads the gardener into the meshes of the usurer—the foolish fly into the spider's web—and to ultimate ruin. Step by step you will rise from the foot of the ladder to the height of lasting prosperity; but the pretender who surreptitiously usurps a high position will come to a sudden, and perhaps deserved fall.

CHAPTER V.

HINTS IN MARKETING.

SECRETS OF SUCCESS EXPOSED.

"Doing the right thing at the right time."

THE all-important secret might be told in a few words: "Cater to the demands of the market." Produce just such articles as the market calls for, and offer them for sale at just such times as people want to buy. The more favorable the combination of circumstances of your own selection—market, locality, soil, and methods—the brighter are the chances of success. Start in modestly to fill a want already existing. Try to have your vegetables in the market a few days, or even a few hours sooner than your competitor. Take to market only the choicest, and keep the poorer stuff out of your customer's sight, thus making a reputation for yourself and your wares, and your success will be at once assured and permanent. Study the peculiarities of your market, and try to hit the periodically appearing demands for certain articles. The best at the right time brings the profits.

It is hardly ever advisable to attempt educating people's tastes. Give your customers exactly what they want; and only after having gained a firm footing among them, or gained a reputation for yourself, would it be wise to begin, cautiously, the work of creating a demand for better things by exposing them in tempting display to people's attention. There is a rule of fashion in markets as well as in attire. When a certain kind of vegetable or fruit is popular in a certain market, it will sell quicker and at higher prices than even a better kind with which people are not acquainted. The process of educating people's taste is always an exceedingly slow one; and the gardener should not make the mistake of growing any thing new and superior, but as yet unknown to customers, in the vain hope of gaining an advantage over his competitors, unless the superiority lies in outside attractiveness—large size, fine color, perfect shape, etc.—and thus appeals to the sight. High quality alone, without "catchy" appearance, is at a discount in the open markets.

Uniformity is one of the chief essentials in making produce attractive and salable. Particular pains should be taken to have

Hints in Marketing.—33

all the vegetables in one bunch or package—the radishes, beets, turnips, celery, or whatever they may be—as near like each other as careful selection can make them. Have everything clean and attractive. If the articles to be marketed are of uneven size, grade them with greatest care, and put the larger ones in

Radishes, Properly Graded.   Radishes, Not Graded.

one package, and the smaller ones in another. Careful sorting and packing is just as necessary as skillful growing.

Regularity of supply is still another point of importance. No matter how good and how abundant your produce may be,

Strawberries, Mixed and Graded.

it will not be appreciated by your customers unless you furnish them regularly just what they want, and when they want it. This inspires confidence and reliance upon you, and insures permanent patronage even at higher prices than customers would be willing to give to the man who offers his wares spasmodically, at irregular intervals, or at rare occasions.

It is well worth taking to heart what one of South Jersey's most successful market gardeners says on this subject:

"If you are catering to the appetites of the town's people, and desire to extend your list of vegetables, plant but sparingly of such varieties as have not yet come into general use, until the demand for them is created.

"Even to-day there are hundreds of families in every large town, and thousands of farmers upon whose table spinach, kale, cauliflower, salsify, and a long list of other vegetables, both toothsome and healthful, has never appeared. To encourage this trade takes time, patience, and no little outlay in labor and cash.

"It has been, and always will be, that each market has its favorites who can sell more at the same price than other growers. If to dispose of your load to-day, you sacrifice the price you would be sure of to-morrow; if to-morrow you find yourself compelled to make further concessions in order to sell your products, you may be sure the necessity for making concessions will continue from day to day, until the prices of all goods in your line are depressed below the line of profit to yourself and all other gardeners; and you will have lost the esteem and goodwill of your competitors without being better thought of by dealers and customers.

"Retailers like to deal with producers whose word is as good as their bond. They desire to be sure that in every basket, box, or barrel the uniform goodness of the contents reaches clear to the bottom. They like men who, when taking orders to-day for to-morrow, can be depended upon to live up to their engagements; whose vegetables are always washed clean, tied tightly, arranged neatly, and whose call can be counted upon with never-failing certainty every week-day, and under all conditions of weather."

CHAPTER VI.

MANURES FOR THE GARDEN.

I. STABLE MANURE AND HOW TO MANAGE IT.

"Of nothing, nothing comes."

THE market gardener can produce in a single season enormous, almost incredible quantities of vegetables on an acre of ground when systematically and continuously cropped. The quality of most of this produce depends on its succulence and tenderness, and its money value is greatly influenced by its size and earliness, all of which features are the result of rapid, thrifty growth, which in turn, is only made possible by the presence of an abundance of available plant food in the soil, especially of the nitrogenous element, which is the chief promoter of succulent growth, in bulbous root, leaf, and stalk.

The prices which the gardener obtains for his products, compared with those realized by the farmer for grain, hay, potatoes, etc., are such that he can much better afford to use large quantities of manure, and especially pay out money for them, than the farmer with whom it is only too often the query whether he can profitably use *any* kind of manure which he has to buy. There is considerable doubt in my mind that wheat, oats, corn, and products of this sort can be raised at present market rates with profits worth speaking of when manure, whether yard or concentrated, has to be bought at the figures usually paid by the market gardener. The latter, as a rule, finds that the more and the better manure he uses, whether bought or home-made, from stable or factory, the larger will be his profits. Manure, good manure, and plenty of it—that is the corner-stone of successful market gardening.

This assertion is not likely to be disputed. But there are economical or methodical ways of using it, and there are wasteful ones. It is not always easy to determine, in which shape, in what quantities, and to what crops manure can be applied so it will do the most good. The importance of the subject demands our earnest consideration, deep thought and study; but we should look at the question entirely dispassionate, without preconceived preferences in favor of one manure, or prejudices against the other. There are gardeners who claim every thing for stable manure, and find no good in "fertilizers;" and there are others who put their whole reliance in the latter. As in most other cases we will find the "golden mean" by far the safest course to pursue.

Stable manure is yet the favorite article with the masses of gardeners. If reasonably free from weed-seeds and properly handled, it is a perfectly safe and reliable fertilizer, and when made from grain-fed animals, as most likely the case in city stables, well worth $2.00 per ton, if it can be drawn without incurring additional expense, or at a time when no other work is pressing. One ton of ordinary, mixed, fresh farm or stable manure contains about 8 lbs. of nitrogen, 10 lbs. of potash and 4 lbs. of phosphoric acid. At current retail rates for these plant-foods, their chemical value would be about as follows, viz.:

8 lbs. nitrogen at 16 cents,	$1 28
10 " potash at 5 cents,	50
4 " phosphoric acid at 5 cents,	20
Total,	$1 98

When thoroughly rotted this manure contains a still larger percentage of the plant foods, hence is not only more valuable for that reason but also on account of its readiness for application, and immediate availability. When we further consider the mechanical effect of this manure, the opening and loosening of the soil, allowing air and warmth to enter it more freely—we will not be apt to underrate its value.

A different thing it would be, if in addition to first cost, we were obliged to incur much extra expense in hauling it a considerable distance; if we were to employ teams, and hire men. I think I would use good stable manure in moderate quantities if the aggregate cost amounted to $2.00, and very sparingly at a higher figure. The manure account is a big item with the rank and file of gardeners near the cities who use from 50 to 100 tons of stable manure to the acre annually. As we shall see later on, the application of even the smaller amount is excessive, and often a sinful and preventable waste.

COMPOSTING MANURE.—Raw manure is not in condition for the market gardener's purposes, except in rare cases. It may do for sweet corn, and comes in play for heating hot-beds, or raising mushrooms; but for general garden crops it must be composted, and made as fine as possible. There need be no loss of fertilizing materials or elements if the compost heap is properly made as shown in illustration next page. Pile it up in a square heap with perpendicular sides and flat top, four or five feet high, and as wide and long as may be required. Let it come to a heat, and fork the mass over from time to time until it is in the desired condition. It takes time and labor, adding to the original cost, and in deciding on the price he can afford to pay for raw manure originally, the gardener will have to take this feature in consideration.

These heaps may be made during autumn and early winter right on the arable land, and the material will generally be ready to be spread upon the soil where wanted, when the time for planting it with spring crops has arrived. It is absolutely necessary that these heaps be of considerable depth, not less than four feet, in order to prevent the rain-water from leaching clear through, and washing away valuable food elements.

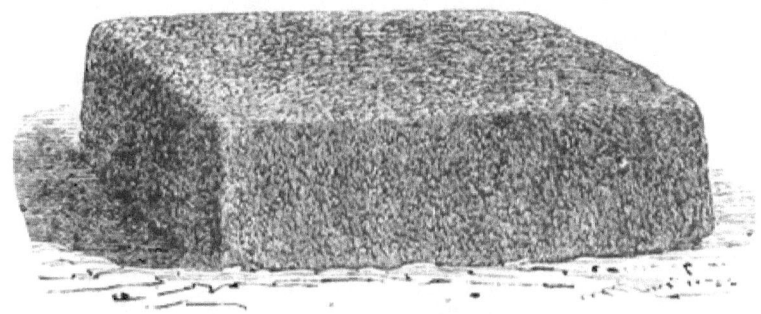

Composting Stable Manure.

It will be all the better if compost heaps of this kind can be made under shelter, and especially if liquids from the barnyard, or soapsuds from the wash house, or similar liquid wastes can be occasionally poured upon them. The compost heap, while in process of construction, is the most appropriate dumping place for vegetable rubbish of all sorts, the carcasses of animals (larger ones cut in pieces), house and kitchen slops, and other waste materials. Refuse matter of this kind often adds greatly to the value and effectiveness of the compost.

What we should avoid most scrupulously, however, is the addition of any material containing live weed seeds, or of vegetable rubbish infected with plant diseases. The best way, indeed the only safe way of purifying old tomato and potato stalks, celery tops, etc., that had once been attacked, however slightly, by blights or other diseases, is to burn them to ashes, and this cannot be done too soon for the safety of succeeding crops. Even manure from animals fed on blighted or scabby vegetation, tubers, and the like, should be rejected for gardening purposes.

In many of our inland villages and cities quantities of good manure from livery stables, from the premises of suburban owners of a family cow, poultry, and other animals, from blacksmith shops, etc., can be had for the hauling, or at a mere nominal price. A dairyman, three miles from here, has great heaps of old cow manure which he is glad to sell for 30 cents a one-horse load (say a ton) or 50 cents a two-horse load (say two tons). Often the nearby gardener has quite a bonanza. The opportunities are too good to be missed. When work is slack, and roads good, the time cannot be put to better use than for hauling manure, day after day. Put it on thick; it will pay. I usually buy my manure supply from the Buffalo Stockyards. I have to pay more for it than is asked by the dairyman already mentioned. But the station is only half a mile from the place. I find it too expensive to have to send three miles after a load when we have other work to do.

CHAPTER VII.

MANURES FOR THE GARDEN.

II. COMMERCIAL FERTILIZERS—THEIR VALUE AND USE.

"Prove all things; hold fast that which is good."

COMMERCIAL fertilizers are coming more and more in general use with market gardeners, and are now quite extensively substituted for stable manure—and that not without good reason. If we examine a good high-grade commercial fertilizer, analyzing 5 per cent. available nitrogen, 8 per cent. phosphoric acid, and 8 per cent. potash, we will find that one ton of it contains, besides less valuable ingredients:

100 lbs.	nitrogen, estimated at 16 cents,	$16 00
160 "	phosphoric acid, at 6 cents,	9 60
160 "	potash, at 5 cents,	8 00
	Total,	$33 60

Such a fertilizer probably retails at $35 to $40 per ton, and is fully worth it. All this large amount of plant food, and perhaps one-half more, can be drawn in a single load, while it will take ten such loads of stable manure to supply the same amount of nitrogen (and that in a far less available condition), sixteen such loads to supply the same amount of potash, and forty to supply the same amount of phosphoric acid. On an average, therefore, the substitution of the commercial fertilizer for barnyard manure will save 14-15 of the labor and expense in hauling and in application, besides all the additional trouble and labor of composting.

In a further comparison of the two manures we come to the following results: A moderately liberal application of compost requires 50 tons to the acre. This means the application of 400 lbs. of nitrogen, 500 lbs. of potash, and 200 lbs. of phosphoric acid, at a cost of $100 to $125, not taking in consideration the large expense of handling and applying it.

Men most liberal in the use of commercial fertilizers apply, and recommend to use, one ton per acre, at a cost of less than

(39)

$50, expense of handling and application included. Many after having tried a one-half ton application find fault if the results do not give as good a showing as a $150 application of compost. This is not common sense.

Soils that have been utilized for the production of garden crops for many years, and are yet filled with humus from previous applications of compost, usually contain considerable potash and phosphoric acid, which elements of plant food, in these heavy dressings of yard manure, are always applied greatly in excess of the needs of crops, and permitted to accumulate in the soil. The nitrogen alone, however, is taken up by the plants, or leached out of the soil as fast as rendered available. When we consider that nitrogen is the chief generator of stalk and leaf, and promoter of rapid and succulent growth, and that the conversion of unavailable forms of nitrogen into available nitrates (the so-called nitrification) is exceedingly slow in the early (cooler) part of spring, we have the explanation of the effectiveness of a manure application holding 400 lbs. of the most important substance of plant nutriment, and of the often comparatively meagre results obtained from a dressing of fertilizer having only one-quarter or less of that quantity of nitrogen. Bone meal, although rich in phosphoric acid, which is not superabundant in stable manure, and therefore frequently used in alternation with the former, generally with excellent results, has the same scanty supply of nitrogen as the high-grade complete fertilizers. This nitrogen in commercial fertilizers, however, is generally in a more readily available form than that in yard manure; and, all points taken in consideration, a rotation of the several manures should be adopted as it has proved far preferable to the exclusive or continued use of one or the other of them alone. The heavy tax that the demands of the crops impose upon the gardener can often be materially lightened in this way.

Some of our best gardeners go much further. They use what stable manure is made on the place, and put all the money to be expended for manures in complete commercial fertilizers, and nitrates (spoken of in next chapter). I have grown excellent vegetables of all kinds on poor soil by this system of feeding the crops; but I miss the quickening and loosening effect upon the soil which is found in an occasional ration of compost. Hence I prefer the rotation system of manuring, and if for some reason it should become necessary or unavoidable to use commercial fertilizers uninterruptedly, I would at least grow and plow under an occasional green crop, such as clover, black peas or southern cow beans, peas, weeds, etc., merely for the purpose of adding decaying vegetable matter to the soil, and thus opening it to the ingress of air and moisture. Its state of concentration fits the commercial fertilizer especially for application to growing crops, or to second and succeeding crops planted between rows of vegetables still standing.

This question has still another aspect. Market gardeners obtain the bulk of their manure supply from city stables, and the demand for the article has raised its price to a figure forcing the shrewd gardener to consider whether he can afford to use the article or not. Here we have a case where supply is not influenced by demand. Nearly the same quantity of manure would be produced in cities whether it is disposed of at $2.00, or at 10 cents a load, or whether the owner were compelled to pay some one $1.00 a load to take it off the premises. The competition of buyers makes the article too high-priced for their own welfare. Use more fertilizers, and less manure from the city stables, and let the decreased demand force down the excessive prices.

Even distribution over the area to be enriched is the chief point of importance in the application of all concentrated manures. This can be attained in no easier and more perfect way than by the use of a good fertilizer drill, such as for instance is attached to the Empire grain drill. The box holds about one bag (200 lbs.) of fertilizer. Place the bags at convenient distances, scatteringly, over the area to be fertilized, fill the receptacle of the drill, and commence operations, refilling as needed. In heavy applications it may be necessary to go over the area repeatedly, and preferably in different directions, either crosswise or diagonally across the preceding application. If such a drill is not at hand, as very likely the case with the market gardener, the stuff may be sown after plowing, and a thorough harrowing be given afterwards. In sowing a ton to an acre, which is a pretty heavy application, the operator will have to make close bouts, scatter with full hand, and then probably be compelled to repeat the operation crosswise of the first sowing, in order to put on the full quantity.

For convenience in sowing by hand it is always advisable to moisten the fertilizer before it is applied. Empty a bagful on a tight barn floor, or in a tight wagon box, spread the fertilizer out in an even layer, then sprinkle water over it; next put on another layer of fertilizer, apply water as before, and finally shovel the whole mass over until it is thoroughly mixed, and uniformly damp. It can then be sowed without filling the air around the party whose hands scatter it, with the disagreeable dust.

There is no reason to fear ill results from "too much" fertilizer, provided it is evenly distributed or thoroughly mixed through the soil. Stinginess in this item is poor economy.

CHAPTER VIII.

MANURES FOR THE GARDEN.

III. NITRATES, WOOD ASHES, AND OTHER SPECIFIC FERTILIZERS.

"Cheapest is what serves its purpose best."

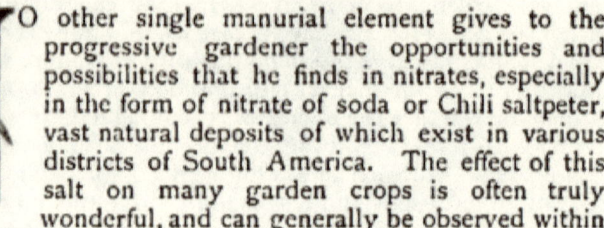NO other single manurial element gives to the progressive gardener the opportunities and possibilities that he finds in nitrates, especially in the form of nitrate of soda or Chili saltpeter, vast natural deposits of which exist in various districts of South America. The effect of this salt on many garden crops is often truly wonderful, and can generally be observed within a few days after its application in the darker foliage and remarkably thrifty growth. It is readily soluble, and its nitrogen in the exact form best suited for immediate absorption by the roots of plants.

The body of gardeners move but slowly, and adopt new things and means reluctantly. So while the merits and possibilities of nitrate of soda have often been pointed out in the columns of the agricultural press, the great public, fortunately for the progressive few, knows nothing about it, a circumstance which gives it into the hands of the shrewd manager to excel his slower competitor with ease, and to beat him in every market. The gardener who refuses to use nitrate of soda especially for his early crops, neglects to take advantage of one of his very best opportunities.

We must bear in mind that the natural process of converting unavailable nitrogenous matter into soluble nitrates is very slow in early spring; that, in order to furnish as much as early crops require at this time, we were compelled to apply the enormous quantities of stable compost with its excess of mineral elements of plant food; and that the deficiency cannot be supplied by the so-called complete concentrated fertilizers containing only 100 lbs. of nitrogen to the ton, except when applied in large quantities. In nitrates we have just the element of plant-food needed, and by applying it in small quantities about as fast as the plants can utilize it, we have it in our power to stimulate a thrifty growth of foliage at comparatively slight expense, and at a time when the product will bring the most money in market.

Nitrate of soda contains about 16 or 17 per cent. of nitrogen, but this in a most soluble form, so that it would not be safe to use it in large quantities at a time, for what is not at once converted into plant structure, will gradually sink through the soil as it would through a sieve, and be lost. The most economical and most satisfactory method is the application of not over 100 lbs. to 150 lbs. per acre repeated at intervals of about two weeks. If lumpy, it should be pounded fine before applying it. Scatter it over the ground when the foliage of plants is perfectly dry, as it is apt to scorch the leaves otherwise, or still better, apply just before or during a rain, when it will be dissolved and carried into the soil at once. Sprinkling over the land in solution is a safe but generally less convenient mode of application. It costs from $40 to $50 per ton, and can be obtained from the large fertilizer manufacturers.

Sulphate of ammonia, a by-product of gas works, contains about 20 per cent. of nitrogen; but this is in a more stable form, as it has to undergo the transformation into nitrate before being readily available. Its effect is naturally slower, but more lasting, and it can be applied in larger quantities, or in single applications, without fear of loss. It may take the place of nitrate of soda during the warmer part of the season with gratifying results, and in combination with that salt at any time, the latter for immediate effect, the former as a more gradual source of supply.

The price of sulphate of ammonia is a trifle higher than that of nitrate of soda. Undoubtedly we have in these two salts the cheapest forms of available nitrogen, and ready means to produce immediate and often astonishing results. I cannot refrain from repeating the statement, that the gardener who scorns the use of these nitrogen compounds will have a hard stand against the competition of growers who put on the market the crisp, succulent and early vegetables that can be so easily produced in all their perfection by the judicious application of nitrate of soda and sulphate of ammonia.

Hen manure might have been mentioned in the chapter on stable compost. It is especially rich in nitrogen. A ton when fresh contains more than twice, and a ton of the dry article more than four times the quantity of nitrogen contained in a ton of common stable manure. This will give an idea of its value for the garden. I always compost it with loam, muck, coal ashes, leaves, etc., apply after plowing (broadcast) and stir it into the surface soil by means of harrow, cultivator and rake. My neighbors sometimes ask me what new variety of spinach, parsley, etc., I have in my family garden, and request me to procure some seed of it for them. Yet the " new " and wonderfully thrifty vegetable most likely is none other than one of the standard sorts they have in their own garden, the only difference being that my ground was manured with one ton per acre of high-grade complete fertilizer, and a good top dressing of composted hen manure, with frequent but very light applications of nitrate of soda, while my neighbors grounds were fed with extravagant quantities of stable compost. The same method of feeding crops has always enabled me to grow celery and other plants, and celery for the table also, in great perfection.

Every year's experience has added strength to my conviction that in nitrate of soda and well-preserved poultry manure we have the most valuable because most quickening and most effective fertilizing substances within our reach. The former has an especially sure and wonderful stimulating effect on spinach, beets, cabbage, cauliflower, and more or less so on other crops, while poultry manure seems to benefit almost all vegetation more uniformly, but always to a remarkable degree. Let no gardener despise these two manures, or neglect to take advantage of every opportunity to procure them whenever they are procurable at a reasonable price.

The exact amount which the gardener can afford to pay for them depends on their quality and state of preservation. Fresh hen manure, reasonably dry and from well-fed hens, contains in each ton about

32 lbs. nitrogen, estimated at 16 cents,		$5 12
30 " phosphoric acid at 6 cents,		1 80
16 " potash at 5 cents,		80
Total value,		$7 72

This is the value of the clear droppings. Usually there are foreign additions, such as dry soil, muck, sifted coal ashes, or other materials used as absorbents, which always justify a lowering of the valuation. If wet and leached, such manure may not be worth half of the figures given. We must take all circumstances in consideration when attempting to estimate the commercial value of these domestic manures. I only wish to emphasize that poultry manure is worth saving in best condition. Don't use wood ashes or lime as absorbing materials under the perches and on the henhouse floor. They drive out ammonia. Dry muck is best, and an occasional sprinkling of kainit will tend to preserve the ammonia. The kainit also adds potash, with which this kind of manure is less abundantly supplied than with nitrogen and phosphoric acid.

In cotton-seed meal we have another nitrogenous manure of special value for the market gardener, but as yet very little appreciated or used. A ton contains about 132 lbs. of nitrogen,

30 lbs. of phosphoric acid, and 20 lbs. of potash, and is worth fully $20.00 as manure. When mixed and composted with stable manure it increases the comparative amount of nitrogen of the latter, and therefore its effectiveness. Gardeners who keep stock should feed cotton-seed meal to the fullest extent that it is safe to do. It then gives double returns, namely, in increase of flesh, and improvement of manure. Where nitrate of soda, on account of distance from source of supply and consequent high cost, cannot be used advantageously, cotton-seed meal can often be had at a comparatively low price, and should then be used in place of the nitrogen compounds.

Potash in any special form is hardly ever needed for the crops on common garden land, since stable compost and the average high-grade complete fertilizer supply an abundance, and often an excess of it, to the crops already. A different thing it

Spinach Fed with Nitrates, etc., and as Usually Grown.

is with peaty and mucky soils. These have already an abundance of the nitrogenous element, although mostly in fixed combinations, and hence in an unavailable form. On the other hand, the mineral elements are scantily supplied. Stable manure would add a comparatively large amount of nitrogen at great expense to the already vast store, and but small quantities of phosphoric acid and potash. Such lands, for that reason, can be made productive in the cheapest and quickest way by applications of phosphoric acid and potash, in the form of a plain superphosphate, or bone meal, in combination with wood ashes. The alkaline nature of the latter neutralizes injurious acids, and helps to make nitrogen available. Unleached wood ashes can be applied at the rate of 100 bushels and more per acre with perfect safety, and leached ashes in much larger quantities. As means of protecting crops against the ill effects of a prolonged drought, however, wood ashes have no mean value on any soil. I will refer to this subject in a future chapter.

The question is often referred to me: "Will it pay a renter to apply manures on land that he will or may have to vacate the next season?" This can have but one answer. It stands between the use of manure and the unsatisfactory outcome of the business. No manure—no paying crop. But in case of pending removal, it will always be safest to use the quick-acting commercial fertilizers, and nitrate of soda in preference to the slower and more lasting stable manure. The nitrate of soda is all and entirely utilized for the next crop, or leached out of the soil, and of the commercial fertilizer only an inconsiderable part will be left to increase the successor's crops, if the soil is as thoroughly cropped all through the season as it should be. Stable manure is apt to donate only a part of its plant-foods for the production of the same year's crops, and much of the expensive material would probably be left for the benefit of the renter's successor.

CHAPTER IX.

GARDEN IMPLEMENTS

AND HOW TO USE THEM.

"Only the best is good enough."

IT is not many years since the spade was considered the first requisite in the garden. Now we know that a good two-horse plow does the work of turning the soil not only much faster, and with less labor to man than spade or spading fork, but much better at the same time. Good plows are now on sale at every hardware store, and used by all intelligent farmers. In fact there are more good plows than good plowers; for simple as the operation seems to be, but few people know how to do it to best advantage. Straight lines and even furrows require much less work than crooked lines and irregular furrows. There is a knack about this natural to some people, but not easily acquired by the average "hired man," and the gardener, if he desires to have the work done well, must do it himself or

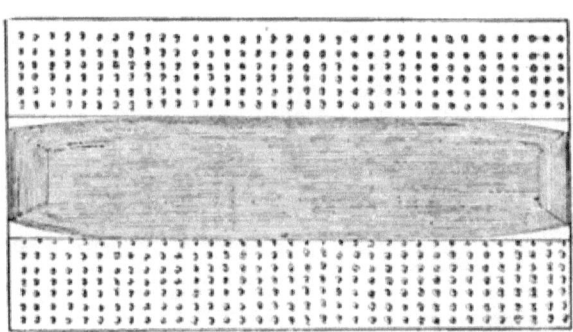

Sample of Faulty Plowing.

instruct his men how to do it. Suppose we have a strip of land to plow of shape as here shown, and situated between strips of standing crops. Even a poor plowman will find little difficulty of striking out the furrow in centre, and to go on all right for awhile; but as the plowing progresses, and the team naturally

(47)

crowds towards the plowed ground when nearing the end of long furrows on each side, the corners become rounded, and when the piece is all plowed clear to the sides, the four corners will still be left untouched, and must be finished with an immoderate amount of turning, and at last will be poorly done, or left partly unfinished. A good plowman will strike his last furrow exactly on the very edge of the piece.

The market gardener also needs a good, light one-horse plow, to plow up smaller patches for second and third crops, in cultivating and hilling-up celery, and for various other uses. Every hardware dealer keeps them.

Subsoiling is not absolutely necessary for warm loam with porous subsoil, but generally of considerable benefit for soils resting on a heavier and compact lower stratum. Such a plow following in the furrow made by the common plow, is intended to lift and break the layer next under the top soil. It is not often used in the home garden. Among modern harrows we have some most excellent tools designed and suited for special purposes. The "Cutaway" is a deep cutting implement, and in many cases can almost take the place of the plow, but it is hardly necessary for the market gardener. The "Disk" is another good farmer's harrow, and doing thorough work, especially on freshly-turned, tough sod; but an "Acme" will answer as well as any other for breaking up and fining the mellow lands in the garden. In an emergency almost any of the older-style, plain steel-tooth harrows may be used. The "Thomas' Smoothing" harrow, however, is so useful and effective in finishing off a piece of land for sowing seeds, in killing weeds in corn and potato fields early in the season, that neither farmer nor gardener can well afford to do without it. The diligent use of this implement will bring the soil in fine tilth, and often leave it in moderately good shape for sowing or planting, but it will always be advisable to apply the finishing touch with a Meeker Disk harrow, which does as good work as a steel-rake, and much faster and more conveniently. We also need a good spade; a spading fork; sharp, light hoes; dibbers, etc. The latter are simply pieces of hardwood, with an iron

Cutaway Harrow.

Acme Harrow.

Garden Implements—49

point and a convenient handle. The new style of dibber, here illustrated, consisting of a flat steel blade with handle, is a great improvement on the old tool, and I hope will soon be put on sale generally. The home gardener, who generally sows seeds by hand, needs a marker, which may be a cheap, home-made affair, constructed from a piece of scantling 4 by 4, with three or four sharpened strips of inch board securely nailed on in front, or mortised in, so that the pointed ends are 15 or 16 inches apart. Two poles are adjusted for handles. The marker may be made reversible, with another set of teeth, but only 12 inches apart, pointing in the opposite direction. The market gardener will also need a tool of this kind for marking the rows where he wishes to plant onion sets, or to set lettuce plants, etc. The distance between the teeth must be regulated according to his purpose. A marker of this kind is here illustrated. It has the disadvantage, however, of compelling the operator to walk backwards, or at least sideways. If you want long rows as straight as is always desirable for neat work, it would be better to adjust a set of handles in the rear, by which one person can steer the implement while another draws it along horse-fashion. This style of marker opens the furrows just about deep enough for sowing in them onion, beet, carrot, radish, lettuce, spinach and other ordinary garden seeds by hand.

Old-style Dibbers.

New-style Dibber.

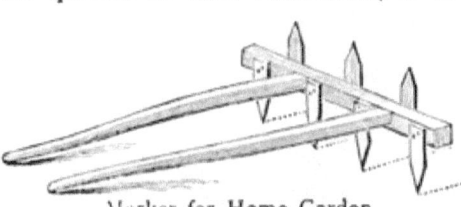

Marker for Home Garden.

To mark out rows for plant setting, especially as required in the new onion culture (described under "Onion" in Chapter XXVIII.), we prefer a tool that will indicate the rows by light marks, not by deep furrows, and can be pushed ahead, enabling one person to make as straight rows as can only be made by two with the first-described garden marker.

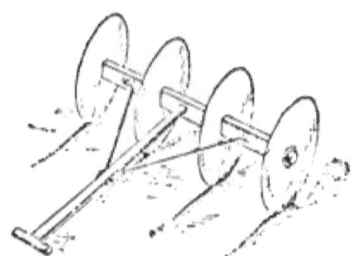

Wheel Marker.

Some time ago I devised the marker last shown on the preceding page. If well made, it does good work. Take one-inch boards, cut to a circle and slightly bevel the edges. The wheels revolve on an iron rod, and are held at the desired distance by pieces of 4 x 4-inch scantling, through the centre of each, lengthwise, is bored a hole of corresponding size. A handle fastened to the centrepiece and braced by iron rods completes the tool.

Cut and description of another marker, which I find very convenient and serviceable for the same purpose, are taken from my "The New Onion Culture" (third edition). "It is an ordinary wooden garden roller, such as any one can make out of a piece of chestnut or oak log three or four feet long, with iron pins driven in centre on each side, and a simple handle attached by means of two pieces of old wagon tire.

A Roller and Marker.

"Bore holes into the face of the roller, one foot apart (three holes for a three-foot roller, or four for one four feet long), and put in pins. To use this tool as a marker, make each of these pins hold a small rope encircling the roller, by driving the pins into the holes beside the ends of the rope. More than one row of holes can be used to change distances if required for other vegetables. Strips may be tacked lengthwise of the roller to mark places in row for setting plants."

Of the many other devices for furrowing and marking garden land I will only mention the one which I am now using almost to the exclusion of all others, and which is a contrivance as simple and convenient as we can ever hope to make it. It is simply an attachment to the Planet Jr. drill or wheel-hoe. The illustration shows the combined drill and wheel-hoe rigged as a furrower. If wanted as a marker for plant setting, we turn the narrow hoes backward. The crosspiece, to which the outside hoes (marker teeth) are attached, may be made of iron or of hardwood, and is bolted to the plate as shown.

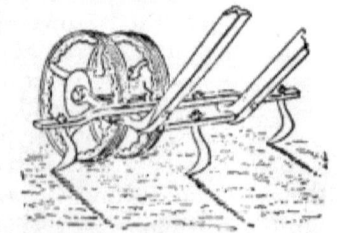

Planet Jr. Combined Drill and Wheel-Hoe as Marker.

This description may possibly induce the Planet Jr. manufacturers to offer these crossbars as an attachment to their hand drills and wheel-hoes.

Indispensable in the market garden, and still more so in the farm garden, and convenient to have even in the home garden,

Garden Implements.—51

is a good seed drill. There are a number of good and serviceable ones now in the trade. The Planet Jr. garden drill shown in illustration on next page, affords a safe, easy, and perfect method of sowing smaller seeds over large or small areas. The intelligent farmer who has learned to appreciate the mangels, and carrots and other root crops as winter food for cattle, sheep, hogs and horses, and makes it a practice to plant largely of them every year, is not unacquainted with the merits of the garden drills, and often would not consider his assortment of implements complete without a good garden seed sower.

I am not greatly in favor of combined tools, but if the home grower is bound to have a seed sower and wheel-hoe combined, the Planet Jr. combined drill, wheel-hoe and cultivator will give him what he wants. Among separate garden seed sowing devices besides the one already named, we have Matthews' market gardener drill, the Model drill and others.

A later addition to our seed sowing devices is the Planet Jr. hill dropping seed drill. It places the

Planet Jr. Hill Dropping Seed Drill.

hills as desired, 4, 6, 8 or 12 inches apart, but can be changed to a drill sower, and the reverse, in a moment. It has a complete marker, does not sow when going backward and can be thrown entirely out of gear in a moment.

There is also an extra attachment for sowing onion seed for sets in a band four inches wide.

Still another tool is the Planet Jr. hill dropping and fertilizer drill, which, as a drill, does exactly the same work as the hill dropping drill, and in addition gives us a chance to sow fertilizers in the drill, either under or above the seed. The fertilizer hopper holds one peck. This tool may be used to sow either seed or fertilizer alone, and will come handy in many instances.

There are also larger fertilizer drills on the market. The possession of one of them will be a great convenience to every gardener or farmer who makes a practice of applying concentrated fertilizers in the drills for potatoes, corn, peas, beets, etc. Some of these implements are also serviceable for drilling peas, corn, etc.

52—How to Make the Garden Pay.

But the tool of all tools, the modern weed-slayer, the great labor-saver, the greatest horticultural blessing of the age—that is the modern wheel-hoe. This above all others frees the gardener from undesirable work, cuts down the labor account one-half, and makes tillage, both in the home and market garden, light and pleasant. It is quite a number of years ago when it was first introduced, but fortunately for the progressive gardener for money, the slow moving majority has not yet recognized its value. The advantages connected with the possession of one of these tools cannot be over-stated, nor emphasized too strongly,

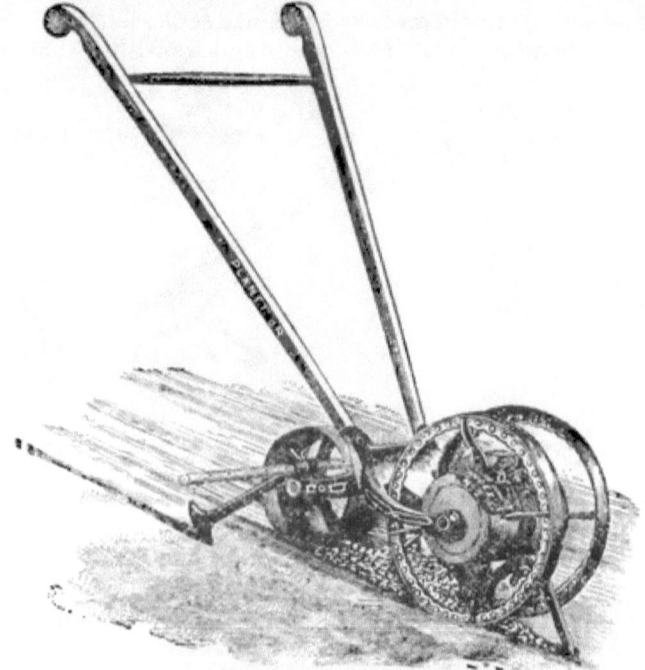

Planet Jr. Garden Drill.

nor told too frequently. Without the wheel-hoe's help the gardener of to-day cannot hope to hold out against his progressive competitors. It is the tool that more than anything else has cheapened the cost of production in garden stuff. The most perfect implement of this kind, at present, is the "Planet Jr. Double Wheel-Hoe," illustrated in next Fig., a cultivator, rake and plow combined, in fact an all purpose tool of tillage, and good to whatever use you put it. It can be made to hoe both sides of one row, or between rows, in level culture and in throwing the soil either to or from the row. This tool banishes the old hand hoe from the garden to a certain extent, and reduces

Garden Implements—53

the unpleasant task of weeding to a minimum. Let no gardener suppose that he can safely get along without a wheel-hoe. In the home garden this implement makes a pleasure of what

Planet Jr. Double Wheel Hoe.

otherwise is a job dreaded by all. Now the half-grown boy runs the wheel-hoe up and down the rows of vegetables " for fun " and recreation, and accomplishes in one-half hour what a man with a hand hoe could not perform in a whole day. As a separate attachment to this we have the Onion Set Harvester, illustrated on next page. As its name indicates it is used in harvesting onion sets, also in cutting spinach for market. Similar cheaper tools have also been put on the market, such as the Planet Jr. Single Wheel-Hoe, Gem of the Garden Cultivator, Gregory's Finger Weeder, and others. They all answer their purpose very well, but the Planet Jr. Double Wheel-Hoe stands at the head, and I advise you to use no other. People who garden

Planet Jr. Cultivating with Rakes.

on a modest scale are often tempted to purchase a combination tool—drill and cultivator combined, such as Planet Jr. Combined Drill and Wheel-Hoe, seen at work hoeing both sides of the row below, and as a cultivator on next page. Such a combination has serious objections, however. Its double purpose necessarily makes it complicated, and less effective in either capacity, and whenever you use it you are wearing out two implements at the same time. If you think you can afford but one tool, by all means sow seeds by hand, and buy a separate double wheel-hoe. The home gardener may manage to get along without a garden drill; the market gardener will find it decidedly inconvenient, and very likely unprofitable to attempt it.

Hoeing Between Rows.

A GOOD HORSE HOE can now be purchased at any hardware store. For cultivation between the rows of cabbages, beans, corn, tomatoes, vines of all kinds, etc., we want a tool with five or more narrow (1¼-inch) blades or hoes which will leave the soil level and as smooth as a harrow. There are various styles of cultivator harrow which do excellent work. When I take everything in consideration, however, I prefer the Planet Jr. horse-hoe to all others. It is a "general purpose" tool on our grounds. We attach the five 1¼-inch blades, and use it for hoeing purposes, or the furrower and marker, for marking corn and potato fields, or the side hoes and rear plow, for hilling, etc. The Planet Jr., always unsurpassed as a tool for general tillage purposes, is always the leader in improvements. As now made, it has a patent lever expanding frame which can be closed to five inches, or opened to twenty-four;

Onion Set Harvester

Combined Drill and Wheel-Hoe.

a side adjustment for the handles by which they may be set from one side to another; a lever wheel by which it may be changed to any depth in an instant, and such a variety of adjustable teeth that we are enabled to do just the kind of one-horse cultivation most desirable.

Ordinarily we use the set of 1¼-inch blades, as they do the best work in stirring the soil. For many reasons an even surface of the soil is most desirable, and we want no ridges and furrows. Hilling is required only in rare cases, such as the last cultivation of potatoes, or in the celery field; and the hilling blades can then be substituted for the two narrow outside blades.

People who grow corn, potatoes, beans, peas, and similar crops on a more extensive scale, will find a great help in the Breed weeder, especially on loose and mellow soils. It is less

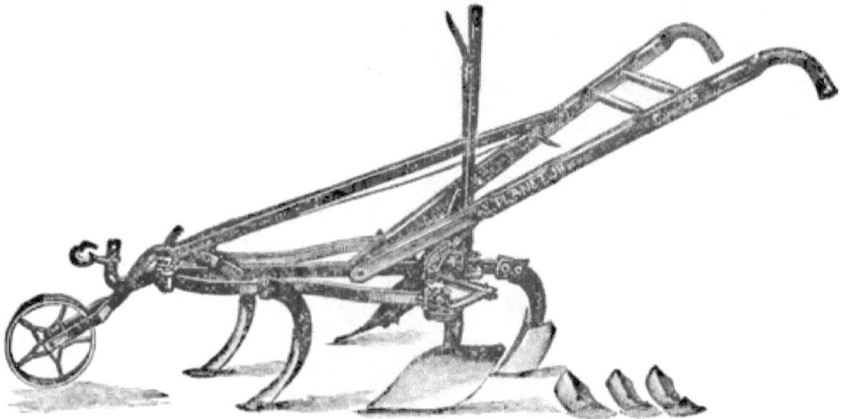

Planet Jr. Horse-Hoe.

suited to clay soils which are liable to bake after a heavy rain. The implement is a scarifier, and built somewhat on the principle of a modern hayrake. Its timely use prevents weed growth both in and between the rows, while the deeper rooted cultivated plants slip through the wire teeth unharmed.

If I further emphasize the necessity of having the hand-hoes bright, clean, and sharp, and hung in the proper angle to a light, smooth handle; of keeping the steel and cutting parts of all implements bright, and well oiled when not in use, and all tools in their places under cover, little else remains to be added on the subject of tools of tillage. Implements for special use, such as asparagus bunchers, spinach cutters, hand-weeders, etc., will be mentioned elsewhere. It is hardly necessary to speak of wagons, etc., as their selection depends on local fashions, and special purposes. A good manure-spreader may be a convenient implement; but I question whether it can be considered indispensable in even a large market garden. With the use of many implements of tillage, such as the various styles of hoes, spades, shovels, forks, etc., the question of "best" is often dependent on the habit of the user. Some people after having once acquired the "knack" of handling a certain tool to advantage will do much better work with it than with a superior or more modern one. The employer must humor the whims of the hired help in such cases, and give them just the tool that they have learned to use with skill and to best advantage.

The improvement of gardening implements, both large and small, is still going on at a rapid rate. The leader of to-day may be crowded into second or third rank to-morrow. This keeps the progressive gardener on the alert all the time to enable him to profit by any new device that may be of unusual merit, and to keep ahead of his competitors. On the other hand I can hardly advise the gardener of moderate means to invest in every new implement as soon as put on the market under high claims. Progressiveness in this respect may well and profitably be tempered with quite a considerable amount of conservatism.

CHAPTER X.

COLD FRAMES.

THEIR CONSTRUCTION AND USE.

"This is an art that mends nature."

COLD frames are simple affairs—box-like structures covered with sashes. The latter are the chief part, and involve the real expense in the construction of such frames, but being a staple article of commerce, and manufactured with special machinery in special factories, can now be bought at (or ordered through) any supply store at moderate prices. They usually cost $2.00 each, ready glazed and painted, and perhaps can be had cheaper in large quantities. The usual size is 6 feet in length by 3 feet in width, and the frames are made to correspond, namely 6 feet wide and 3 feet in length for every sash to be accommodated.

The selection of site is important. The proper place for frames is in convenient proximity to the water supply, and also

Arrangement of Cold Frames.

in a position sheltered from the north and west, facing south or south-east. A close and tall hedge of evergreens affords a most excellent protection, but if such does not happen to be where it can be utilized for the purpose, a tight board fence, at least six feet high, must be built at the north side of the beds and extending their whole length. A building, hedge or board fence at the west is also desirable. In this comfortable situation construct your system of frames, making it as easily accessible as convenient for operation, and as snug generally as circumstances will permit. The frame is set on top of the ground, no excavation being required. The back is made of boards 12 inches wide, nailed to stakes driven in the ground at the ends and middle of each board; the front consists of boards only 8 inches wide, and fastened to stakes in the same manner, at a uniform distance of 6 feet from the first. When the necessary end pieces are adjusted we have a close fitting box, 4 inches lower in front than at the back. Such a system of frames, in process of construction, is shown on preceding page.

The number of sashes required by the market gardener depends on extent of business and area, and still more largely on the particular line of work in which he is engaged. For general market garden purposes it may take 20 to 25 sashes to each acre of ground, but when frames are extensively used for the production of vegetables, such as spinach, lettuce, carrots, beets, parsley and soup celery, or in the special line of growing plants for sale, the number of sashes required will be proportionately larger. Some gardeners devote their energies almost exclusively to cold-frame products.

In some cases it is more convenient to buy the sash frames unglassed, and put the glass in them on the premises. In this emergency, as also in the work of repairing and patching old

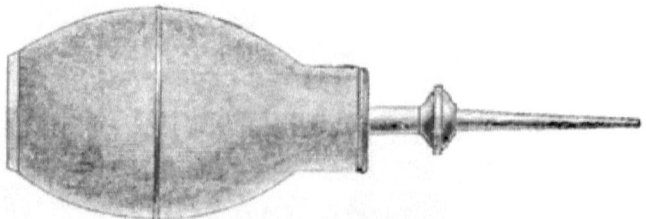

Improved Putty Bulb.

sashes, the newer method of putting on putty in liquid form, and by means of a putty bulb, can be recommended as quite convenient, and preferable to the old way. The mixture used for this is composed of one-third white lead, one-third common putty, and one-third boiled oil, all by measure not by weight. Mix oil and putty thoroughly, add the white lead, and strain. If too thick, as liable to be in cold weather, add a small quantity of benzine or turpentine. Paint the sash ; then fill the bulb with the liquid putty, run a little of it along the sash bars, then bed the glass on it, and run more of the liquid along the edges of the glass, next to the bars; allow it to harden and you have a neat and tight joint.

USE OF FRAMES.—Let us suppose that the cold frames are available in the autumn for regular work. The first use to be made of them is in wintering cabbage, cauliflower and lettuce plants for the extra early crops. Some gardeners sow the seed directly into the frames in rows a few inches apart and thin afterwards. A better way, undoubtedly, is to sow the seed in open ground, about 15th of September, and transplant four weeks later to the frames. It is of greatest importance that each plant should have its just allowance of space. Cabbage and cauliflower plants should have 5 or 6 square inches each (plant in rows 3 inches apart and 2 inches apart in the row), and lettuce plants somewhat closer (1½ inches apart in the rows). The general tendency with gardeners is to plant too thickly—and this is a prolific cause of failure, or of poor plants. A good practice, also, is to make two sowings in open ground, about September 15th and 20th, to be sure of plants. If the first sown get too large, the others will be just right. Cabbage, cauliflower and lettuce plants are quite hardy, and can endure considerable cold weather without injury. The sashes must be put on by the time winter sets in, and the chief point of importance afterwards is unceasing and untiring attention to proper ventilation. We should bear in mind that the object is not, to grow plants during the winter, but to keep them on a perfect stand-still (dormant), and make them so hardy that they will at once start into lively growth when planted out in spring, even in rather cool weather, and be able to endure late severe freezes without check. For this reason a moderately low, not a warm temperature is required in the frames, and also a considerable amount of exposure. On cold but clear winter days, and when the temperature is not lower than within a few degrees of zero, the sashes should be partly raised, by tilting at back or front, or by partial removal, or in any other convenient way. This requires considerable attention and good judgment. During moderate weather the sashes had best be removed entirely. Constant watchfulness, and doing the right thing at the right time, will insure good plants. Only in a climate with severe winters are shutters or mats required for additional protection. What they are, and how made, is told in next chapter. Deep snow should not be left very many days upon the sashes, unless the ground in the beds was frozen at the time of its fall. Early removal is the safer treatment.

With all the progress that we have made of late in horticultural art, and in spite of all the efforts put forth by good writers and publishers in behalf of the distribution of horticultural knowledge, it is a fact that the production of good plants is the exception, and that failure, wholly or in part, is the rule. Hence we often find the liveliest demand for well-grown wintered plants at paying figures, $4.00 to $5.00 per 1,000, being the usual price, which gives an average of $2.00 to $2.50 for the plants covered by one sash.

One of the most successful gardeners says: "I would prefer such wintered plants at $10 per thousand to spring (hot-bed) grown plants as a gift—not to speak of the worthless plants that are shipped every spring by the hundred thousand from the South, and palmed off on the public as cold-frame-wintered plants." If, on account of failure or neglect, the frames are not provided with plants, and these are needed for early use, the next best method of growing them is the following: pack a layer of fermenting horse manure all around the cold frames, and sow the seed in them in February; or still better, use hot-beds as directed under proper heading.

Another, and a very important use of the cold frames is for the production of spinach, radishes, parsley, soup celery, carrots, beets, etc., for early market. Spinach may be sown in the autumn, and marketed during the winter, or as soon as the crop is large enough, and prices acceptable. The frames can then be replanted with the same or some other crop. Vegetables thus grown in cold frames often find ready sale and remunerative prices in April or May. The extent to which the gardener can engage in this work depends on local conditions, and these must be consulted. Make the soil in the frames very rich by mixing it freely with good compost. Watering the beds with weak solutions of nitrate of soda generally has marked results in producing quick growth, heavy development of foliage and excellent quality, especially crispness and tenderness. Always sow the seeds in rows across the beds. Early "marketableness" and the greatly desired uniformity can only be secured by attention to proper thinning, and this should be given just as soon as the young plants are large enough to show individual thrift and other qualities, so the most promising may be left, and the undesirable ones removed. Growing crops under glass is an expensive business on account of the glass and the attention it requires, and space is valuable. Hence, to attain satisfactory results, we must aim to cover the whole area under glass with vegetable growth, yet without undue crowding. Not a single square inch of the available area should be left unutilized, and yet not a single plant checked in its development for lack of space. This is a matter requiring considerable care and judgment, and without these failure is more certain than success.

The results of a series of careful experiments made by observing and inquisitive growers of cold frame crops right in my immediate neighborhood seem to speak in favor of the distances named in the following table, as most profitable for this special purpose, viz.:

Sow spinach in rows 8–9 inches apart, thin to 2 inches.
" beets " 7 " " " 3 "
" carrots " 6 " " " 2 "
" radishes " 4 " " " 2 "
" soup celery " 6 " "
" parsley " 6 " "

Under no circumstances would it be safe to make the rows still narrower, or leave the plants closer in the rows. If you vary from these distances, by all means make them larger. Instead of planting the radishes by themselves, however, it is generally preferable to sow one row between each two rows of any of the other vegetables. This makes the rows as close as three inches apart in some cases; but the radishes will be off in time for the other stuff to occupy the space when it is needed.

The usual time for sowing these crops is about March 1st for New Jersey, and correspondingly earlier or later further south or north; in other words, from two to four weeks sooner than the same vegetables could be sown in the open ground. This is late enough to insure safety from injury by the tail end of winter; it is also early enough to hit the time of brisk demand, and realize the best prices. The aim is to get these crops from one to four weeks ahead of the earliest out-door supply. The competition from the South is generally not very formidable, as their modes of cultivation, perhaps their soil and climate, and certainly the long shipment always lower the value of vegetables from there in the eyes of consumers and dealers. The near-by products often bring high prices when the southern supply goes a-begging.

This also is the case with head lettuce, so-called. This, like the other crops, is grown in cold frames during the latter part of winter for marketing in early spring. Many gardeners make it a practice to have a number of spare frames without sash, but covered during winter with litter to keep the ground from freezing. When the time arrives that the cabbage and lettuce plants in the regular frames can get along without glass protection, perhaps by March 1st, the spare frames are made ready, planted with lettuce plants from the wintered supply, and these set six or seven inches apart each way. They are then covered with the sashes taken from the cold frames containing wintered plants, and tended in a similar way as the plant frames by giving ventilation when needed. Aim to stimulate early and full development of the crop in every way possible. Applications of nitrate of soda, either dry or in solution, or of liquid manure hardly ever fail to pay well. If it is thought risky to leave the wintered plants, from which the sashes were removed, entirely without protection, simple home-made frames covered with common muslin (or with the waterproof cloth now made for the purpose), might be substituted for the glass sashes, and the plants kept thus protected during the night until danger is past.

WATERING THE BEDS.—It is not necessary to apply water at this time very frequently, except quite late in the season, and during clear weather; but when done the application should be thorough—no mere sprinkling will do. The most convenient method is by means of force pump or pressure, and rubber hose. Later the rains of heaven should be called into service whenever they happen to occur at an opportune period. The careful manager, by speedy and entire removal of the sashes from the beds, can often save much labor otherwise required for watering the crops by artificial means.

In many localities, especially where the seasons are comparatively long, as in New Jersey, the cold frames after having done duty in the production of vegetables, may then be further used for growing late tomato plants, or for finishing and hardening off tomato plants raised in hot-beds. Market gardeners in districts where tomatoes are grown in field culture for the canning establishments, often have considerable call for plants up to July. It is true such plants must be sold low, often at no more than $1.50 per thousand; but as they are grown as a second or third crop, and 600 to 800 of them may be grown under each sash, this feature adds quite considerably to the profits of running cold frames.

Forcing cucumbers is another industry in which the cold frame is made to serve a good purpose. After the lettuce or crop of wintered plants is cleared off, a few cucumber seeds are planted in center of sash. When the vines are up, ventilation is given as needed, and the sashes removed entirely as soon as the season has pretty well advanced, and the vines begin to crowd the sashes. This crop, coming, as did the other, a few weeks in advance of the earliest out-door supply, generally brings remunerative prices. Melons can be grown in a similar way.

The exact dates of planting, what crops to grow, and to what extent for each—all these are questions of local bearing, depending on climate, season, demand of the market, and usual price of products. In every one of these enterprises constant thought and study, earnest consideration of these questions in all their intricacy and various aspects and bearings, and pretty good judgment, are first requisites of success. On these the whole matter hinges, much more than on rules and instructions which at best can be only of a general rather than special character.

Southern climate often permits the use of cold frames where hot-beds would be required at the north.

By taking advantage of the additional protection during the night that mats or shutters afford, tomato and even egg-plants can be grown without bottom heat. This question, however, must also be left largely to the judgment of the individual grower, who is acquainted with his local conditions.

The use of cold frames in starting lima beans, cucumbers, melons, etc., by planting on squares of inserted sod, which are to be transferred to the open ground when the season has sufficiently advanced, will be referred to at another occasion.

CHAPTER XI.

MANURE HOT-BEDS.

THEIR CONSTRUCTION AND USE.

"A little leaven leaveneth the whole lump."

IN outward appearance and arrangement hot-beds resemble the cold frames described in preceding chapter. In the cold frames no artificial heat was employed, while the hot-beds have what is called "bottom heat." The material most generally used by gardeners for producing this heat is fresh horse manure.

The proper place for the hot-beds is in same plot with the cold frames, near the water supply, and under the shelter of a hill, building, or tight, tall fence or hedge. Make an excavation a little more than six feet wide (for sash of common length), 24 inches deep, and as long as needed to accommodate the desired number of sashes, running east and west, or northeast and southwest. Set stakes half a board length apart on each side, and enclose the excavation tightly with boards clear from the bottom up, to hinder the intrusion of moles, rats and mice. The north side may be 12 or 18 inches high above the surface, the south side six inches lower, so as to give the sashes the needed slope to carry off rain and snow water, and the sun all the better chance to reach the soil, and stimulate plant life under the sashes. When the frame is in place, a strip of inch board, wide enough to serve as rest for the sash edges, and having a two inch upright in the centre, as shown in illustration, is then fastened across where each two sashes meet.

Cross-bar for hot-bed.

The preparation of the manure, although quite a simple matter, is still a mysterious subject for many gardeners, and the knowledge of the simple principles involved in this question is not general. Many growers fear the uncertainties connected with this method of heating beds. The yeast fungus, which is the cause of fermentation, if once introduced into a manure heap suitable to its growth, spreads quite rapidly, and soon has the whole mass in a state of heat. Horse manure is the best because richest or "hottest," for this purpose, and sheep manure comes next. The manure made from animals fed highly with grain, bran, oil meal, etc., is most suitable. It should contain plenty of urine-soaked litter; and the addition of half its bulk of dry forest leaves, especially after they have been used as absorbents in the stables, is always of advantage. The object in view is the production of uniform and immediate heat all through the bed, and for this reason the spores or seed of fermentation should be spread all through the manure heap, and the latter thus tempered—leavened, as it were. To do this, draw the manure to a convenient place near the hot-beds, and pile it up in a conical heap, leaving it there until fermentation has well started in. In very cold weather it may be necessary to cover the pile lightly with straw, hay, or other loose litter to prevent freezing from the outside before the heating has begun. Before fermentation becomes too lively, as indicated by escaping steam, the heap may be forked over again, and piled up as before for a few days to heat, or thrown immediately into the pit, taking pains to mix the fermenting part all through the whole mass, and to break up all lumps. If the manure is already very

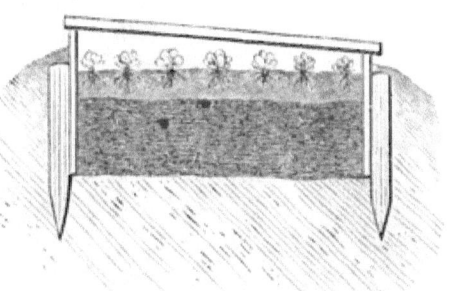

Hot-bed cross section.

hot at this time, tread it down firmly; but if fermentation has only just set in lightly, leave the manure in the pit somewhat loose, and fill up clear to the top of frames. In settling, a depression is apt to form all along the middle of the bed, and right there the manure should be packed more solid than at the sides. Now put on the sashes, and leave until fermentation has again become quite active all through the bed; then tread down solid, even off where needed, and cover with soil about six inches deep. Soil, to be in best condition for this purpose, should have been prepared the fall previous, and be kept safe from freezing until wanted. It must be rich and fine, and consist of about one-third well-rotted compost, and two-thirds good loam, rotten turf, etc.

The beds should now be left until the soil has become

warmed through, and the weed seeds near the surface have had time to germinate. Then remove the sashes, rake the surface thoroughly to kill the weeds, and make a smooth and fine seed-bed; and you are ready for planting or sowing seed. The illustration on preceding page represents a cross-section of bed.

Sometimes the manure, especially if poor, *i. e.* from poorly-fed animals, refuses to come to a heat. Then all you have to do is to make it richer by mixing it with hen manure, bone dust or by throwing hot soapsuds, rank liquid manure, etc., upon it. This treatment will generally bring it to terms. One good load of manure is about sufficient for two sashes.

The depth of the manure in hot-beds is variously given as 18, 24 and 30 inches. This is a question hinging on locality, season and plants to be grown. For general purposes in a climate like that of New Jersey or southern Pennsylvania, and late in February, or beginning of March, an 18-inch layer of fermenting manure may do; but in a severer climate, earlier in the winter, or for the production of pepper and egg plants, or other plants requiring considerable heat, the manure should be 24 to 30 inches in depth, and the pit be dug deep enough to answer these conditions. The first use in the season made of the hot-beds is in growing lettuce for early market. They are got in readiness and planted by middle of January. Plant about 6 or 7 inches square, cover the beds with straw mats or light shutters during cold nights, and give ventilation in clear, warm days. Radishes are grown in same way. Watering, if not done by means of a stream forced through rubber hose, is facilitated by means of a long-spouted watering pot or sprinkler. When the crop is taken off, the beds may be used same as cold frames.

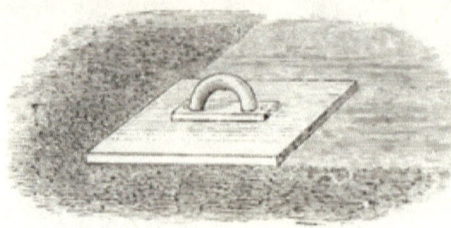

Firming Board.

STARTING EARLY PLANTS.—The chief and most important use of hot-beds is for the production of egg plants, tomato and pepper plants, also of cabbage plants for early planting when the needed supply of cold-frame-wintered plants is not at hand. For starting tomato, egg and pepper plants, the beds are generally put in readiness in February or March, and the seed sown rather thickly (best in regular rows), lightly covered with fine soil, mold or pulverized moss, and firmed by lightly patting the soil with some convenient implement, as the back of rake or hoe, or with a piece of board with handle, made especially for this purpose, of the shape shown in engraving.

In watering, a fine rose sprinkler, or a coarse spray nozzle and tepid water should be used. It is not safe to let the soil get dry, or to neglect ventilation on warm clear days. During cold nights, especially at the extreme North, the beds will need additional protection by straw mats or board shutters. The liability of the weather to suprise us with sudden changes must keep the grower always on the alert. It is never wise to withhold protection for the night because the evening is warm, or neglect the bed for the day because the morning is cloudy. Sometimes in a dark day, when ventilation does not seem to be required, the sun will suddenly break through the clouds at midday, threatening to burn the plants if the sashes are not speedily removed or raised. In short, hot-beds require constant and careful watching.

SHUTTERS AND MATS.—The shutters used for additional protection are made of half-inch stuff, and of size of sash. A stack of them piled up when not in use, is here illustrated.

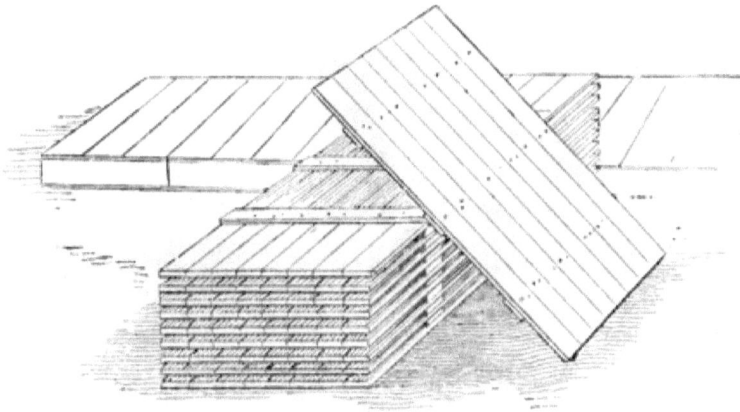

Stack of Shutters.

The straw mats can also be made by the most unskilled person from long rye straw tied with tarred string. Their manufacture is a simple thing indeed. Make a frame 7 by 4 feet, as seen in engraving, and tightly stretch four or five parallel stout tarred strings, ten to twelve inches apart, from top to bottom. Have as many balls of lighter tarred string, and fasten one end to each upright string next the bottom, leaving the balls in front of the frame. Now lay a whisk of straw, cut sides out, in the junction of the strings at the bottom, and fasten it there by twisting each of the smaller strings once around the straw and the upright string. Next put on another whisk of straw, and continue until frame is full, and the mat finished. The whole expense connected with these handy conveniences and effective means of protecting early tender plants in frames is a quantity of nice, clean, bright rye straw and some tarred string. The labor required in making them does not count for much as the work can be done in a convenient outbuilding, or under a shed during rainy days at leisure. In the course of a season a large supply of such mats may be made, and as they can be rolled up, stored and handled conveniently, and besides give the very best of protection against cold, they are greatly to be preferred to

Frame for making Straw Mats.

board shutters. Rye cut before the grain has formed makes the best material for mats, and the gardener in need of them will find it a good plan to have a piece of rye grown and cut at the period named for this very purpose.

FLATS, ETC.—When the plants are large enough—perhaps in five or six weeks—they are transplanted in other newly-made hot-beds giving space enough for their full development, or 2 to 4 inches square. This is often done (and a superior way it is) by putting an inch or so of sand or soil upon the new manure, and placing upon this foundation, close together, shallow boxes called " flats " into which the plants are set at the proper distance. If plants are to be retailed by the dozen, it is well to make the flats hold one dozen plants each, or of various sizes and containing various quantities as may be desired by the purchaser. More and more ventilation is given as the season advances, and the plants must be perfectly hardened off by exposure, transfer to open cold frames or otherwise, before they can be safely placed into the open ground. This is a matter of greater importance than most people imagine. Millions of early started and well-grown plants are annually set out, that in transplanting before they have been properly accustomed to the hardships of outdoor life, receive a check from which they do not recover soon enough to prevent much later plants, or even natural seedlings, from getting ahead of them, and producing fruit much the earliest. The proper hardening off of plants is one of the secrets of success, and perhaps a leading one, in the production of early crops of garden fruits.

SOIL FOR FLATS.—The most important item of annual expense connected with running manure hot-beds is the manure used for fuel. But, after all, this costs nothing in reality, since it loses very little fertilizing substance by the process of slow combustion in the hot-bed, and when dug out next fall, or in the spring following, is worth fully as much to the gardener as when first put in, if not more. It went into the pit—a raw and unreliable manure; it comes out—a fine, rich compost that can be used with advantage for feeding any of our garden crops, or may be compounded with sand, muck, loam, etc., thus giving us the very best soil for forcing vegetables under glass. I must warn, however, against the only too common practice of making the soil for flats, in which vegetable plants are grown, excessively rich. Over-fertile soil encourages sappy, succulent, tender growth, which is not wanted, because little able to endure the hardships of transplanting and outdoor life. We prefer a nice fibrous loam of medium fertility, such as you can procure by piling up sods from a rich old pasture, or from fence corners, for a sufficient length of time to have them well rotted and thoroughly fined. It may take a year, and repeated turning and spading over, to get these sods in the desired shape, but the fibrous loam thus obtained is, for the purposes of plant raising, well worth all the trouble it causes to get it. If additional plant foods are thought to be necessary, 10 or 15 pounds of superphosphate (dissolved bone) and a few bucketfuls of unleached wood-ashes, or a larger quantity of leached ashes, may be added to each load of compost without fear. Strong, stocky growth of plants is and must be our aim, and the sod loam will be sure to give it.

In forcing succulent vegetables for the table, such as lettuce, radishes, onions, rhubarb, etc., we want the bed soil very rich. The mixture already spoken of comes handy. Early in the summer we always make a compost heap as follows: One load of muck, one load of sand, one load of old cow or horse manure. To this is added a quantity of old sods (from pasture or fence corners), old hot-bed manure, manure from spent mushroom beds, etc. All this material is worked over at least once a month with spade, shovel, spading fork or hoe, until reasonably fine and uniform all through. In late fall it is sifted and put upon the benches of the greenhouse, or if wanted for hot-beds and cold-frames in spring, into the cellar or any place where we can get at it at the proper time.

If we neglect to make provisions for the needed supply in good season, we may find ourselves in sore straits to find just what is wanted in the winter with the ground frozen solid. It may then be necessary to look for a supply in the cellar, under barns, sheds, other outbuildings, or under the manure heap. Cart from any source at hand, mix and sift, through a coarse sieve first, and through finer ones as the stuff becomes drier and finer.

While the item of expense alone is decidedly in favor of manure hot-beds, there are, on the other hand, serious inconveniences, and sometimes obstacles connected with it. The right kind of manure is not always to be easily obtained, or not in the required quantities; the heat is only partially under the control of the gardener, and the whole thing connected with many uncertainties, especially for the less experienced manager. Then there is the annual digging, and composting, and refilling, and with all these inconveniences, your fuel will last only for a few weeks. For this reason I have always looked with somewhat of disfavor upon manure as fuel for hot-beds, and have had an open eye for a more steady and controllable heating method. In some respects I consider the fire hot-bed a great improvement on the manure hot-bed.

CHAPTER XII.

FIRE HOT-BEDS

AND THEIR CONSTRUCTION.

"Nothing is denied to well-directed labor."

THE cognizance of the weak points in the common manure hot-bed has led progressive people to try wood and coal heat in beds otherwise similarly constructed. The heat is generated in a simple furnace at the lower end of the bed, and distributed by an ordinary flue beneath the bed, running its entire length, and ending in a chimney at the opposite end. To promote the equal distribution of heat under the soil, the flue at a little distance from the furnace may be divided in two or three

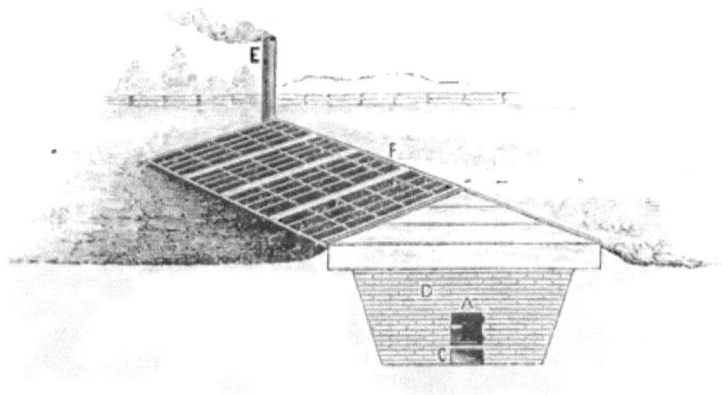

Fire Hot-Beds.

parallel branches or pipes, uniting again before they enter the chimney.

For reasons of better utilization of the heat, and convenience of management, it is preferable to make these beds intermediate between hot-bed and common greenhouse. For many years I have had such beds under my observation, and found that they

(71)

can be run very successfully and economically, and are now run so in many places for forcing lettuce, radishes, etc., followed by egg plant, tomato, pepper or sweet potato plants. A bed of this kind is shown in illustration on preceding page and consists of a double row of sashes forming a gable roof.

The proper place for the structure is near the cold frames or regular hot-beds, and running in same direction of compass. A trench, see illustration, is excavated in centre of bed, slanting from the surface of the ground where it is nearly as wide as the bed, to the bottom where it need not be over half that width. The furnace end should be on lower end of bed and from three to four feet deep. From there the flue rises gradually, say one foot to every ten in length, until it enters the chimney at the end opposite the furnace.

The fire-place may be constructed of fire-brick. Its height is about two feet, ten inches of which are the ash-pit below the grate; its width about twelve inches, and the length of grate twenty-eight or thirty inches. The bottom of the flue immediately in the rear of the furnace must be somewhat above the level of the grate, say 6 or 8 inches, to prevent ashes and cinders from getting into the flues. The first 8 or 10 feet of flue must be constructed of brick; the remainder may consist of terra-cotta as used as a substitute for brick chimneys, or even of 10-inch tile drain.

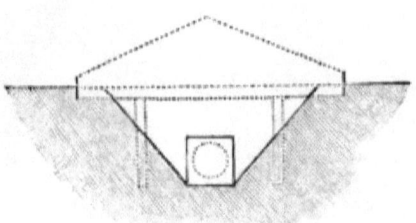

Trench for Fire Hot-Bed.

The chimney may be of brick or of terra-cotta, whatever the builder prefers. A pit immediately in front of the fire-place, to the depth of bottom of ash-pit, allows the operator to tend the fire, and when not in use, is kept covered by a slanting door. A solid frame-work, well supported underneath, holds a floor of plank or boards for the soil, and a frame for the sashes to rest upon. The most common mistake made in the erection of a fire hot-bed is right in this frame-work. Few people seem to bear in mind that this has to carry a considerable weight, and being exposed to the influence of constant dampness, is liable to decay and give out very soon, unless the timbers are strong, well-put up, and of a kind not easily affected by moisture. The whole arrangement of the bed is so simple that anybody of ordinary understanding should be able to put it up without difficulty. The gardener's common sense will dictate to him the details not mentioned. The greatest objection to a hot-bed of this kind— tendency towards dryness of atmosphere, and necessity of frequent

Fire Hot-Beds.—73

watering—may in a measure be overcome by placing shallow pans upon the flue under the floor of bed, and keeping them constantly supplied with water.

The Michigan Agricultural College has recently built a fire hot-bed which comprises some very meritorious features, and the description given by C. S. Crandall in "Popular Gardening" well deserves a place here. "Our fire hot-bed," says Mr. Crandall, "was not alone a hot-bed, but combined a small forcing house where we could work under the glass, and a tool room twelve feet square. Depth of excavation, and position of furnace is indicated in illustration. The hot-bed, six feet by sixty feet, was excavated full width, one foot deep at the chimney end and three feet at the

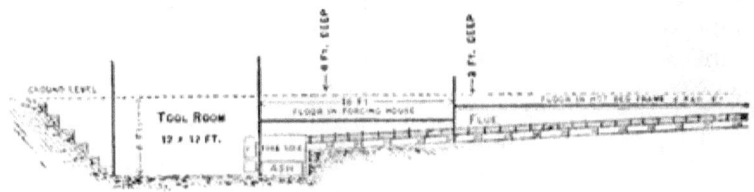

Length Section of Fire Hot-Bed.

other, and was fitted with frame same as for an ordinary bed. Then narrowing the trench to two and one-half feet, it was continued twelve feet to the furnace, where it was lowered six feet from the surface, and continued on this level for furnace bottom and tool room floor. Seen from above, the excavation would appear as in next figure.

"The dotted line indicates the outline of forcing house portion. This was 11 feet wide. The outer walls consist of pieces of two by four-inch scantling set into the ground, boarded on both sides, and the top capped with 2 by 6-inch scantling, on which the rafters and sashes rest. These walls project above ground about 18 inches, and are banked to the top on the outside with earth. Upright pieces of scantling placed against the sides of the

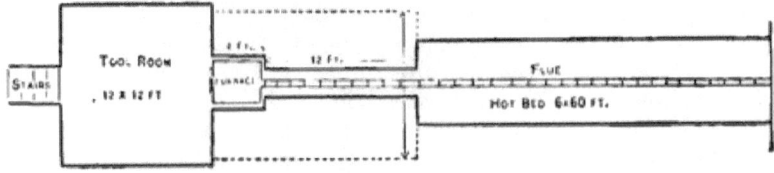

Ground Plan of Fire Hot-Bed.

trench served as supports for the rafters. Five sashes are used on each side. The adjoining tool room wall formed one end, the other was double-boarded down to the hot-bed frame, with which it was connected.

"The trench was boarded up as high as the ground level, and the bottom floored over, a few inches above the flue, thus forming a passage between the beds. The beds were covered with boards, and on these were placed our seed and plant boxes. In the hot-bed frame the floor made of inch-boards was laid level, being close down to the flue near the chimney end, and nearly two feet above it at the other end. The sides were extended above the floor 14 inches in front and 18 inches at the back, giving slope sufficient to carry the water off the sashes. At intervals of six feet, and alternating from side to side, spaces were left between the floor and the sides for the passage of warm air to the plant space above.

"On a portion of this floor earth was placed to the depth of eight inches, and some seeds sown here, but nearly all our plants were started in the forcing house in boxes, and as it became crowded, the boxes were transferred to the hot-beds, placing the tender sorts at the end nearest the furnace, but cabbage and similar plants near the chimney.

"The tool room, used also for the storage of coal, potting soil, etc., was walled with brick and covered with a shingle roof. The furnace was built of brick. A frame with doors to fire box and ash pit formed the front, and was set even with the inner face of the tool room wall, and held in place by rods built into the furnace wall. The fire box, lined with fire brick, was 30 inches long, 15 inches wide, and 18 inches high in the centre. The ash pit, 8 inches deep below the grates, had same width and length as fire box. We used a single flue of 6-inch sewer pipe running straight from furnace to chimney. This was supported on brick, four inches from bottom of trench, and the joints were made tight with fire clay and mortar.

"On starting the hot-bed we found a difficulty in the excessive radiation from the flue joints nearest the furnace. This was obviated by encasing the first twelve feet in an outer brick flue, which was allowed to open into the air chamber under the hot-bed. The dryness of heat obtained by this method of heating renders necessary the maintenance of pans of water over the furnace, and at intervals along the flue. The experience of the year proved so clearly the utility and convenience of our forcing house that we removed the hot-bed frame and converted the whole length into forcing house, excavating full width of eleven feet, and running two flues, one under each trench."

"Plants can be successfully grown in fire hot-beds, and in many cases at less expense than in manure-heated beds. For a forcing house, such as I have spoken of, the same sashes, the same furnace and flues required for a hot-bed can be used. The only difference is in the additional lumber necessary for the frame, and the extra labor of construction. So I would suggest to anyone contemplating a fire hot-bed, that they carefully calculate the cost of both hot-bed and forcing house, and then do not let a reasonable difference in cost prevent them from choosing to build the forcing house. Very many cheap houses of this character, varying somewhat in construction, according to the taste and means of the owner, are built every year. Their utility has been demonstrated, and their cost is within the means of gardeners who now depend entirely upon hot-beds."

I have given this detailed description, not to advise the reader to build exactly in the same way, but to make him acquainted with the true principles underlying the construction and management of fire hot-beds and similar structures, general rules which he will be wise to follow pretty closely while the arrangement of minor details can be left to his individual taste and preferences.

Fire hot-beds in some respects are undoubtedly a great improvement on the old-style manure hot-beds. Yet I believe there is still room for further improvement. Hot-water boiler and pipes may yet play a very important part in the make-up of the hot-bed of the future. As the old flue had to give way to hot water and steam pipes in green-house heating, so will the fire hot-bed have to make room for the hot-bed heated by hot water or steam. Flues will have to go; but it looks to me that the hot-bed of the future may be a hot house or forcing pit, and not a hot-bed at all. But whether the one or the other, now that we have cheap iron furnaces, some of them self-feeders, for hot water heating, I can see no reason why the flue beds with their dry heat should be used. Hot water gives us an easily-controlled, uniform and altogether unobjectionable heat, and can be used with perfect safety, and for any purpose of forcing and plant-growing with far less attendance than a fire hot-bed will demand. The hot-water heating system has the further advantage, that it dispenses with deep trenches under the beds and with the frame work needed for fire hot-beds, which is so liable to give out in consequence of the supports rotting away. The only excavation worthy the name is that for the boiler or furnace, while the pipes can be imbedded one foot below the surface of the hot-bed soil, or otherwise arranged in the same way as will be described for the modern forcing house.

In some instances the waste steam of factories has recently been utilized for heating hot-beds and pits. Wherever the gardener finds opportunities of this kind, he should try to make the most of them.

CHAPTER XIII.

COLD VEGETABLE HOUSES.

HOW TO BUILD AND HOW TO MANAGE THEM.

"Make the most of it."

THE management of cold frames for forcing vegetables naturally involves considerable inconvenient outdoor work during the season of raw and chilly winds, cold rains and snows; and progressive market gardeners have sought to relieve themselves of the unpleasant job, and at the same time of a part of the real hard backaching work connected with it, by the substitution of plant houses for plant beds. Such structures which afford glass protection not only to the crops but also to those who work among them, have recently come in use among Eastern market gardeners, especially within marketing distance of the large cities near the Atlantic Coast, and generally give entire satisfaction to the owner, not only with respect to the personal convenience of doing the work in them, but also from a financial standpoint. Next figure presents a full view of a house of this kind—in reality nothing more nor less than a piece of ground covered and enclosed by a simple frame-work which supports a roof of common hot-bed sashes. The sun rays and the protection that the glass affords are the sole reliance of the grower for the heat needed to produce his crops. Such houses, of course, will do very well in a climate like that of the coast section from New York city southward; but where the winters are much longer and severer, and clear days less the rule during the winter months, artificial heat will probably be indispensable.

The construction of the building is very simple. Each side of the roof consists of two tiers of common (3 by 6) hot-bed sashes, the peak being 8 feet high, making the building about 20 or 21 feet in width, and three feet for every four sashes in length. The sides are two feet high, and made of common rough boards (of double thickness with building paper between) nailed from the inside to short stakes driven into the ground at suitable intervals. Banking with earth nearly up to where the sashes begin, is a commendable practice. The end facing south or east is glass, while the opposite end is made of boards, preferably of

Cold Vegetable Houses. — 77

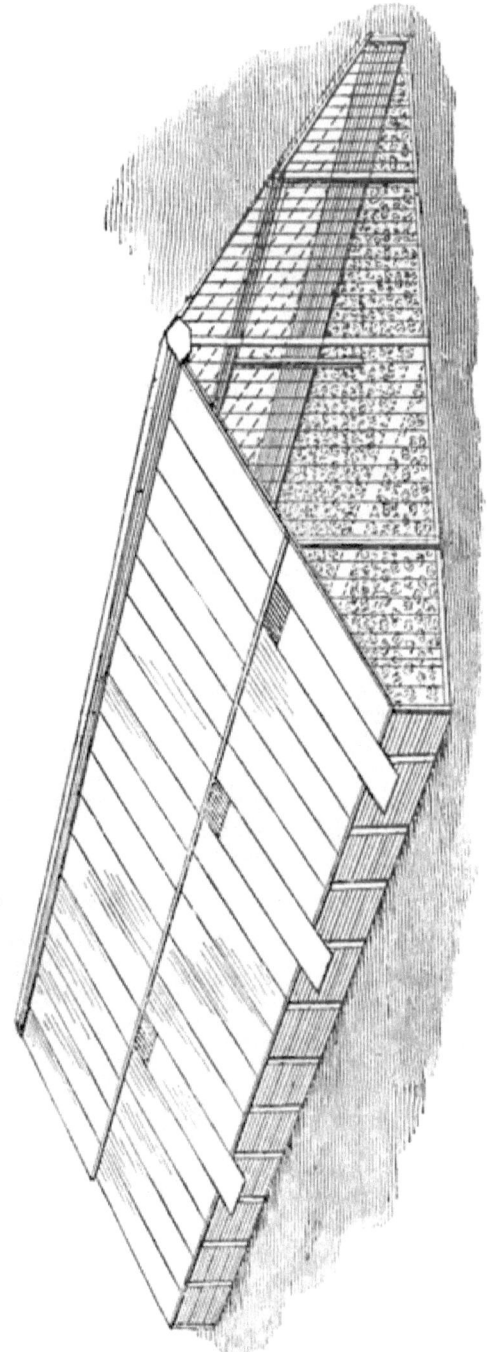

Cold Forcing House in New Jersey.

double thickness, like the sides, and with a layer of building paper between. The door is tightly fitted in this end. A row of stakes or posts capped with 2 by 3 (or 3 by 3) scantling under the

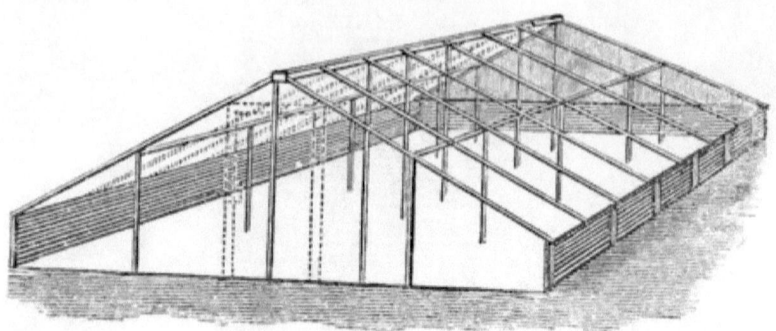

Frame of Cold Forcing House.

junction of the two tiers of sashes on each side, and a similar support for the peak, give a solid foundation for the rafters and sashes, and a cap for the peak completes the structure. The frame appears as shown in illustration. The sashes are fastened to the rafters in such a way that they can easily be taken off to be stored away at the beginning of the warm season. Every other one of the lower tiers should be arranged so that it can be slid down, to give ventilation as required, and be held in place by a simple iron button, as illustrated. I need hardly say that it is of greatest importance to have the whole structure snug and tight, for success depends mostly on the effective retention and utilization of the heat accumulated. As little as possible of it should be allowed to escape.

COST OF HOUSE.—One of my former neighbors in New Jersey has two such houses in successful operation, and he is still adding to his area under glass. They are forty sashes, or a little over 120 feet, in length each, covering at least 2,500 square feet of tillable ground. The 160 new sashes for each, ready for use, were bought for $300. The lumber and the frames and glass for the south end cost about $100, and figuring the labor of putting up at another $100 (in the present case there was no cash outlay connected with it, as the owner and his help did all the work themselves): we have an aggregate expense of $500 for each building, or $100 for each 5 square feet of tillable ground. The cold-frame

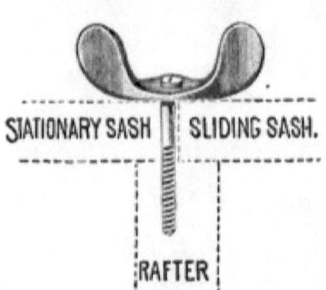

system, it is true, gives us about 7 square feet of glass-covered area for the same money, but considering the waste space (near the front side of frame for instance) and other disadvantages, the difference in cost of the working surface is hardly worth mentioning. The forcing house, on the other hand, gives us a comfortable place to work in, a chance to work to best advantage in a natural position, instead of lying over the beds on our stomachs, and to work on days when the weather would not permit keeping the beds exposed, or working outdoors without great inconvenience. Considering all the points—the chances for continuous cropping, the full utilization of all available space, the ease of management, and the convenient method of planting, sowing, weeding, etc., and the satisfaction generally which it affords—I do not hesitate to pronounce the house a model of cheapness and convenience. It may not economize the heat as well as if built lower, and in the shape of the heated forcing houses described in next chapter, yet its shape is preferable for many reasons. Comfort, convenience, avoidance of backache, etc., are worth as much to the gardener as to people in other pursuits of life. The satisfaction which the possession of such a house affords is alone worth a good deal. There are people of means who would rather have a more costly and more elaborate affair. These when intending to build a forcing house, should consult agricultural architects, and the catalogues of manufacturers of greenhouses and greenhouse supplies. I have no advice for them. The house which I have described will also be suitable for localities with longer and colder winters, but it will need artificial heating, and this can easily be provided by putting in a furnace and a system of hot-water or steam pipes. Two one-inch steam, or two-inch hot-water pipes around the sides and south end will probably give all the heat required for the purpose of forcing hardy vegetables.

GROWING THE CROPS.—The cold house being put up and ready for use by the first of November or December, the whole tillable ground is made very rich by the free application of fine compost, thoroughly spaded or forked in, with perhaps an additional top dressing of composted and thoroughly fined hen manure. If the soil is of a clayey nature, and the compost does not make it sufficiently porous, spread a few loads of sand over it, and mix the whole by spading or forking over. The gardener can afford to prepare the ground well, for his 2,500 square feet are calculated to give larger returns in cash than a hundred times that area of farming land can be expected to do. The first crop to be grown, same as in cold-frame forcing, is spinach. The rows are marked off 8 or 9 inches apart crosswise of the house, and the seed sown in the usual way, leaving a path through the centre from door (at north end) to rear. Watering should be attended to when needed, and whenever done should be thorough, so as not to require over-frequent repetition. In theory the plants are to be thinned to 2 inches apart in the rows. In practice they are usually left to grow as they come up; and with good seed, a thorougly prepared, almost perfect seed-bed, and the water supply under entire control, the gardener can sow thinly enough that the plants will not be unduly crowding each other, and yet cover the entire space—for this latter, as in cold frame management, must be the foremost aim. Stimulate the growth by all legitimate means, give ventilation when needed, and generally treat like plants in cold frames. Cut, barrel and market the stuff when the demand is brisk, and prices good.

Towards the end of February, or early in March, every spot cleared from spinach is at once prepared for the next crop, which may be lettuce and radishes. These vegetables are planted, and generally handled and marketed same as if grown in cold frames, always bearing in mind that they should stand thick enough to cover and utilize every available inch of space, yet without undue crowding. On this point hinges the measure of success. And don't forget the early thinning of the radishes to two inches apart. Boston Market lettuce is yet a general favorite for glass culture. Of radishes, the early round varieties, especially Earliest Scarlet Erfurt, Round Dark Red, Maule's Earliest Scarlet, etc., can justly be recommended for this purpose. All these, under stimulating treatment, can be put in market in between four and six weeks from the time of sowing, so that the house, wholly or in part, will be ready for another crop early in April. This next crop may be cucumbers, egg plants, tomatoes, or whatever promises to give best returns at the time of maturity. Cucumbers (Long Green or White Spine) are usually the crop selected. They are planted in hills five feet apart each way, leaving two or three plants per hill, soon cover the entire area with thrifty and generally healthy vines, and produce cucumbers a number of weeks in advance of the earliest grown in open air, hence at a time when they always bring a good price. When the vines begin to bloom, the sashes are removed, first partly during the day, then entirely both day and night, so that insects have all the chances needed to fertilize (pollenize) the fruit blossoms, and the gardener has no need of using artificial means for the transfer of the pollen to the embryo fruit.

If tomatoes or egg plants are the crop selected, the aim must be the same as with a cucumber crop, namely, to get the fruit into a willing market a few weeks sooner than competition from outdoor growers begins, thus getting the benefit of consumers' sharpened appetites and readiness to pay a remunerative price for the product. Lorillard and Ignotum, and possibly many others, are suitable for glass culture. They can be planted reasonably close—say 2 feet each way—and should be trimmed to single stalk, and trained to stakes or strings. The removal of the sashes at the proper time, as with the other crop, will give the dry atmosphere needed for "fruit setting."

PROCEEDS FROM SEASON'S WORK.—Some of my readers will desire to have some estimate of the money that can be realized from the various crops produced during one season in a building as described, and covering 2,500 square feet.

The spinach crop, if well grown, should not be less than 30 barrels. I have seen 40 barrels taken off a cold house of this size, and am sure that 50 can be grown easily enough. To be on the safe side we call it 30 barrels. Late in February, or early in March, it usually brings from $2.00 to $3.50 at wholesale in the New York City market. If it nets the grower $3.00 the crop gives him $90.00. Next comes the radish crop, consisting of at least 5,000 bunches, netting 2 cents each, or $100.00 in the aggregate. Lettuce, if grown instead of the radishes, wholly or in part, will bring approximately the same figure. The cucumber (or tomato) crop may add $75.00 more to the net proceeds, which sum up as follows, viz.:

Spinach, 30 barrels, at $3.00	$ 90 00
Radishes, 5,000 bunches, at 2 cents,	100 00
Cucumbers,	75 00
Total net proceeds,	$265 00

Deducting from this sum the amount of interest on investment, with $35.00, and legitimate wear and tear, with $30.00, or $65.00 in all, we have for our season's work in the one cold house the net amount of $200.00. In most cases the proceeds will be larger, since I have purposely put the returns low enough, and the expenses high enough, in order to be on the safe side in either direction.

I will only add that the cold forcing house as here described, is a contrivance which gives the gardener an opportunity for employment at very fair paying rates during a time of more or less enforced idleness, thus also enabling him to keep a good hired man, if he has such, permanently the year round, instead of discharging all hands at the beginning of winter, and beginning with an entirely new set of raw hands next spring.

CHAPTER XIV.

FORCING HOUSES OR PITS.

SIMPLE, SENSIBLE STRUCTURES, SUCCESSFULLY MANAGED.

COST, CONSTRUCTION, ETC.

"What you do, do with your might."

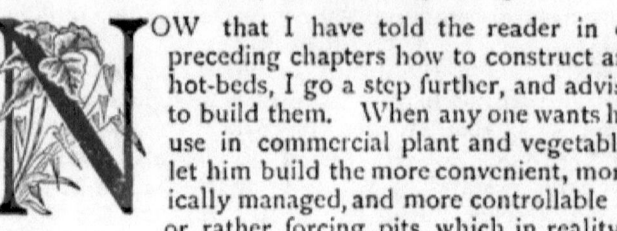

NOW that I have told the reader in one of the preceding chapters how to construct and manage hot-beds, I go a step further, and advise him not to build them. When any one wants hot-beds for use in commercial plant and vegetable growing, let him build the more convenient, more economically managed, and more controllable hot-houses or rather forcing pits, which in reality are somewhat intermediate between hot-bed and hot-house, and now in use by some of our leading market gardeners. Of elaborate, fancy, and therefore expensive structures, I shall not speak. Cheapness in construction of his buildings and in their operation must always be a leading consideration with the average market gardener, but he can combine quite a large element of convenience and comfort with it. If he values convenience sufficiently to forego for its sake slight advantages of economy, the cold house, which I have previously described as "a model of cheapness and convenience," can easily be arranged for a forcing house as already suggested. When run as a regular hot-house, for forcing lettuce, strawberries, cucumbers, tomatoes, etc., during the winter, more heat and consequently more piping or greater boiler capacity will be required than if used merely as related for the cold house, but for the purposes of propagating and plant growing, it will certainly be preferable to have the whole system of heating pipes underground, in order to warm the soil somewhat in the congenial fashion of the manure hot-bed. In growing plants for sale, we consider the root the chief part, and for root development bottom heat is essential. With lettuce and spinach, and all the other forcing crops except radishes, the grower wants top, and is not in the least concerned about the root, and in that case he will prefer to let the heat come upon his plants from above, in the natural way. It is a general principle that bottom heat favors root growth, heat from above top growth, and we must make our arrangements in accordance with the intended use of the forcing house.

(82)

Economy and absolute safety will always be the weightiest considerations with market gardeners. I think the great merits or advantages of the hot-houses or forcing pits in use, for instance, by my friend, Mr. Theo. F. Baker, of Cumberland County, N. J., and of the similar structure erected by Mr. R. Bingham, of Camden, N. J., will be readily appreciated by every reader, and give many of them a clue to the satisfactory solution of the problem: How shall I build a hot-house?

THE MODEL FORCING PIT.—A sectional view of the most sensible forcing pit yet constructed is here presented, the greatest difference in outward appearance between it and the cold-house shown on page 68, being in the arrangement of the sashes. In the cold-house, as described, the four tiers of sashes form a single roof and a single building, while the sash arrangement in

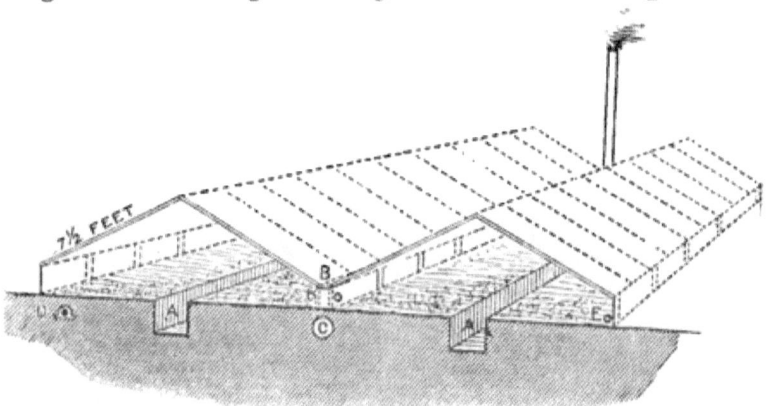

Market Gardener's Forcing Pit—Sectional View.

our forcing pit divides the house in two sections lengthwise, making, we might say, two parallel buildings of it, the roof of each being formed by two single tiers of sashes. In the former we had a pathway in the centre of house, and an opportunity to walk all over, and work upon the beds. The forcing pit, on the other hand, has two alleys or walks (AA), one under the centre of each roof, dug into the ground 18 inches wide, and 18 inches deep; and standing in these the operator, reaching over to each side, in same way as in any green-house, manipulates the beds and plants. The sides of the alleys are either walled or boarded up. The beds or "benches," as in the cold-house, are even with the surface of the ground, but the glass is pretty close to them, as the peak of the roofs is only 4½ feet above the level of the ground, and consequently 6 feet from the bottom of the alleys. The sashes should be 7 or 7½ feet long, and of any convenient width, although the common size of hot-bed sash (3 by 6) might be made to answer. Large-sized glass is preferable, say 12 by 16 inches. The sides, consisting of boards nailed to stakes, double if possible and banked up, are only one foot from level of ground to eaves. The width of the whole double structure is 26 feet. In the centre, at B, where the two roof sections meet, the sashes rest on a plate or plank 2 inches thick and 12 inches wide, gathered out ¾ by 8 inches to catch and carry off the water, and these centre planks, as shown in engraving, rest upon

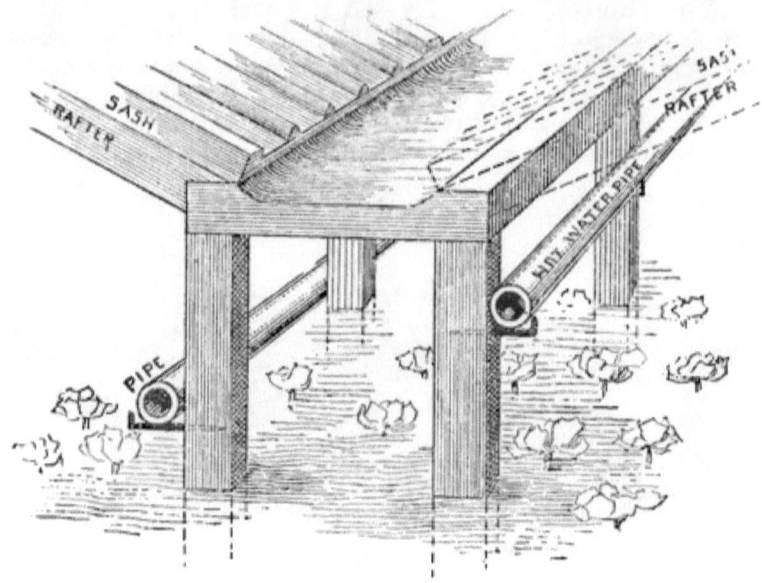

Centre Plank and Support.

two rows of 2 by 3 inch posts, 2½ feet long and 12 inches above the beds. These posts in each row are 4 feet apart.

METHODS OF HEATING THE PIT.—The old method of heating by means of a brick (or similar) flue has a slight saving in the expense of construction in its favor, but it requires a much greater running expense, especially in the items of fuel and attendance. Hot-water and steam heating give us superior advantages for the one single drawback of greater cost of construction, to such an extent, indeed, that the gardener who lays the least claim to progressiveness, has only his choice between the hot-water and the steam system. While the battle between the advocates of hot water and those of steam is still raging, I can state it as a fact, that either method may be made use of with perfect success. Florists and gardeners who work on a very extensive scale, and can afford to employ a night watchman, generally favor the steam system, and claim that it not only saves fuel, but also gives the operator better control of the heat, since there is but very little of it stored up in the circulation; but nearly everybody admits that hot water is preferable for small houses, especially on account of safety, the pipes distributing heat just as long as the water in the boiler is hot, whether actually boiling or not.

My own preference is for hot water; but the use of a large boiler with low pressure will render steam heating also perfectly safe and probably satisfactory; only be sure to have the boiler low enough, the chimney high enough, and the pipes at such gradual inclination from the boiler upwards, that the condensed water will freely return to the boiler and not accumulate in any part of the pipes. If the latter is the case, the trouble makes itself known by what is generally termed "hammering," which is a sound repeated at regular intervals somewhat like that made by striking a hard article against the pipe. The use of steam also involves a smaller outlay than that of hot water, since one-inch pipes will do, and are often preferred for the one system, while two-inch pipes are usually considered the smallest suitable for the other.

The boilers used for steam heating are generally bought second-hand, of four or five-horse power, such as have faithfully served for high pressure, and are condemned for that purpose. Hot-water and steam furnaces and boilers of any desired size, from the simple self-feeding, base-burning water heater, to that for heating buildings covering many thousands of square feet, may be bought at reasonable figures from manufacturing firms who make a specialty of them, as Hitchings & Co., of New York City, and others.

MR. BAKER'S METHOD OF HEATING.—Mr. Baker's forcing pit is constructed on the plan given on page 83, 26 feet wide by 100 feet in length. The boiler is a second-hand four or five-horse power, and at an outside temperature of zero has to carry about 5 pounds of steam in order to maintain a temperature of 65 to 70 degrees inside. Two-inch pipes conduct the heat from the boiler, one line of pipe running up on each side of the house, and both returning through the centre back to the boiler. The furnace room is an excavation 10 feet by 12 feet, and 6 feet deep at the north or northwest end of the house, walled up or cemented, and covered with a roof. Length of pipe required is 450 feet. The entire cost of a structure of these dimensions, boiler and pipes included, amounts to $450 for the material, to which the cost of steam-fitting by a plumber will have to be added. Any man of ordinary intelligence can do all the rest of the work on the house.

86—How to Make the Garden Pay.

For the purpose of vegetable forcing, the pipes are laid all above ground, as shown at *E* and *B* page 83. If wanted for starting seedlings, and for general propagating purposes, however, the pipe had better be placed from 10 to 12 inches under the surface, encased in an ordinary 3-inch drain tile, as shown at *D*, or perhaps still better in the manner employed in Mr. Bingham's house, and shown on this page. Mr. Baker tells me that he has been most successful in growing lettuce, radishes and such vegetables by running the pipes above the benches, fastened to the outside posts, and in the centre the same way, thus heating the air and letting it warm up the soil in Nature's own way, rather than drive out the moisture by bottom heat, which he thinks is the chief cause of "damping off" and of mildew.

Mr. Bingham's Method of Heating.—The house here shown is constructed exactly like the one shown and described on page 83, but 124 feet in length. The paths or alleys *A A* are

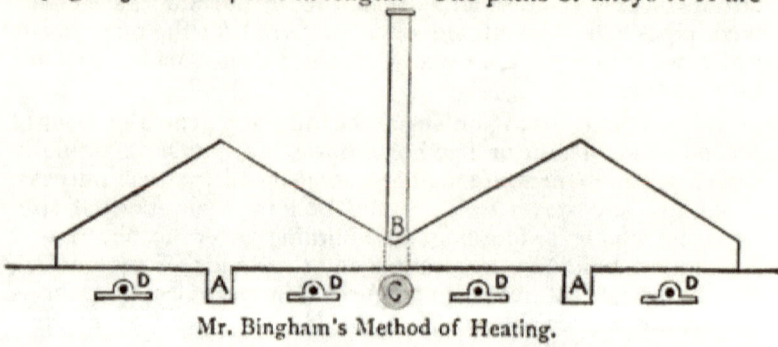

Mr. Bingham's Method of Heating.

somewhat narrower so that the outside benches are 5 feet 8 inches in width. The boiler is second-handed, with upright flues and 19-inch grate, rated four-horse power. The direct heat from the furnace is perfectly utilized by means of an under ground terra-cotta flue *C*, 10 inch diameter, which runs from the boiler room to the smoke stack *B* at the north end. The steam pipes are placed from 18 inches to 6 inches under the centre of each bench, as shown in *D D D D*, resting on a concrete and covered with a 5-inch horse-shoe tile. The concrete is made of one part Portland cement and 5 parts gravel, laid two feet wide and two inches in thickness. Two lines of 1- or 1¼-inch pipe under each bench would be an improvement, but the heat radiation is good, and the surface of the benches warmed pretty uniformly, certainly much more so than by Mr. Baker's plan of simply encasing the 2-inch pipe with a 3-inch tile. With the hot-water system the distance of underground pipes from the surface should be more uniform, but a double line of pipes in this case is still more desirable.

While theory and the opinion of expert growers give preference to heating from above ground for forcing purposes, Mr. Bingham has, practically, most excellent success with the underground system. "The ground is thoroughly warmed several inches deep," says Mr. B., "and retains the heat much better than the air, which comes in contact with the cold glass. By keeping our source of heat lower, we get a much larger per cent. of its value than by air-heating systems. Theoretically we claim to save 50 per cent. of heat which is wasted by other plans, and our trial has practically proved it." This is a matter yet open for investigation; but in the meantime it will be advisable to place the pipes in the cheaper, handier and entirely safe way in use in Mr. Baker's forcing houses, when the house is intended chiefly or wholly for forcing vegetables. There is no objection, however, to introducing the underground system for one of the benches, as shown at *D*, page 83, mainly for plant growing and propagating purposes, as also to try forcing for the comparison of results between the two systems.

Provision has to be made for ventilation. The simplest method consists in hinging every alternate outside sash, so that it can be lifted, or in arranging it as explained for the cold plant house, allowing every alternate outside sash to slide down or be removed entirely. Mr. Bingham's house is also constructed in such a way that the caps, rafters and sashes can be entirely taken off during the warm season, and stored in a convenient place under shelter. At the approach of another forcing season, the benches can thus be enriched and otherwise prepared for cropping as easily and conveniently as beds in the open ground.

I do not think that a simpler, cheaper, and safer forcing house could be conceived than one built on the same general principles here described. It combines the best features of the hot-bed and the greenhouse, and will tend to elevate the undertaking of growing vegetables and plants during the winter and early spring from drudgery to be dreaded to a pastime and pleasure. The cost of heating a house of this kind is inconsiderable—a few tons of coal go a great ways, and the management of the furnace is so simple that any boy can tend it. The vegetable crops are grown in the same way as described for the hot-beds. Lettuce is the first crop, and can be gotten ready for market from Christmas on. This is followed by radishes, or any other vegetable which the market may usually call for, or by strawberries, and perhaps later on, by egg-plants, tomatoes, peppers, etc. Boston Market, a strain of Tennis Ball, is yet considered the safest lettuce variety for early winter forcing. Mildew and aphis (or green louse) are the two dreaded enemies of the crop, and must be fought with the means named in the chapter on "Insects and Plant Diseases."

88—How to Make the Garden Pay.

DRAINAGE FOR BOILER PIT.—Sunken houses, like Baker's and Bingham's, are out of the question where an outlet for drainage water cannot be secured at least six or eight feet below the ground surface. The boiler pit has to be dug deep enough for the top of boiler to be below the point where the flow pipe enters the greenhouse. On porous subsoil nothing need be feared, but if the soil does not allow the speedy absorption of surface water, either some sort of artificial drainage, below bottom of furnace or boiler pit, has to be provided, or the house must be elevated, and the walks put on top or above the ground rather than sunk into it.

BEGINNER'S GREENHOUSE.—The little greenhouse here illustrated in perspective was intended solely for amateur purposes, and in this respect I consider it nearly perfect. But I find it fully large enough for a modest start in market gardening, and if a somewhat larger house should be preferred, a few feet might easily be added to its length, at little additional cost. It stands

Small Double-Span Greenhouse.

on the ground level, with furnace pit dug about four feet deep and good chances of drainage just below this. The building is heated by means of one of Hitchings & Co.'s base-burning water heaters (No. 22), and four lines of two-inch gas pipe, requiring a moderate amount of coal, and but little attention. The whole building, heating apparatus and all, was put up at a cost of about $250, and a little of my own work and supervision. Each span is ten feet wide and sixteen feet long. The woodwork, posts and boards excepted, consists of southern cypress, and was purchased, ready for putting together, from one of the firms advertising such lumber in the columns of horticultural journals. The structure is attached to permanent posts reaching below the frost line. The sides are double-board walls, with sawdust packing. The three thicknesses of board, two thicknesses of building paper, and a four-inch layer of dry sawdust allow very little waste of heat. The walls are as high as the benches, and the side posts extend eighteen inches above the plates or wall caps, and support the side gutters. This eighteen-inch space, all along the sides of the building, is closed in by means of hinged sashes. The gable ends, except the one at the northeast and which joins the furnace room, and is simply boarded up, have vertical bars (1⅜ by 1¾ inches) resting on the gable plates and extending to the end rafter. In one of the gables, facing the dwelling house, is the large door with sash top. The middle gutter is supported by posts inside the house, and all three gutters have a slight deviation from the horizontal line in order to give rain and snow water a better chance to run off.

If desired, a house of this kind might be roofed with hot-bed sashes. I have used permanent sash bars, placing them fourteen inches apart, and the regular greenhouse glass of double thickness. The latter, both on the roof and at the gables, is "butted," that is, simply placed together edge to edge, not lapped. Care is taken to select panes that fit well together. When the glass is once carefully laid, you have a roof that is as

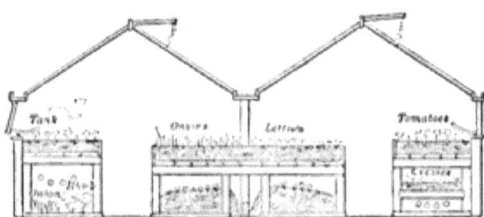

Cross-Section of Greenhouse.

perfect as any glass roof can be made. The glass lies smoothly and evenly on the projection of the sash bar, and is held down firmly by the cap. We use a little soft putty in which to bed the glass, but none on top of the glass. Everything, of course, is made snug and tight. The top ventilators, of which there are four (each 14 by 16 inches) and the hinged side sashes should also be well and closely fitted in, so that there will be no leaks of heat during cold nights. All the ventilators are worked by iron lifting rods of simple construction.

The heater stands in a pit north of the east span, the chimney is close to the heater and extends somewhat beyond the ridges of the house. We must be sure to have good draught and security from catching fire. One end of pit is partitioned off for a coal-bin. The location and arrangement of benches and pipes may be seen in the illustrations representing cross-section and ground plan. If you have no idea of the arrangement of pipes, and how to get them together, it will be advisable to employ a regular plumber. I always do such work myself.

90—How to Make the Garden Pay.

By the help of a plan drawn on the one-inch-to-the-foot scale, you or the party who is to furnish you the piping can get the correct length of every piece of pipe, and make a list of all

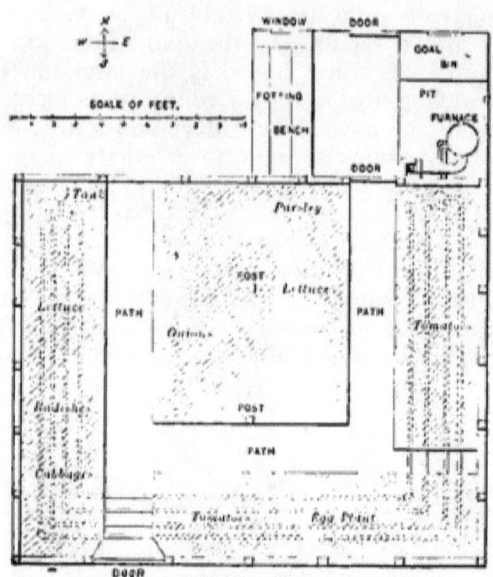

Ground Plan of Greenhouse.

the fixings needed; and when you have all that, it is easy enough to put the whole thing together.

OTHER HOUSES.—Many other plans might be given. Those found in the preceding pages are merely samples on which I

Section of Hillside House.

have tried to demonstrate the leading principles. Some people may have a good location for a cheap lean-to placed directly against the south side of some building; others for a hillside house, plan (cross-section) of which is here given. I do not think it necessary to go into all the details of construction, heating, etc. Any person intending to build a greenhouse of any kin should not only study works on greenhouse construction, but also visit the greenhouses in his vicinity, and talk with the men who run them. Many good suggestions may be gathered by such a course.

CHAPTER XV.

EARLY PLANTS FOR THE HOME GARDEN.

VARIOUS MEANS AND DEVICES FOR EVERYBODY.

"A will—a way."

FOR the average-sized kitchen garden only a comparatively very small number of early plants are needed, so few, indeed, that people often come to the conclusion it is cheaper to buy them than to raise them, especially when plants are to be had as cheap as they are now. Yet we cannot always, nor even often, get what we want. Professional plant-growers frequently are very careless about the seeds they sow. The plants are for sale, and a tomato plant will sell, if well grown, no matter what fruit it will produce afterwards. So in the purchase of plants we always run a risk, and at best have to deal with uncertainties. Then we may wish to try a new tomato, or pepper, or egg-plant, etc., and plants of high-priced novelties cannot often be purchased. Furthermore, while poor plants, grown in crowded hot-beds, and consisting of much stalk and little root, are abundant and cheap, really first-class, well-grown, well-rooted and well-hardened plants are generally rare, always dear, and often not on sale. Take it on the whole, therefore, I think every home gardener who takes the least interest in his garden, will of necessity have to dabble in the business of plant growing. He can go at it in a variety of ways.

Where a sunny kitchen window is at disposal for the purpose, some tomato, pepper and egg-plants can easily be started in a box or in boxes placed in front of it, as shown in illustration. A common soap box, obtained from the nearest grocer will furnish material for two or three such boxes. Suitable soil is prepared by mixing one-third of well-rotted compost and two-thirds sandy loam or rich garden soil, and of course it should be got in readiness in the autumn before the ground freezes. The boxes are filled with this nearly to the top, and the seeds sowed thinly in shallow furrows. Each variety should be plainly labelled, or the name written on outside of box facing each row. Sift a little sandy loam, leaf mould or pulverized dried peat moss upon the seeds, pat it down gently to firm the seed, then water with hot water from a fine rose sprinkler, and as often afterwards with tepid water as the soil becomes dry, and needs it. Thus treated the young plants should make their appearance in about a week's time. A few cabbage, cauliflower and lettuce plants may be grown in a similar way, but the box should be set in a colder room, or in a less sunny exposure. It generally falls to the lot of the good housewife to care for such plant boxes, and in most cases she will enjoy the task. The chief aim must be to make the plants strong and stocky by giving each sufficient space, and thin out the surplus at an early stage of development. Tall, over-grown things are not desirable. Where there is sufficient window room, and if possible, any way, the plants should be transplanted once or twice, and more space given at each time. Nothing is more serviceable than empty tomato cans (with a hole punched in the bottom) for setting in tomato and egg plants, one in each, from there to be transplanted to the open ground. The true lover of a good garden, and the man who has a large family to supply with vegetables, will sorely miss the convenience and aid of a hot-bed, and the best thing for him to do is to invest the amount of $4.00 or $6.00 in sashes, and put up a little frame. The excavation may be made for only one-half or two-thirds of the bed, if this is three sashes in size, so that a part of it is managed as hot-bed, and the other as cold frame. Plants must be ranged according to their degree of tenderness, and beginning at the hot-bed end, as follows: egg-plant, pepper, tomato, cauliflower, cabbage and lettuce; and ventilation given more freely and frequently on the cold frame side than on the other. For directions as to general management I can only refer the reader to Chapters X and XI.

Plant Box in Window.

The well-to-do home gardener who can afford to spend a little time and money for the privilege of running a miniature green-house or forcing pit, which will not only give him an abundance of plants such as he may desire, but also a chance to raise a few nice, crisp vegetables in the winter months, may construct a building, answering one of the two sections of the forcing pit described in preceding chapter. Such structure is here shown, and will need no detailed explanation. Hot water will be found the proper method of heating, and a base-burning water heater that manufacturers furnish for from $25.00 upwards, will do good service.

The people of Hammonton, New Jersey, use a boiler of this kind for heating the brooders in their chicken houses, and it may be arranged somewhat in the same manner, and as shown in next figure. When the house is all made snug and tight, and where winters are not exceedingly severe, it seems that a single pipe for each bench,

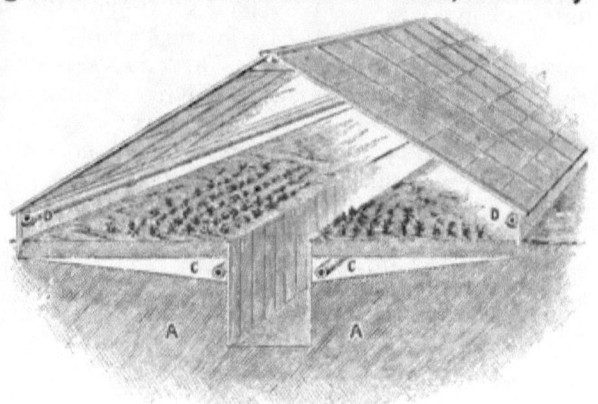

Amateur Green-House.

either in an air-chamber under it to provide bottom heat, or near the outside would be fully sufficient.

To make the arrangement perfectly clear, I will say that the barrel B is used merely to give pressure to the water in the stove; C is the faucet for drawing water from the barrel; D the faucet for emptying water out of stove, pipes and barrels. E is a cock for letting out air from the pipes in order to prevent it from interfering with the water circulation. F and G are cocks by which the connection between stove and water pipes can be broken. If one of them is shut, the circulation stops, and the pipes will gradually cool off. If it should be desired to heat or boil the water in the barrel, it can be done by shutting off the two cocks, F and G, and opening the one in the vertical pipe leading from the upper heating pipe to the barrel, thus completing the water circulation through boiler and barrel. An arrangement of this kind, simple and inexpensive as it is, sometimes may come handy, even if not entirely necessary for the regular purpose of green-house heating.

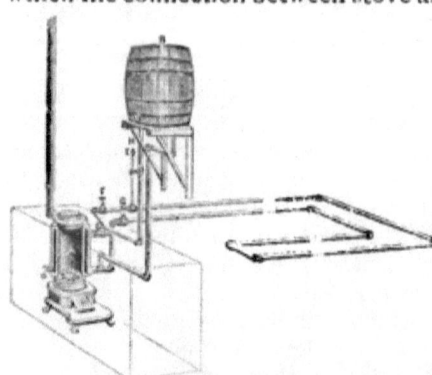

Base-burning Water Heater and Arrangement of Pipes.

CHAPTER XVI.

DRAINAGE.

WHERE NEEDED AND HOW DONE.

"The ability to overcome obstacles is a certain guarantee of success."

THE best garden soil—that adapted for the production of early vegetables, and composed of a dark, sandy loam resting on a porous subsoil —needs no artificial drainage. My experience with red sandy subsoil in New Jersey was highly satisfactory. The soil water moves freely up and down through subsoil of this character, and the air has a chance to warm it deeply and quickly. The possession of such land (without a single underdrain on it) gives advantages against which the proprietor of clayey loam underlaid with stiff blue clay will find it utterly impossible to compete successfully, no matter how much money he may expend for drainage. Whatever may be said in favor or greater fertility and the retentiveness of clayey loam, and the leachy character of "lighter" soil, the fact remains that vegetables grown on the former will be days if not weeks later than on the latter. This only shows the importance of selecting a more or less sandy loam with porous subsoil for general gardening purposes, and of steering entirely clear of clay on clay foundation. Muck resting upon blue clay meets with the same objection. Still such cooler soils, when properly drained, can generally be utilized with advantage for certain crops, such as for instance, onions and celery. If a piece of such land belonging to the gardener is yet in an undrained condition, he should lose no time to make it available, and often exceedingly profitable by preparing a thorough system of drainage. In some cases an otherwise fine garden soil is underlaid with a fairly porous loam which, however, offers some obstruction to the free passage of surface water. Then drainage will improve it wonderfully, and perhaps render it equal to the best garden land in earliness and productiveness.

The first concern is to find an outlet $2\frac{1}{2}$ to 4 feet below the lowest part of the field, as a starting point for the main ditch that is to be carried right along the lowest line of the surface across the whole field, with a gradual rise of not less than

½-inch (more is better) to the rod. The laterals begin from this main, are 2 or 2½ rods apart, and closer if it can be afforded or is thought necessary, 3 to 4 feet in depth, and also rise gradually at least ½-inch to the rod. As the only object is to places the tiles into the bottom, we have no need for wide ditches, and in order to save labor, aim to make them as narrow as possible. With the improved ditching tools now on sale in every hardware store, such drains can be cut quite conveniently to the depth of 4 feet with only one foot across on top and 6 inches at the bottom. The work is begun with common spade, shovel and if needed pick-axe, perhaps with the assistance of a common plow and subsoil plow; but the last 12 inches of depth are dug with the long narrow spade shown at the left in engraving, and the finishing touches given with the draining scoop shown in centre of same figure. This scoop, which is drawn towards the operator, only finishes the perfect cleaning out of the bottom, correcting faulty grade, etc., and leaves a concave bed for the tile. Scoops of this kind are made in different sizes to fit the tile. Too much care cannot be bestowed on the grading. To secure perfect working order, and durability of the drains, their every part should have a slight incline towards the outlet; and everything that might tend to obstruct the continuous flow of water in the tiles must be carefully guarded against. Common sense in the whole matter must dictate the details, and will be found a safe guide throughout.

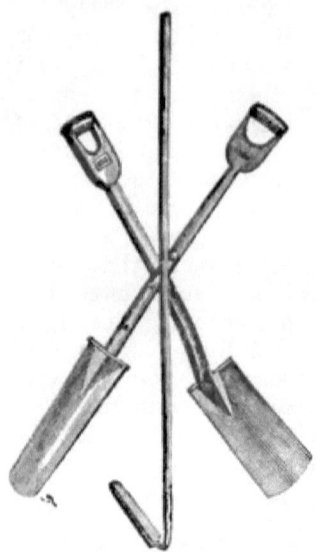

Set of Draining Tools.

SIZE OF TILES.—The amount of water that runs off in an even and continuous stream, after the first rush from the newly ditched field, determines the size of tile. Two-inch tile are generally preferable for the lateral drains, while the main must have a size fully capable of carrying off the water that collects from the laterals above, at the time of greatest supply. The flow from a well-arranged system of underground drains, when in perfect working order, is pretty nearly uniform through the whole year, only of greater volume in winter than in summer. For water containing iron larger sizes are necessary, as the deposits adhere, and are liable to fill up the tile after awhile. The extreme upper end of the main, for a short distance, may be arranged as a lateral, and laid with small tile, but it should then be made larger by using

Drainage.—97

3 or 4-inch tile, and for the lower half or one-third 6-inch and perhaps even larger sizes may be necessary. The number and length of laterals, and amount of water passing through them, determines this question.

LAYING THE TILES.—Next to perfect grading of the bottom, the effectiveness and permanency of the whole draining operation depends on the careful laying of the tiles. The work should never be entrusted to a raw hand, unless the latter is endowed with an unusual amount of common sense, skill and intelligence. It is much safer to employ a man used to such work, and pay him good wages by the day, not by the rod or job. It is not safe to run the least risk of having this important job slighted. Laying the tile should follow immediately upon the levelling (grading) of the bottom, and in order to perform this task without stepping into the ditch, a six foot pole with a $\frac{1}{4}$ inch iron rod fastened to the end and bent in the form of an elbow, is used to handle section

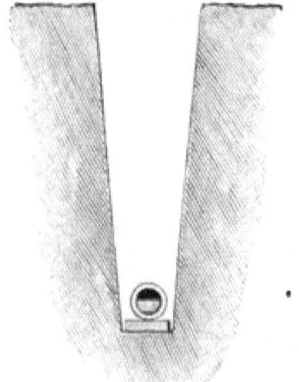 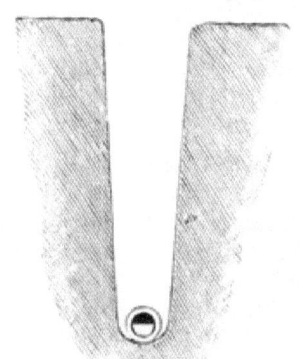

Tile on Soft Bottom.   Tile on Clay Bottom.

after section of tile, and placing it in its proper place. The ends should be closely fitted together, and clay subsoil firmly packed around them to hold them in their place, until the ditches can be filled up again to the top. Fine surface soil or anything that will decay, should not be put immediately in contact with the tiles. It is also essential that the point of discharge in the laterals should be a few inches above the level of the main, to insure a good flow. It is obvious that the tile can be laid directly upon the bottom of the ditch when the subsoil is perfectly hard and solid, especially if of stiff clay. Soft muck or quicksand in the bottom of drains makes it necessary to rest the tiles upon a line of narrow (6 inch) boards placed in the drain, as here illustrated. In some instances tile cannot be readily obtained, at least not without paying heavy transportation expenses, and other means of constructing the drain have to be found. I have used board troughs with excellent results. The poorest kind of lumber may be utilized for this purpose. Two boards are nailed together at right angles, and held firmly in place by strips nailed diagonally across.

Usually such troughs are laid directly upon stiff clay bottom carefully graded, or upon a line of boards placed upon soft bottom, pointed side up, as here illustrated. This construction, however, is decidedly faulty. The water has a chance to spread out quite widely. Consequently it moves with very little force, and will continually deposit sediment, gradually filling up the trough. If he trough is inverted, as shown in the next illustration, so that the water runs in a narrow and deep little stream, it will have sufficient force to carry all the sediment along with it.

(Faulty Construction).

Stones and pebbles, where plentiful, can be used to good advantage also; but to get a properly constructed drain with such material, the inexperienced owner will always find it safest and cheapest to have the work done by somebody that understands it. Tile is always best, and drains thus made will be of more lasting value. All stone drains are quite liable to get choked up after awhile, since it is almost impossible to keep the soil from washing and working among the stones, and finally fill up the throat.

THE ADVANTAGES OF UNDERDRAINING.—As one of the most beneficial results of good underdraining on many soils, the crops are given more root room.

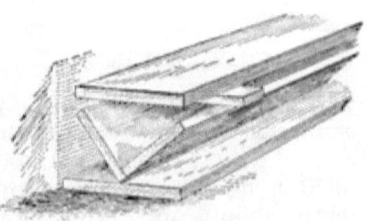
Board Trough
(Proper Construction).

The roots of almost all our garden crops (and field crops also) thrive in moist soil, but not in that which is wet or water-logged, and they are stopped when they come to the soil water. Underdraining lowers the soil water level, allows the roots to go deeper, and therefore gives them more room to work in. Each plant needs a certain amount or weight of soil for its best development. If it can feed deeper it will not require as much surface, and hence plants in well-drained soil can be planted closer than in undrained land. But good drainage gives still other benefits. It warms the soil by admitting air more freely, lengthens the season at both ends, and by promoting the circulation of air and moisture, furnishes chances for chemical action by which insoluble plant food is rendered available.

But, after all, tile drains, if ever so well laid, cannot be expected to last forever, and often they give out quite unexpectedly, making it necessary to take up parts of them for repairs In an emergency of this kind it is quite convenient to know the exact location of every drain, and to be able to find it without having to dig over a large area. A map showing the location of every tile drain put down, with distances marked in rods and feet, will be of great advantage, and a valuable assistance sooner or later.

SURFACE DRAINAGE.—An opportunity for the easy escape of surface water, especially during the winter, is a good thing for all soils, and urgently needed on tile-drained, level lands which otherwise are liable to be saturated at times to such an extent that the drains are unable to carry the surplus off as fast as it accumulates. Beds that were kept high and dry all winter by plowing during the fall in ridges allowing the surface water to run off at once in deep dead furrows, are always ready for planting earlier in spring, and then usually give better crops than land just plowed level. Good surface drainage, in short, is an advantage not to be ignored, even on land supposedly well tile-drained. I would always advise to plow such land in the fall in narrow beds, giving the dead furrows a suitable outlet. It will pay.

CHAPTER XVII.

IRRIGATION.

SURFACE-SOAKING AND SUB-EARTH FLOODING.

"More powerful than art is Nature."

IRRIGATION, while a necessary and common practice under the rainless skies near the Pacific coast, is hardly ever thought of at the east. I have made a few trials on a somewhat limited scale, and the results fully convinced me that the chances are not rare where the eastern gardener might employ some system of irrigation with as telling effect. The first requisite, of course, is a sufficient water supply, one which can be controlled or made available without great expense. The amount of liquid needed for thorough work—and this alone gives satisfactory results—is so immensely large, that I have little respect for any source of supply of less ·magnitude than a pond or small stream. I cannot do better than quote from a paper read before the American Horticultural Society, by Mr. J. M. Smith, Wisconsin's noted and successful gardener, and President of the Wisconsin State Horticultural Society: "A few things should be remembered by those who contemplate artificial watering. Suppose that you have one acre of cabbage that you wish to water. To do this fairly well requires at least 30,000 gallons of water, and this will need to be repeated at least once a week until rain comes. To make strawberries do their best in dry weather, requires considerably more than for cabbages, and to be put on oftener. To merely sprinkle the ground when it is very dry, is, in my opinion, a damage rather than a benefit. It has a tendency to form a thin, hard crust, both air- and water-tight. Neither the damp air nor the rains will pass through it, neither will a light shower. It requires a heavy rain to dissolve it. Thus you shut out the benefits to be derived from the cool, damp night air, the heavy dews that we often have, also the little sprinkles of rain that are almost sure to come occasionally. For a couple of years after my water-works were put up, I was at a loss to understand why our watering had so little effect. I had a piece of early cabbage that was suffering for want of rain. The men were told to put on water until the ground was thoroughly soaked for at least six inches deep. They

(100)

did so, and I learned two things by it. One was that a thorough watering would make the plants grow; the other was that it took a great deal of water to make it thorough.

"Hence if you water at all, do it well. No system of artificial watering that I have ever tried is equal to rain from the clouds. I do not state these things to discourage any one, but because I believe them to be facts that should be known to those who contemplate some improvements of this kind. My waterworks cost me nearly $1,000, and I have no doubt but that they have more than once paid for themselves in a single season."

SURFACE IRRIGATION.—Where a pond or other body of water is available, so that a stream can be run directly to the highest line of the field, irrigation is a very simple matter. Make light furrows down the slope, 8 or 10 feet apart, between the rows of plants, and let the water run down in one after another, long enough in each, to soak up the ground pretty thoroughly to the lower end, before turning off the flow into the next furrow. The application should not (or need not) be repeated until the ground becomes quite dry again, but it is absolutely necessary for best results, and lasting effects of the operation, to cultivate the ground thoroughly just as soon as the surface is again dry enough for such work. Always make the water channels in the higher places, as the lower ones are apt to take care of themselves. In irrigating a $\frac{1}{8}$ acre lot of celery one season, between 6,000 and 8,000 gallons of water were needed to give the ground one thorough soaking, but this had a most excellent effect on the plants.

Very much, of course, depends on the nature of the soil. A loose, porous loam, resting on porous subsoil, will drink in rapidly almost unlimited quantities of water, and allow it to percolate, from any point of discharge, over a wide area. Consequently the channels into which the water is turned and made to flow down the slope, gradually soaking in and away, may be ten, twelve feet or a rod and more apart, even on considerable of a slope. On soils which do not allow the percolation of water quite so freely, the channels must be nearer together, and their course more nearly, or almost quite, on a level.

In some cases water from a near supply (pond, stream, etc.) may be conducted to the highest part of the field in a box ditch, and from there distributed through holes bored into the side boards, opening and stopping them up as the case may require.

A natural water supply, above the field, however, is not always at command. In that case, it may be advisable to secure it by letting a windmill or steam pump raise it from a pond, stream or well into large tanks, from which it is to be distributed over the field by means of hose, or by a combination of iron pipe and hose, or in other ways that may suggest themselves to the intelligent gardener.

HOME-MADE HOSE.—A method of surface irrigation practiced by Mr. H. A. March, a well-known gardener and grower of cauliflower seed, of Washington State, deserves more than a passing notice. The following are the details of his plant as described by himself:

"On the south side of our farm, we have a never-failing spring of water that gives us about 45,000 gallons every 24 hours. It is situated about 20 feet higher than any of our tillable land. This water is brought down in open troughs to the tanks on the upper side of the field to be irrigated, holding 20,000 gallons each. We turn the water into the tanks in the heat of the day, and the sun warms it up to about 60°.

"To distribute the water, we use a hose made from 12-ounce duck. We take a piece 30 feet long, and cut it lengthwise into three pieces, which makes 90 feet of hose about 2½ inches in diameter. We fetch the edges together, double once over, and with a sewing-machine sew through the four thicknesses twice, which makes a hose that will stand a six or eight-foot pressure. To make it waterproof, we use five gallons of boiled linseed oil with half a gallon of pine tar, melted together. Place the hose in a washtub, turn on the oil hot (say 160°), and saturate the cloth well with the mixture. Now, with a clothes-wringer run the hose through with the wringer screwed down rather tight, and it is ready to be hung up to dry. A little pains must be taken to blow through it to keep it from sticking together as it dries. I use an elder-sprout about a foot long with the pith punched out. Tie a string around one end of the hose and gather the other end around the tube and fill it with wind, then hang it on a line and it will dry in a few days and be ready for use. It will last five or six years.

"To join the ends, we use a tin tube 2½ inches in diameter by one foot long. It is kept tied to one end of the hose all the time. To connect them, draw the open end of the hose over the tube of the next joint and tie it securely. When ready to irrigate our celery we take the hose in sections convenient to carry, lay it from our tanks to the third row from the outside and down this row to the end of the field. Then the water is turned on.

"To connect the hose with the tank, we take a hardwood stick 15 inches long, bore a two-inch hole through it, and with a hot iron burn it out smooth on the inside, work one end down until it will fit into the end of the hose next the tank and tie it securely; then work the other end down so that it will fit tightly into a 2½-inch hole. With a 2½-inch auger, bore a hole in the tank on the side next the field you wish to water, two inches up from the bottom—then no sediment or dirt will wash into your hose. Push the plug into the hole; with a mallet give it a few gentle taps, and the work is done. We now have our water running, and it can be carried to any part of the field for any crop that needs it."

The crops most markedly benefited by irrigation, be this from the surface or from underground, are cabbage, cauliflower, celery, lettuce, radish, and perhaps strawberries and onions. There are many instances where the increase of a single crop, due to artificial watering, has more than paid the original cost of the whole irrigation plant.

SUB-EARTH FLOODING.—One of the simplest, cheapest, and most effective methods of subirrigation has been in use for years in some celery, cauliflower, and onion fields near Mount Morris, New York. This is a tract of deep, rich, sandy muck, 30 or 40 acres in extent, situated at the foot of a hill, and slightly

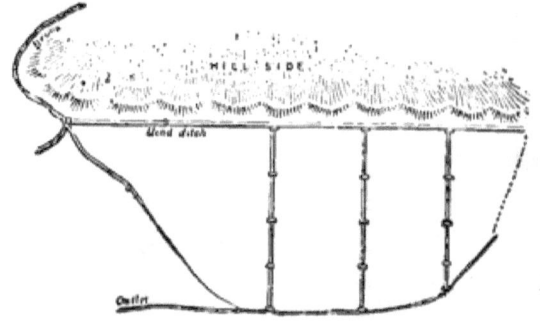

Plan of Irrigated Field.

sloping away from it. A little brook flowing down the hillside and passing by at one corner of the tract furnishes a moderate and never-failing water supply. A deep ditch is dug all along the foot of the hill on a dead level, forming the head of the lowlands. Another ditch, parallel with the other, forms the boundary on the lower side, and the two ditches are connected by a number of parallel cross-ditches, as shown in illustration. All these ditches are provided with flood-gates to dam up the water when required. Ordinarily all the flood-gates, except the one at the head of the upper main, are kept closed, and the water flows along in its natural course unobstructed. When the soil begins to get dry, however, and shows the need of water, the mountain brook is turned into the head ditch, and the latter is allowed to fill up almost to overflowing. This alone will give the whole strip next to the head ditch, several rods in width, a pretty good soaking in a comparatively short time. Then by opening the flood-gates at the head of the cross-ditches the water is turned into the latter, allowed to rise to the top at the next set of flood-gates, and by overflow and soaking in, well distributed over another strip parallel with the head ditch. Then these flood-gates are raised and the water allowed to flow into the next section of the ditches, etc., until the whole tract of land has had a thorough soaking. Just as soon as the surface has become again dry enough for cultivation, horse cultivators and hand-wheel hoes are at once brought into action.

There are other tracts of sandy muck or other porous soils in various parts of the country offering just or nearly as favorable opportunities for a similar method of sub-earth flooding as this tract near Mount Morris, New York, and wherever found they can easily and with little expense be made to produce large crops of celery, onions, cabbage, cauliflower, and other garden crops. Such land, properly arranged, is easily worth, for these purposes, a clean $1,000 per acre.

Celery Irrigated by Tile Line.

SUBIRRIGATION BY TILE.—Another system often mentioned but rarely employed, is that of placing tiles in close, parallel, shallow ditches all through the field, so the tiles are just out of reach of the plow. The water introduced into these tiles, one line after another, from some source, soaks up the land from below the surface, otherwise in the same fashion as by surface irrigation. This method is especially suited to stiffer soils, on which surface soaking would be liable to do more harm than good, in consequence of leaving them, after drying, hard and baked as a brick. On such soils, however, the tile lines should be just about on a dead level. The water escaping at the joints soaks in rather slowly, and should be given all the chance required to do so, otherwise the greater bulk would run off to the lower end of the tile line and leave only little for the upper end. The exercise of good judgment will be necessary in arranging each particular spot for this style of subirrigation.

I have tried a tile line right along the centre of my patch of early celery, planted closely on the plan of the "New Celery Culture." A cross-section of bed is shown on preceding page. There is a box at the upper end into which the water is poured directly from a barrel on wheels. The barrel holds about 60 gallons, and is drawn by single horse. We get the water from the creek close by. Even with slight fall we have to turn the water into the box quite slowly, or else see it run to the lower end much faster than is desirable. On the whole we call this plan of irrigation a success.

SUBIRRIGATION FOR GREENHOUSE BENCHES.—Recently the principle of watering crops by means of underground tile lines has been applied to the greenhouse benches, for forced lettuce and radishes, apparently with the best of success. The idea originated in the fertile brain of Prof. W. J. Green, of the Ohio Experiment Station.

The bench is made solid and water-tight, or nearly so, by the free use of white lead or cement, and lines of two-inch horse-shoe tile, with an elbow at one end, are laid two feet apart in the

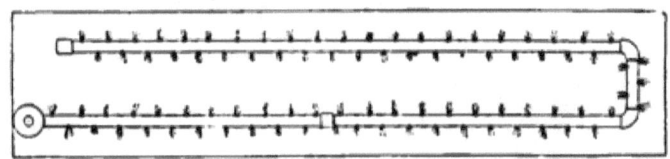

Iron Irrigation Pipe in Bottom of Bench.

bottom of the bench, which is then filled with soil in the ordinary manner. The even distribution of water will be facilitated by having the tile lines across the bench, and therefore the runs of water short. If the lines are laid lengthwise, requiring long runs, a nice leveling and adjustment of bench and tile line will be necessary, so that the water will neither run too freely at first, nor be carried too fast to the further end.

One of my benches has been arranged for subirrigation by means of a five-quarter-inch gas-pipe laid on the ordinary plank bottom in the manner shown in accompanying sketches. The two parallel pipe lines are two feet apart. Quarter-inch holes are drilled through the pipe four or five inches apart, alternately on opposite sides. The further end is closed, although not perfectly tight; the other end is turned up and receives the water through a funnel, or directly from the hose. The bench bottom is not absolutely water-tight, being made of ordinary matched two-inch pine-plank. Neither lead, cement, nor paint has been used. This has saved work, time, and expense, and the arrangement seems to work well.

I find the following advantages in the new method of water-application: (1) Ease of application; (2) certainty of thoroughness in watering; (3) exemption of plants from disease. Overhead watering in amateur houses, when it has to be done by means of the ordinary garden-sprinkler, is a tedious task. In the new arrangement we simply pour a few bucketfuls of water into the funnel and the work is not only done, but done well. This method of application also enables us to use washing suds, manure-water, and similar liquids which we would not like to put on the plants from overhead, either from considerations of cleanliness or for fear of clogging the sprinkler.

Watering beds with the sprinkler is rarely done thoroughly. A bucketful of water sprinkled on in the usual fashion will make a good-sized bed appear soaked, while, in fact, the application may not have reached beyond an inch deep, leaving the lower portions dust-dry. Such, indeed, is not an uncommon condition of many benches and flats in the glass-houses of amateurs. Subirrigation gives us reversed conditions. On a bench, which one bucketful of water applied by surface-sprinkling would render

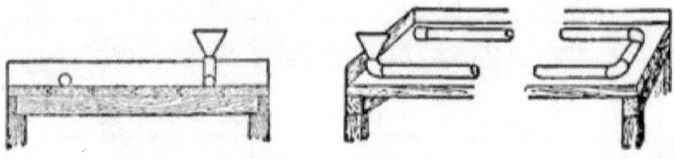

Subirrigated Bench.

apparently quite wet, you may turn two or three bucketfuls through underground pipes, without bringing moisture enough for a respectable show to the surface. The consequence is that almost everyone, without exception, would apply a greater quantity of water by subirrigation than by the old overhead sprinkling method. Herein, I believe, may be found one of the chief reasons for the greatly increased growth of certain crops observed as the result of subirrigation. It is only an experience similar to the one made in the application of fertilizing substances on potatoes and other crops. Quantity of application is the deciding factor rather than the mode of application. Lettuce and onions are especially subject to this influence. On an ordinary bench, and in nicely prepared, porous soil, I can produce almost double the growth of these vegetables in a given time by doubling the ordinary overhead applications of water. It is surprising what large quantities of water lettuce will take and delight in. Amateurs seldom give it enough for best effect. With a subirrigation arrangement this will be different. The application does not quickly show on the surface, and consequently it is naturally more abundant than under the old method. The roots of the plants are kept well supplied with moisture all the time, and the growth, therefore, is rapid and healthy.

When watering beds by subirrigation, it will occasionally be desirable for the gardener to examine the soil at the bottom of bench, in order to be able, judging from its condition, to properly gauge the quantity of water to be turned on. A home-made soil-tester, like the one here shown, will come quite handy in such an emergency. It is simply a tin tube with a wooden pestle, built something on the principle of the boy's pop-gun. The tube is pressed down into the bench, then withdrawn with the core of soil remaining in it, and finally the core pushed out by means of the wooden pestle, ready to be examined.

Another style of underground watering of greenhouse lettuce—the simplest and cheapest of all, and just as effective as any other—consists of turning water into four-inch flower-pots sunk into the bench in the centre between every four plants. Cross-section of bench thus arranged is here shown. A few dozen pots reach over quite a bench and may be sunk in their proper places at the time the plants are set. On account of its great simplicity, I prefer this method to the other for my uses.

The principle of subirrigation is now also applied to watering seed flats or pans. Overhead water applications to small

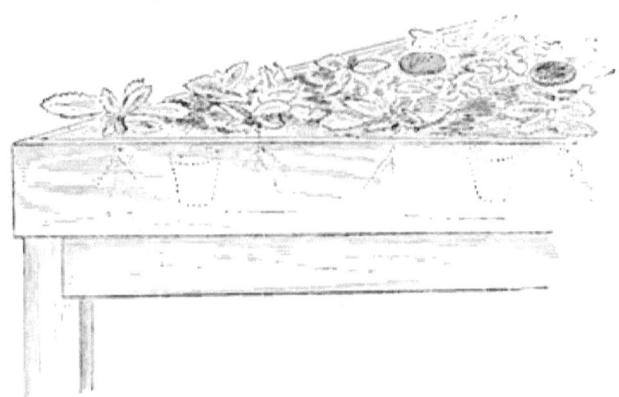
Subirrigation by Flower Pots.

seeds or small plants in seed pans has always been objectionable and risky. Every objection is met and every risk avoided, however, when we place the flat into the "water-bench," a shallow, water-tight box or pan containing about an inch of water, and letting it remain until thoroughly saturated from the bottom up, then taking out and replacing by others. The water application in this method is a thorough one, and yet it does not disturb the surface of the flat, damaging plants or washing out seeds, as overhead sprinkling often does.

AQUACULTURE, OR THE NEW AGRICULTURE.—Reports of wonderful crops produced on slopes of soil by no means rich, under a new system, called by the inventor (A. N. Cole) "aquaculture" (water culture), or new agriculture, at one time attracted considerable attention; but since this method is quite expensive, and possible only under certain conditions, namely, on a slope with impervious clay subsoil, it is not of general utility nor excessively meritorious. Mr. Cole gave the following description of it: "A ditch is opened on a water level along

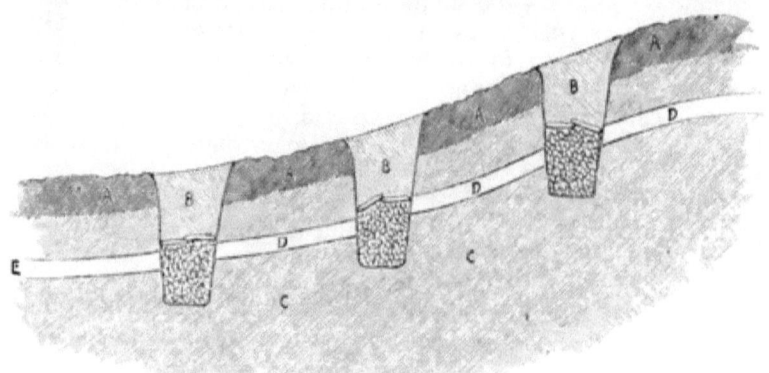

Slope Subirrigated after Cole's Method.

the hillside or slope, say a yard wide, and from three to five feet deep. At the bottom of this ditch are loosely placed cobble and blocky stones, for a foot or two, then flat stones are laid over these, then a quantity of smaller stones; these are covered over with weeds, briars, brambles, fine brush, straw, corn stalks, or other available material, to prevent the fine earth from falling among and filling the crevices between the stones. A heavy coating of manure may follow, and then the excavated soil is spread over it, and a terrace is graded if desired. Whatever course the trench may take, the surface of the hard pan at the bottom of the ditch must never vary from a water level. A series of such ditches, one above the other, are dug a rod or so apart and similarly filled, over as large a surface as is to be improved, each forming an elongated reservoir, which will be filled by the watercourses cut off, or by the melting snows and early rains;

and if the subsoil is firm clay, or hard pan, it will be retained, and as the surface soil dries, absorbed by capillary action, and brought within reach of the roots of vegetation.

"The connecting overflow trenches should be in the subsoil, and filled with fine stone to the depth of a foot at least, and shingled with flat stones in the same manner as the reservoir trenches. This shingling should be of sufficient depth to escape the plough or the deepest spading. The head of the overflow trenches at the base of the slope should be at least twelve or eighteen inches above the bottom of the reservoir."

Cross-section of slope thus subirrigated is presented in engraving. A is the surface soil; B, the reservoir trenches; C, the subsoil; D, the connecting overflow trenches (which might be laid with tile where that can be had conveniently and cheaply), and E, the outlet of drainage trench. I have given this for information more than in the expectation that many readers will make practical use of it.

CHAPTER XVIII.

INSECTS AND OTHER FOES.

THEIR WAYS OF DOING MISCHIEF AND HOW TO KEEP THEM IN CHECK.

"Eternal Vigilance—the Price."

OF all the obstacles to the successful production of choice garden vegetables, none has ever shown itself in a more serious aspect than the multiplication of injurious insects. The problem how to get rid of them often sorely puzzles the ingenuity of even the best gardener. Frequently our plants come up nicely, and we are pleased with their apparent health and thrift, and perhaps pride ourselves on our skill; only to find, at our very next visit to the garden, soon after, that the whole plantation is badly damaged, if not already ruined beyond any chance of recovery, by an unexpected attack of insect foes. Occasionally we have to admit our utter defeat.

The question how to deal with insects is a serious problem. The best of talent has been, and still is, engaged in the attempt to find a satisfactory solution. Columns upon columns on the subject have of late been published by the agricultural press. Lectures upon lectures on insect lore have been delivered by specialists, and bulletin upon bulletin touching upon this matter are issued by the Experiment Stations, and sent out by the thousand, and yet I am asked more questions on "insects and what to do for them," than on any other subject. So I will endeavor to give pretty plain and full instructions.

As a general rule it may be stated that the most satisfactory, and often the only effective measures are those of a preventive character or tendency. The aim should be to keep our crops entirely out of reach or observation by their insect foes, and success in this can more generally and more easily be achieved by a judicious system of rotation ("wide" rotation, as I am tempted to call it), than by the application of drugs, etc. The gardener knows, or should know, the exact location of the breeding places of the various bugs and beetles. Where their food plants had been grown the year before, right there we may confidently expect to see the foes reappear this season. In last year's cabbage and radish patches the flea beetle will be found plentiful this year; and where we had cucumber and squash vines then, we will find the yellow-striped squash beetle, the black squash bug, etc. Wherever circumstances allow, therefore, each crop should be planted at considerable distance from any place where the same or a similar crop was grown the year before. This practice, although it may not prevent insect visits entirely, must at least put enough of the depredators off the track to materially moderate the amount of damage coming from that source. For the home garden, and for smaller operations generally, such a course cannot often be followed, and other means of protection have to be sought.

Foremost among preventive measures stands the often employed practice of hiding the plants, in boxes or open frames, or under mosquito netting, or by surrounding them with other quicker-growing plants (buckwheat, beans, etc.), which not only serve as a screen, but also disguise their scent. Strong-smelling substances, such as carbolic acid, kerosene, turpentine, etc., are also quite frequently used to hide the natural scent of the exposed plants, thus removing one of the chief means by which insects are enabled to find their food plants. Another quite common preventive consists in covering the endangered plants with some substance (plaster, lime, etc.), that is distasteful to their enemies, and this, unless they come in excessive numbers, or are exceedingly hungry, is often effective in driving them off. Either hand-picking and mashing, or poisoning, must be resorted to where preventives cannot be employed, or have not proven effective. That all the natural enemies of our injurious insects—birds, toads, snakes, cannibal insects, such as the useful and pretty little ladybird, the colosoma (ground or tiger beetle), the soldier bug, etc.—should be encouraged and given shelter, need hardly be mentioned. A list of the most destructive and common insect enemies and the most improved ways of preventing their mischief, will be found in the following :

ANTS (*Formica*).—Although not generally directly destructive to garden vegetables, they are sometimes quite obnoxious in consequence of their manner of throwing up hills. Destroy their nests by pouring boiling water, or hot strong alum water over the hills. The ants can also be trapped very easily by placing a coarse sponge moistened with sweetened water near their haunts, thus attracting them in large numbers. When the sponge is black with the creatures, throw it into boiling water; then wash it out and reset the trap. Poisoned molasses placed near their haunts, will also soon make an end to their existence.

APHIS OR PLANT LOUSE.—Of the hundreds of species of green, black, and blue aphis in existence, quite a number are troublesome to the gardener. Fortunately the whole tribe is quite tender ; and lettuce, cabbages and cauliflowers seriously infested, perhaps almost wholly covered by these lice, are sometimes entirely cleared of them by a cold spell or a hard rain, etc., and for this reason their injury to such crops in the open ground is less feared and serious than to those under glass, where they often become a real source of danger.

In tobacco we have a simple preventive and remedy. Apply tobacco dust freely, both directly to the soil, as a means of prevention, and upon the infested plants as a cure. Strong tobacco tea, made by steeping tobacco stems in water, if sprinkled or sprayed on plants, will also quickly rid them of lice. Fumigation (burning dampened tobacco stems two or three times a week) is quite generally practiced, and universally successful as a preventive measure in greenhouse culture.

A simple and effective remedy for this and other injurious insects is the kerosene emulsion, made by churning one quart of soft soap (or one quarter pound of whale-oil soap), one pint of kerosene oil, and two quarts of water, until a perfect union or emulsion is formed. The operation of churning can be performed in an easy and convenient manner by the use of a good force pump, forcing the liquid back into the vessel containing it. The emulsion should be diluted with two gallons of water, and applied with a force pump and spray nozzle over the infested plants. The fine spray makes the operation economical as well as safe, and if thrown with sufficient force, is more liable to touch all lice. It is sure to kill eggs as well as lice.

Asparagus Beetle, Larva and Egg.

ASPARAGUS BEETLE (*Crioceris asparagi*)—.An asparagus branch infested with this comparatively new insect enemy in its different stages of development, natural size, with enlarged specimen of beetle and larva at the lower right hand corner, is here shown. This insect has a natural enemy in the cat-bird, which feeds on both beetles and larvæ, and sometimes greatly reduces their number. Dusting the infested plants when wet with dew, with air-slacked lime on a quiet morning, is probably the simplest, and a reasonably sure remedy. Hand-picking is a rather tedious operation, and only practicable in a small patch. Cutting the affected tops, removing and burning them is often practiced with good effect. Dusting with tobacco dust, or spraying with the kerosene emulsion, are also reasonably safe remedies.

BEAN WEEVIL (*Bruchus obsoletus*).—This insect has become a really more formidable foe to the grower of beans, peas, and other leguminous plants, than even its much larger relative, the pea weevil. It devours the seeds of nearly all plants of the pulse family with apparent equal relish, but is easily enough managed. Simply throw the beans or peas as soon as gathered and threshed for a few seconds into boiling water. This will kill the larvæ of either weevil contained in them. Seed beans and peas should always be treated in this way to guard against injury to the next crop. Old seed is always free from bugs, and by its use all danger of carrying the pest to new fields in the seed is averted. It may be a good plan to tie up beans and peas intended for seed tightly and securely in stout paper bags, and to keep them over without opening the bags, until the second year. The bugs will then have died without living issue. The larvæ can also be destroyed by exposing the seeds in a closed vessel, box or barrel, to the fumes of turpentine, or bisulphide of carbon, or by mixing with them a small quantity of fresh insect powder.

The Ohio Experiment Station finds that the exposure of the infested seed for one hour to a temperature of 145 degrees Fahrenheit destroys the larvæ without injuring the germinative quality of the seed. An ordinary gasoline stove oven, with a lighted kerosene lamp beneath it, was used in conducting the experiments. Only a very small flame is needed to produce the required amount of heat. To be of most benefit, this remedy must be applied as soon as possible after the beans or peas are fully ripe.

CABBAGE PLUSIA (sometimes called green lettuce worm).—It is the caterpillar of a pretty moth (*Plusia Brassicæ*), and sometimes does serious injury to cabbage, lettuce, celery, endive, sage and some flowers. It is a ravenous eater, and in cabbages and lettuce bores clear through to the hearts, and prefers to feed from the inside rather than the outside. For this reason it is not so easily reached with insecticides as the green cabbage worm. Try buhach and careful hand picking.

CABBAGE MAGGOT.—See Radish Fly.

CABBAGE WORM.—The larva of the cabbage butterfly (*Pieris raphæ*), shown on next page, has for many years been the most serious obstacle to the home production of cabbages, and yet few insect foes are so easily kept in check as this. The butterfly is double-brooded. The first brood is seen flitting about the fields in May, the second in August, and the progeny of the latter causes the most trouble.

The sovereign remedy for this pest is fresh Pyrethrum powder, generally called Persian or Dalmatian insect powder. The imported article, when in full strength, is perfectly reliable, but when stale (and this is the usual condition of the powder on sale in drug stores) gives rather uncertain results. Buhach is a California product, the ground flower of *Pyrethrum cinerariæfolium*, generally fresh, and put up in tight tin cans, and in my experience has never failed to give entire satisfaction. While the imported article may be bought for less money, pound for pound, the California product, on account of greater strength and certain death-dealing effect, is by far the cheaper in the end, and every gardener should try to get buhach in preference to the common insect powder.

Butterfly of the Cabbage Worm.

The remedy can be applied in various ways. When to be used in liquid form, take a tablespoonful of the pure powder, and with a little water work it into a paste, then dilute with two gallons of water, and sprinkle it on the plants with a watering pot, or still better, apply in a fine spray with considerable force, so that every worm will be reached.

A very convenient mode of application for the home garden is that in dry form, by means of a simple dusting apparatus or pocket rubber bellows, as for instance shown in illustration. This,

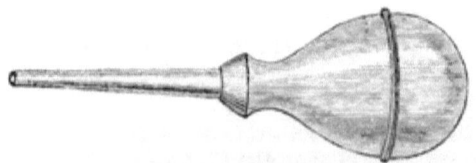

Simple Powder Bellows.

or a similar and just as effectual one, can undoubtedly be had of our friend, Wm. Henry Maule, of Philadelphia, Pa., or most other seedsmen, at a mere nominal price. During the summer months I generally carry one of the bellows charged with a mixture of one part of buhach, and four or five of flour or air-slacked lime in my pocket, and apply a few puffs here and there, wherever I notice the effects of cabbage or similar worms. That puts a sudden stop to their mischief. The whole matter is so simple, inexpensive and certain, and requiring so little time or effort, that I would hardly give any man 10 cents to insure me perfect immunity from worms for each 100 head of cabbages.

Insects and Other Foes.—115

When we have at hand a remedy so highly effective and satisfactory as buhach, there is absolutely no reason why we should search for other means, and I believe it is simply fooling away time to experiment with hot water, ice water, solutions of saltpetre or alum, or with pepper, road dust, or the many other remedies of like nature recommended. Mr. A. S. Fuller also reports that he has had the very best success in killing the worms by sprinkling the infested plants with tar water.

CELERY WORM.—The caterpillars found on celery, parsley, etc., which are the progeny of the asterias butterfly (*Papilio asterias*) can be got rid of by the remedies recommended for the cabbage worm; but since they are hardly ever numerous, I have always disposed of them by hand-picking.

CORN OR BOLL WORM (*Heliothis armigera*).—The moth of this, like the cabbage butterfly, is double-brooded; the first brood generally attacking the very early varieties of sweet and other corn varieties, and the second brood doing considerable damage to the late varieties, so that the intermediate sorts usually escape altogether. The fruit of tomatoes, bean and pea pods, and vine fruits are also occasionally attacked. The only remedy that promises relief, is to hand-pick the first brood of larvæ, found on early sweet corn, and to destroy them, thereby rendering the attacks of the subsequent brood less serious. It is sometimes recommended to bait and catch (drown) the moths by means of a mixture of molasses and vinegar.

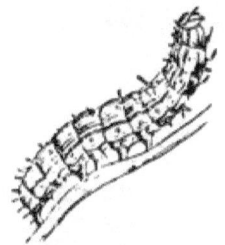

Corn, Boll or Cotton Worm.

CUCUMBER BEETLE (*Diabrotica vittata*).—Of all the insects in the garden, the little creature that wears a yellow-striped suit, and troubles young cucumber, melon, squash and pumpkin plants is probably the worst, and difficult to deal with. Hiding away the whole patch so the beetles cannot easily find it, by changing location (the "wide rotation" spoken of) is yet one of the very best methods; but this cannot well be practiced in the home garden, and here we may often adopt the plan of hiding away individual plants or hills, either by placing a simple frame or bottomless box around them, as here illustrated, or by covering them with muslin-covered plant protectors, or with little pieces of muslin fastened down to the ground at the four

Frame for Protecting Young Vines.

corners, or by similar devices. A ring of buckwheat or beans sown around the vines when the latter are planted, is another expedient sometimes employed for the purpose of hiding the vines. The period of danger is only while the plants are young, especially in seed-leaf, and our first aim should be to push the plants by rich stimulating food, liquid manuring, if needed, past the stage when they are liable to ruinous attacks.

The young plants are so tender and succulent, and there is so little of them, that the first visit of a number of striped beetles usually means little less than destruction to the victims. Treatment must positively be begun in advance of the insects' first appearance.

The usual method, suited especially for larger plantations, but having considerable merit for the home garden also, consists in keeping the plants from the day they first begin to break ground until they are beyond the period of danger, well covered with plaster or bone dust The coating must be renewed promptly whenever washed off by rains or heavy dews. Air-slacked lime is sometimes used, but it is always risky, on account of its still caustic nature. In all cases where plaster is made to serve as insect repeller, I would prefer to have it flavored with carbolic acid, by mixing a pint of the crude article with a bushel of plaster. The acid can do no possible harm, and it always adds to the effectiveness of plaster or air-slacked lime.

Another equally meritorious remedy is the following: Mix a tablespoonful of kerosene in two quarts of plaster, sifted wood ashes, or bone flour, rubbing it with the hands until the oil is well distributed, then sprinkle this over the vines, and repeat as often as required. It is also worth while to try this trick of repelling the marauders by placing little heaps of ashes, saturated with kerosene, turpentine, or carbolic acid, or pieces of corn-cobs, soaked in coal tar, among the vines to be protected. Should the insects find the vines in spite of all precautions, we yet have a remedy to apply, and this consists in spraying the vines with a weak solution of Paris green at the rate of 15 gallons of water to one ounce of poison. Apply in a fine spray, so that the poisonous liquid will reach the upper and lower surfaces of every leaf, and the stems also. If a spraying apparatus is not at hand, a small quantity of poison may be mixed with the plaster or bone dust, and applied dry.

CUT WORMS (*Agrotis*).—A large number of species of cut worms make themselves highly obnoxious to the gardener by the impudence with which they attack and cut down almost every kind of newly-set plants. They are mostly clumsy and greasy-looking caterpillars of some dull shade of color (grayish, brown, greenish), remain in their hiding places on bright days, and come to the surface at night or in cloudy weather, to seek

Insects and Other Foes.—117

what green stuff they can devour. The illustration presents both worm and moth of one of the species.

Cut Worm—Moth and Larva.

Fortunately these worms have many natural enemies, among them the robin, thrushes, quail, wren and other birds, toads, etc., which together keep their numbers down quite well. Fall plowing serves to bring many of the worms to the surface, and to expose them to "bird's-eye view" and perhaps to destruction by frost.

The fresh effects of their night's work can best be noticed bright and early in the morning, and they can then be found near the place of mischief, hunted up and killed. Before a piece of plowed ground is planted, we can often dispose of the majority of the worms by placing pieces of sod, sprinkled with a poisonous solution, at regular intervals over the ground. The remedy is simple, and may be repeated, thus making the way clear for setting plants. Beans are sometimes planted for bait, and in advance of the real crop, whatever that may be. The field is looked over on several mornings after the beans are up and the worms hunted up where plants are seen cut off. The regular crop is planted after most of the worms are destroyed. A practice often resorted to, is to encircle each plant to be set out, with a piece of paper, which should reach down into the soil, as the worm cannot crawl under it, and extend several inches above the surface, so it cannot crawl over it.

The picture shows how this is done, and how the plan works. I often use plant protectors somewhat resembling bottomless flower pots, which I had made for the purpose, as a mechanical obstacle to the cut worm's progress.

Cut Worm and Protected Plant.

FLEA BEETLE (*Haltica*). In this we have another, and often a very troublesome enemy. On soil where cabbage, radishes or turnips were grown the year before, or in the vicinity thereof, these little jumping things appear often in such numbers, that it is difficult to make headway against them. Change of location is, therefore, to be recommended as the chief preventive measure. Ordinarily we can succeed in preventing serious damage to our young plants of the Brassica family, by dusting them, when first appearing above ground, with plaster, air-slacked lime, sifted wood ashes, soot, tobacco dust, or in fact any dust-like material. When the beetles appear in very large numbers, and consequently are very hungry, mere grit will not repel them, and a little admixture of Paris green—one part to a hundred parts of plaster—to such applications will be necessary. The insect is hardy and resistant enough not to appear to be inconvenienced by even the best of buhach in full strength, nor by strong vapors of naphtaline. Little chicks will catch these insects in great quantities, and so will toads when they happen to come across an infested patch.

Of late these insects have appeared in vast numbers in our potato fields, and often entirely ruin the foliage, greatly reducing the crop of tubers. The only remedy that thus far has seemed to give relief, is spraying the vines freely with a strong decoction of tobacco stems or dust. Very likely, also, the free use of dry tobacco dust may drive these beetles away.

GRUBS—*White.* See *May Beetle.*

MAGGOT—*Cabbage, Onion,* etc. See *Onion Fly.*

MAY BEETLE. (*Lachnosterna.*) In the perfect or beetle state, this does not usually damage the gardener's crops very seriously; but its larva, the well known and much feared "white grub" is often very destructive to the roots of strawberries, corn and other garden plants, especially when grown on sod land recently brought under cultivation. Both beetle and larva are shown in illustration. Fortunately these fat grubs have many natural enemies, especially brown thrushes, robins, crows, and a number of other birds; also moles, pigs, skunks, etc. Fall plowing and continued cultivation will soon rid the field of their undesirable presence. It is also recommended to make some artificial breeding place, by covering piles of fresh cow manure with fine earth during latter part of May or June. Many beetles will select these for a place to deposit their eggs, and the heaps may be turned over and spread out exposing the young larvæ to sure destruction by frost, birds and other natural enemies.

May Beetle and Grub.

ONION FLY. (*Anthomyia.*) More generally known as radish or cabbage fly. In general appearance it resembles a small house fly. It is the parent of the maggot, which troubles the roots of cabbages, radishes, onions, turnips, etc., and makes itself

Insects and Other Foes.—119

so exceedingly obnoxious to the gardener. Plenty of lime in the soil, or its free use about the plants, or ashes from the burnt rubbish heap, tend to keep them away. Wood ashes moistened with kerosene oil and scattered around the plants are said to be especially effective in repelling the fly. Change of location is a reasonably safe and simple preventive, and although not an absolute one, should always be employed where practicable. In some years it is almost impossible to raise early radishes and cabbages free from the disgusting worms, and again the next season on same soil, and all over the whole vicinity, the trouble from this source will be so slight as not to be worth mentioning. The insect seems to prefer radishes to cabbages, and either of these to onions, so that the latter, if some cabbages or radishes are planted in the same field with them, will generally escape attack, as all the maggots will concentrate on the cabbage and radish plants. These must be pulled up and destroyed. Where onions are affected, as may be seen by their tops turning yellow, they should also be gathered and destroyed.

During last spring it has been discovered that lime-water is a reasonably sure remedy, where plants are just beginning to suffer. Slack a peck of caustic lime in 20 gallons of water, preferably diluted liquid manure, stir long and thoroughly, and apply to the plantation at the rate of a pint to each cabbage plant, or a quantity sufficient to soak the ground closely to the roots, so that every maggot there at work will be reached by the caustic liquid, the mere contact of which brings sure death to all soft-bodied worms. The occasional application of lime-water to plants in seed bed, and also to those in open field, at least during their earlier stages, deserves to be generally adopted as a precautionary measure.

Parsley Worm, Butterfly and Chrysalis.

PARSLEY WORM.—This is the larva of the Asterias butterfly (*Papilio asterias*), and feeds on the leaves of parsley, parsnip, celery, carrot, dill, and allied plants. It is a disagreeable fellow, with a most disgusting odor, and the best way to treat it is to pick off the leaf-stalk on which it is found, throw it on the ground, and put your foot heavily upon it. Butterfly, caterpillar and chrysalis are shown in accompanying illustration.

PEA WEEVIL.—This is the bean weevil's larger brother, and must be treated in same way. For directions see *Bean Weevil*.

POTATO BEETLE. (*Doryphora decemlineata*.)—This has become far too common to need description. Change of location for the patch can again be recommended as a means to mitigate if not entirely avert its fearful ravages. Paris green will have to be used in nearly every case, however, if serious damage is to be avoided. Hand-picking is seldom reliable, except where the beetles are not usually very numerous. The remedy can be applied either in dry or in liquid form. The beetles, hungry after a long fast, generally appear as soon as the potatoes are coming up, and the first application of poison—preferably in a dry form—should promptly be made, to dispose of this old stock, and prevent not only the destruction of the first tender foliage and consequent weakening of the plants, but also the propagation of the destructive pest.

The preparation of the poison is quite simple. Pure Paris green is mixed with at least 100 times its weight of plaster, flour, or air-slacked lime—the first named preferred. Make the mixture thorough, and if convenient, prepare it a few days in advance. In the absence of better means of application, a simple tin-can, with handle and perforated bottom, will answer the purpose, especially when the plants are yet small. Give each plant, as soon as up, a dash of the dry poisonous mixture, and thus protect it from harm. Later on, when the first brood of eggs hatch, the young larvæ or slugs concentrate in the tender centres of the stalks, and another dash of the poison should be applied without delay, for if neglected more than a few days, the slugs will scatter all over the plants, and make fighting them more inconvenient, necessitating the distribution of the poisonous material over the entire surface of the plant. Repeat the dose as often as required. Various new devices for putting poison in dry form on potatoes, by hand or horse power, have now been introduced, and the grower must select those that suit his case.

The recent improvements in spraying machines, spraying devices, and spraying materials have made the application of Paris green in liquid form safer, more convenient, and generally preferable to that in powder form. It saves us the inhalation of the poisonous dust. The liquid can be applied at any time, whether the vines are wet with dew or not. No scorching effects have to be feared, and the fungicide, if properly prepared, sticks to the foliage closer than a brother. An effective application could not well be made by the old method of using a garden-sprinkler, or any similar "sprinkling" device, without more or less injury to the foliage, in consequence of the uneven distribution over the plant. The liquid would gather here and there in

Insects and Other Foes.—121

drops, especially on the lower end of leaves, and evaporating, leave the poison often too concentrated for the good of the plants. We now avoid this danger by the application of the liquid in the form of a mere mist with our modern sprayers and modern spray nozzles, and by the addition of a little lime to the Paris green water.

A good knapsack sprayer (now to be had for about ten dollars) fitted with a good, improved Vermorel spray nozzle, will answer for spraying smaller patches, up to a limited number of acres. For larger areas, and if it can be afforded even for an acre or two, I greatly prefer the barrow sprayer here illustrated. It is especially designed for spraying potatoes and similar crops, and works to perfection. When the soil is rough or stony, and the task of pushing the barrow and loaded tank rather above the strength of the operator at the handles, a horse or boy may

Barrow Sprayer.

be hitched on far enough ahead to be out of reach of the sprays, and with little effort will pull the machine along. Two rows are sprayed at a time, but if bugs are very plentiful, I would prefer to go between every two rows, and thus spray every row twice, in opposite directions, in order to make the job all the more thorough and effective. An automatic agitator, which, like the pump, is geared to the wheel, keeps the liquid in the tank constantly stirred and prevents the Paris green from settling to the bottom.

Unfortunately, it must be said that the Paris green now on sale in general grocery and hardware stores, although put up and recommended for the very purpose of being used for the potato beetle pest, is by no means of uniform strength, and some of it decidedly weak. The proportions which we formerly used with telling effect, namely, one pound of Paris green to

150 gallons of water, now seem to give little inconvenience to beetles and slugs. I have been gradually increasing the proportion of the poison, and at present use one pound to only 50 gallons of water. But in order to make this entirely safe, and to head off every chance of injury to the foliage, I either combine the Bordeaux mixture (spoken of in next chapter) with the Paris green, thus fighting blights as well as insects by one application, or at least add milk of lime freshly made by slacking two or three pounds of burnt lime, to the 50 gallons of Paris green water. Always mix the Paris green with a little water to a paste before you add it to the spraying liquid.

Potato beetles are very destructive to egg plants, especially when first set out, and then again late in the season, after potatoes have matured, and the beetles find no more food except the egg plants, of which they are very fond. The young plants, when first set out, then still tender and checked in their growth, would fall easy victims to the beetles. They should be closely watched, and the beetles picked off by hand two or three times a day, until the supply seems to be exhausted or engaged elsewhere. Afterwards the larvæ that may hatch from the few eggs deposited on the plants notwithstanding all our efforts, can easily be kept off by Paris green application. A similar treatment is advisable for potato seedlings, or choice early potatoes of any kind. I have seen beetles come on in such numbers, after the potato season in New Jersey, that no matter how many might die from the effects of the poison put on egg plants, their places were at once filled by others, and it was impossible to save the plants from entire annihilation.

RADISH FLY AND MAGGOT.—I might rest contented by simply referring to my remarks under the heading of *Onion Fly*. Let me say, however, that entomologists classify the radish fly and maggot as *anthomyia brassicæ*, and give us three species of onion fly or maggot, namely, the imported onion fly (*anthomyia ceparum*), the native onion fly (*Ortalis arcuata*), and the black onion fly (*Ortalis flexa*). The common cabbage and onion flies, *A. brassicæ* and *A. ceparum*, resemble one another very closely and the same means which will check or dispose of one,

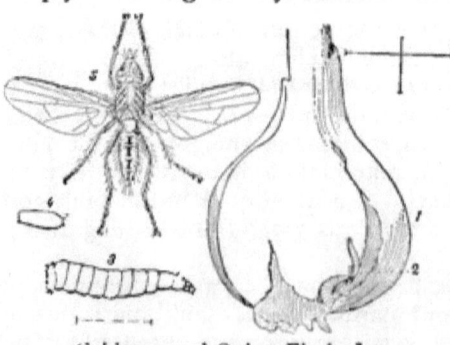
Cabbage and Onion Fly in Its Different Stages.

will also check or dispose of the other. The results of recent experiments seem to indicate that heavy dressings of kainit, muriate of potash, or possibly of nitrate of soda, and other fertilizers have a tendency to drive these pests from our fields, and possibly cut worms and other creeping and crawling things also. I usually make annual dressings of this kind to my garden soils, and I find that my crops suffer less every succeeding year from the attacks of maggots, cut worms, etc. I have yet to mention the collars of tarred paper devised for the protection of cabbage and cauliflower plants against maggot attacks. These collars may be round, square, or six-cornered. They should have a hole in the centre for the stem of the plant. A slit from outside to centre allows the collar to be easily slipped around the plant at the top of the ground. Good results in preventing maggot attacks have been reported as secured by the use of these collars.

SNAILS.—One effective method of dealing with slugs and snails, where troublesome, especially in greenhouses and frames, is to set traps by scattering pieces of orange-peel over the ground. The snails are so fond of this delicacy that they will remain clinging to the peel rather than go back to their hiding places at break of day. Examine the traps every morning, and destroy the marauders.

Sometimes these disgusting, slimy creatures appear in countless numbers, attacking peas, beans, corn, and other crops, and almost utterly denuding the lower parts of the foliage. They keep in hiding during the day, and begin their work of devastation after sundown. I can get rid of them very easily. The knapsack sprayer is charged with water in which a handful or two of common salt, or of muriate of potash, or kainit is dissolved. Lime-water will give the same results. Shortly after dusk I begin the dance, giving the attacked plants a thorough spraying. If necessary, this may be repeated in a day or two. Every slug touched by the spray will be dissolved, and nothing but "grease spots" will be left in the morning.

SQUASH VINE BORER. (*Algeria cucurbitæ*.)—Our first aim should be to repel the moth, and prevent her from depositing her eggs on the plants. Perhaps this may be successfully accomplished by placing corn-cobs smeared with coal tar, turpentine, kerosene, or carbolic acid near the roots of the plants. If we have not been successful in keeping the moth off, we should hunt up and destroy the larvæ (borers) when they first begin to tunnel through the main stock near the surface of the soil. They give the preference to pumpkins, squashes, and similar members of the gourd family, but also attack melon and cucumber vines, riddling the stem near the ground, and often cutting off all communication between top and root. Discover their location and dig them out with the point of a sharp knife. With squash and other plants which readily strike root from the joints, it is the

Layered Squash Vine.

easiest thing in the world to practically prevent all injury. All you have to do is to cover the first joints firmly with fresh soil as soon as the vines begin to run. The plants, as shown in picture, can then be made entirely independent of their original roots.

SQUASH BUG, BLACK. (*Anasa tristis.*)—In July the patches of dark brown eggs may be found on the underside of the leaves of pumpkins, squashes, etc., while the bugs are hidden under rubbish, clods of soil, stones, etc., near the plants. Few things seem to be repulsive enough for them to keep or drive them off the plants, but plaster flavored with kerosene or carbolic acid may be tried. It may at least tend to lessen their numbers. Trapping is yet the only sure remedy. Place pieces of shingles, small stones, or rubbish of some sort about the hills, and examine them for bugs every morning, dispatching them by shaking into a dish containing some kerosene, or mashing them with home-made tweezers consisting of a simple piece of band iron,

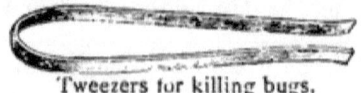

Tweezers for killing bugs.

and bent as here shown. The bug is repulsive and has a most disagreeable odor, but should be fought with persistency.

WIRE WORM. (*Julus.*)—These are the offsprings of various snapping beetles or elaters, hard, smooth-skinned, white or yellowish, worm-like creatures, feeding on potatoes, carrots, the roots of herbaceous plants, etc., and often doing considerable damage to these crops. As beetles, they live on the tender leaves of various plants. The name "wire-worm" is often wrongfully applied to the generally larger and darker-colored centipede or thousand-legged worm. Trapping or baiting is about the only method of fighting them which promises any success whatever. Sliced potatoes or other vegetables are buried beneath the ground here and there over the area to be freed from the pest, and each place marked with a stick, for convenience of examination. Look these baits over carefully every morning, and gather and destroy the worms.

Insects and Other Foes.—125

ZEBRA CATERPILLAR (*Mamestra picta*).—The parent of this worm is the handsome moth shown at *a* in accompanying illustration. The spherical eggs are laid in clusters on cabbage, cauliflower, and other plants early in the summer. The larvæ when young are blackish, but soon change to light green. The young worms cluster together upon the leaves and are then easily disposed of by hand-picking. If left undisturbed, they afterwards scatter over the plants, and the best way to destroy them at this stage is by spraying with kerosene emulsion, kerosene and water in mechanical mixture, hot water, or by the other means recommended for the green cabbage worm. A full-grown larva is shown at *b*. It is marked by broad longitudinal vel-

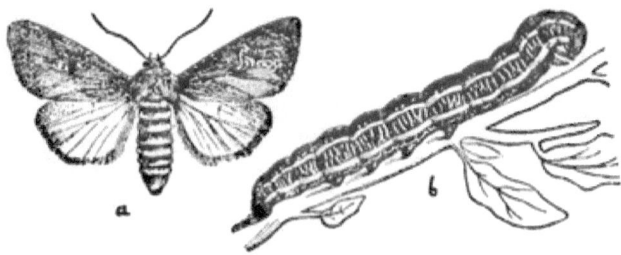

vety-black stripes on the back, and brilliant yellow stripes upon each side, connected by fine, transverse zebra-like lines. When disturbed the worm curls up and drops to the ground.

HARLEQUIN CABBAGE BUG (*Murgantia histrionica*).—This enemy is found only in the Southern States, from Texas along the seaboard as far north as Delaware. The full-grown insect, which is gaudily colored, chiefly in black and orange-yellow, lives through the winter hidden under leaves and rubbish. In the spring, just as soon as it finds any of its food plants, it begins to deposit eggs. The larvæ hatch out in a few days, and at once begin to pierce the leaves and suck the life-sap from the plants, soon killing them. They are timid, and on anybody's approach try to hide. The illustration shows the insect in its various

stages of development, in life-size. Clean culture and the destruction of all rubbish by fire, during fall or winter, are important means of fighting this pest. Hand-picking into pans containing water and kerosene is often resorted to. Wild mustard

126—How to Make the Garden Pay.

is a favorite food-plant of the bugs, and may be sown in patches or between the rows to be planted with cabbages later. The bugs congregating on the mustard may then be destroyed by spraying with pure kerosene.

TOMATO WORM (*Phlegethontius celeus*).—A beautiful sphinx moth is responsible for the existence of the large green worm so often found on tomato and potato plants. This worm, picture of which is shown at *a*, is a voracious feeder, and devours the leaves of the plants at a rapid rate. Whenever you see the leaves stripped, and notice the peculiar castings on the ground, you will find the worm close by. Pick off the leaf on which it is feeding, throw it on the ground, and put your foot heavily upon it, mashing the worm. When plowing, in fall or spring, we

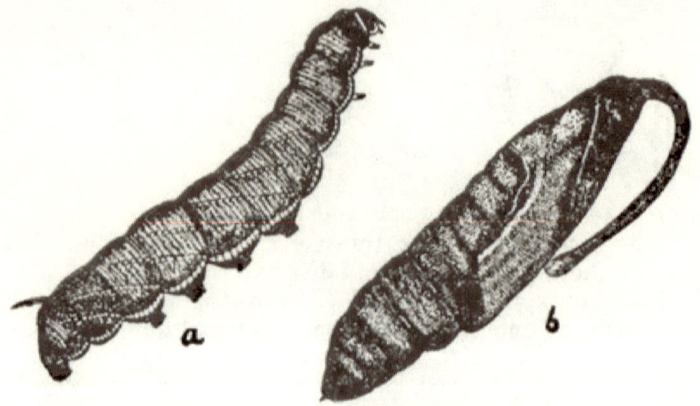

often find large pupæ, such as shown at *b*. They represent the next stage in the development of this insect, and should also be destroyed. The worm or caterpillar is subject to the attacks of a parasite, a small four-winged black fly, which deposits its egg within the worm. The maggots which hatch out of these eggs feed upon the juices of the body, and finally kill the worm. Caterpillars thus infested may be known by the little egg-shaped cocoons of white silk which the larvæ spin upon the backs of their hosts, and should not be destroyed. If left undisturbed, the little flies will soon issue from the cocoons and continue the work of destroying our enemies. It is said that the moths may be poisoned by smearing shingles or pieces of board with molasses, mixed with a little poisoned water and a small quantity of whisky or beer, and nailing them from one to two feet high to little stakes driven scatteringly over the potato and tomato patches.

Tobacco Worm (*Phlegethontius Carolina*).—This is a very near relative of the tomato worm, and resembles it closely in appearance and habits. The moth delights in sipping the sweet nectar from the flowers of the Jamestown weed (*Datura stamonium*), and this weed is sometimes planted purposely in tobacco fields as a catch plant. A little sweetened whisky and water poisoned with arsenic is then introduced into the flowers that invite the visits of the sphinx moth.

Blister Beetles.—Several species of beetles belonging to the same family as the "Spanish fly" so familiar to the drug trade, are known in various localities as "potato beetles," "old-fashioned potato beetles," etc., and frequently do considerable damage to potato fields. The most common among them are the ash-gray blister beetle (*Lytta cinerea*), shown at *a*, the black blister beetles (*Lytta murina* and *Lytta atrata*), shown at *b*; the striped blister beetle (*Epicauta vittata*), shown at *c*, and the margined blister beetle (*Lytta marginata*), besides a number of

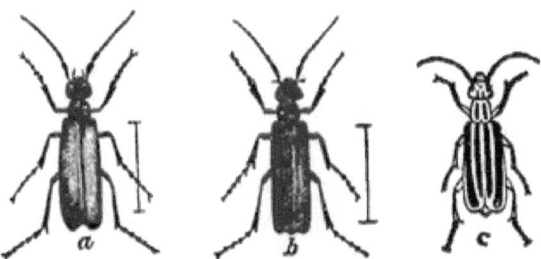

others. Some or all of these species live in their larval stage exclusively or chiefly upon the eggs of grasshoppers, and are therefore of immense benefit to us on this account. Usually blister beetles appear in large numbers in the season following that of an abundance of grasshoppers. In consideration of their services as grasshopper-destroyers, we would prefer to deal leniently with them unless they do much damage by appearing in large numbers. Then men or boys may be sent through the field, who, working with the wind, drive the beetles before them by short flights into windrows of hay or straw previously prepared on the leeward side of the field. These windrows are then set afire and the beetles destroyed with them.

Potato Stalk Weevil (*Trichobaris trinotata*).—This infests potato fields in various sections of the United States. The female beetle (a snout-beetle) places a single egg in a slit about an eighth of an inch long, made in the stalk near the ground. The whitish grub, which soon hatches out, tunnels into the heart of the stalk, usually in a downward direction, causing withering and premature death of the vine. The affected vines should be promptly pulled up and burned, and all vines of an infested field after harvest had better be gathered up and burned.

POTATO STALK BORER (*Gortyna nitela*).—This is the larva of a brown moth, and attacks a number of plants, especially potatoes, tomatoes, corn, dahlias, rhubarb, spinach, also the twigs of trees and bush fruits. Destroy the larvæ wherever found. The insect is propagated largely upon weeds, and clean culture should be given to all crops subject to its attacks.

TWELVE-SPOTTED DIABROTICA, OR CUCUMBER BEETLE (*Diabrotica 12-punctata*).—The slender white larva of this insect attacks the roots of the corn plant in the more Southern States, and is there known as the Southern corn-root worm. The adult beetle feeds upon the leaves of melons, cucumbers, squashes, and a great number of other plants. Paris green, applied as for the potato beetle and brood, is probably the surest protection to such plants against the enemy.

BOREAL LADYBIRD (*Epilachne borealis*).—This seems to be the black sheep of the ladybird family, and the only one of its members which feeds on vegetable crops, especially on pumpkin and squash leaves. In some localities along the Atlantic coast it has already become a serious pest. I made its acquaintance in New Jersey years ago. The beetles average nearly three-eighths of an inch in length, are almost as broad as long, and nearly convex. In color they are bright yellow, or yellowish brown, with four black spots on the thorax and seven on each wing cover. The eggs are deposited in patches on the underside of the leaf, and easily recognized by their bright yellow color. The larvæ are yellow with black branching spines. The beetles are easily found eating in broad daylight on the upper leaf surface, and spraying with Paris green water can be recommended. Destroying the eggs and larvæ early in the season should not be neglected.

RHUBARB CURCULIO (*Lixus concavus*).—The parent beetle is of a dull, grayish-brown color, and usually covered with a yellowish powder. They often gnaw and tunnel holes in the stalks of rhubarb, doing much injury. Its young are raised chiefly on the stalks of yellow and other docks. Keep your fields clean of dock, also pick off the beetles by hand when found on rhubarb, and destroy them.

GRASSHOPPERS.—The three most destructive and most widely distributed species are the Rocky Mountain locust or Western grasshopper (*Melanoplus spretus*), the bird grasshopper or American locust (*Acridium Americanum*), and the red-legged grasshopper (*Melanoplus femur rubrum*). In some years the

Rocky Mountain locust becomes a real plague in the West, stripping whole sections of every vestige of green in short order. Here at the East we sometimes suffer great annoyance by the hordes of the red-legged grasshopper, but seldom considerable real injury. Their natural enemies, especially blister beetles, birds, and various mammals, prevent their excessive multiplication. In the garden we can keep them down pretty well by giving chickens, ducks, hens, and turkeys a chance to fatten on them. If this method is not practicable, or the grasshoppers are too plentiful for the poultry set at them, we may possibly reduce their numbers by driving them out in short flights. Several persons, each provided with a tree-branch or switch, foliage left on at the end, walk up and down through the garden, beginning at one side, and with swinging switches gradually scare and crowd the locusts towards the other side, and finally out and off some distance. This may be repeated several times a day until the period of danger seems to be past. Possibly a windrow or windrows of old straw or rakings might be placed along outside the garden, the grasshoppers driven in and unto them and burned. One of the most practical methods of protecting crops from destruction by excessive numbers of hoppers is by baiting them with poisoned bran. Make a mixture of 100 pounds of bran, three pounds of Paris green, two quarts of old molasses, adding a little water to make the mass stick well together. The hoppers seem to prefer this mixture to green food. Put little heaps of the poisoned bran all over the area to be protected, or simply strew it between the rows of potatoes, corn, cabbage, beans, etc., etc. Cut worms may possibly be poisoned by the same means.

OTHER FOES.—Moles, although living entirely on worms and insects, and never destroying crops directly by eating, often, particularly in sandy and mucky soils, become a source of much annoyance to the gardener by tunneling under the plant beds, lifting out, and killing many young plants, indirectly by exposure and drying up. Good traps may now be had at very reasonable prices of almost every hardware dealer. When persistently kept set according to directions which accompany each of these traps, they will soon reduce the numbers of the burrowing pests.

RATS, MICE, ETC.—When troubling hot-beds, hot-houses, etc., are also easily enough trapped or poisoned. Cheese crumbs are a favorite bait for them; but there is hardly anything that will more surely entice the rodents than Sunflower seed. If a steel trap is used to catch rats, a large piece of very thin muslin should be covered over the trap when set, strewn with cheese crumbs, sunflower seeds, pumpkin seeds, etc., and perseveringly kept set. This will clear the premises of rats after awhile. Woodchucks are frequently very troublesome to beans, and occasionally

130—How to Make the Garden Pay.

to squash and pumpkin vines, corn, etc. One of the surest ways of getting rid of them, is to find the burrows, insert a one-quarter or one-half pound charge of dynamite with a long fuse, stop up every opening, then fire the end of the fuse outside, and leave the animal to its fate. A mixture of tar, sulphur and saltpetre, burned inside the burrow, with all the openings closed, will also hardly ever fail to produce the desired effect.

ADDITIONAL REMARKS.

KEROSENE FOR INSECTS.—Once more I wish to call special attention to the virtues of kerosene as an insecticide. Its mere contact is sure death to most insects, among them to many which do not readily yield to other treatments. Almost all slugs, maggots, worms, lice on plants and animals, and many beetles and bugs and their eggs are readily killed if we can reach them with kerosene. All we have to do is to apply it in such form or dilution that it will do no direct damage to the plants or trees. The Division of Entomology, United States Department of Agriculture, recommends the following formula for emulsifying kerosene:

		Per cent.
Kerosene oil	2 gallons.	67
Common soap or whale oil soap	½ pound.	33
Water	1 gallon.	

Dissolve the soap over a brisk fire in boiling water, and when in solution remove from the fire and add the oil. Churn the mixture for a few minutes by means of a force-pump and spray nozzle, or if these are not at hand, beat with a paddle until a cream-like emulsion is obtained. Care must be taken that the oil is thoroughly emulsified. If free oil is present it will rise to the top of the liquid after dilution and injure the foliage. If well made, the emulsion thickens on cooling into a jelly-like mass, which adheres, without oiliness, to the surface of glass. In making kerosene emulsion use rain-water if possible, or, if the well-water is hard, add an ounce of lye or a little baking (bicarbonate of) soda to the water. For scale insects dilute one part of the emulsion with nine parts of cold water; for many other insects, one part of emulsion to fifteen parts of water, and for soft insects, like plant-lice, from twenty to twenty-five parts of water may be used to one of the emulsion. Milk is considered even preferable to rain-water.

Another method of applying kerosene is in a mechanical mixture with water. Professor E. S. Goff, of the Wisconsin Experiment Station, first hit upon this idea, and this has led to the construction of an attachment to knapsack sprayers by the Mississippi Station which does away with all the trouble of making an emulsion, at the same time with every danger of injury to plants connected with the application of an improperly prepared emulsion. The accompanying illustration shows sprayer with attachment. The latter consists of a separate tank filled with the kerosene and attached to the main tank, but readily detachable. Any proportion of kerosene and water can be pumped from the nozzle by simply turning the stopcocks. The kerosene and water are so thoroughly mixed in the act of pumping that the kerosene is as harmless to foliage as in an emulsion of the same strength.

This attachment can also be used for many purposes other than the mechanical mixture of kerosene and water. In many cases it may be best to dilute fungicide only when applied to the foliage in the act of pumping. For this purpose the attachment will also prove useful. Of course when copper or other corrosive compounds are used in this manner, the small tank should be made of brass instead of tin.

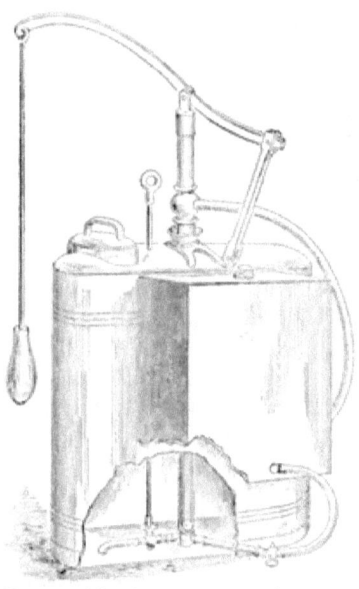

Pump with Kerosene Attachment.

GYPSINE.—The new insecticide gypsine, so called because first used for the gypsy moth in Massachusetts, is an arsenate of lead, and claimed to be fully as effective as Paris green, and superior to it in many respects. It has the advantage of being readily seen on the leaves, so that one can tell at a glance which leaves have and which have not been sprayed. Being lighter than Paris green it does not settle so quickly, and as a result can be distributed more evenly over the foliage. It does no harm to the foliage, even if used in much greater strength than the formula directs, so long as the right proportion of the two ingredients is maintained. There should be an excess of acetate of lead. The insecticide is easily prepared by dissolving eleven ounces of acetate of lead and four ounces of arsenate of soda in 150 gallons of water. These substances quickly dissolve and form the arsenate of lead. The addition of two quarts of glucose or molasses will tend to glue the poison more firmly to the foliage. The cost of making this mixture is slight.

WELCOME HELP.—It cannot be denied that we have a great many good friends and helpers among the creatures that walk, creep, and fly. The average gardener, however, is often entirely unaware of how much of his exemption from insects or of his easy success in fighting them is due to the assistance of friendly creatures, and altogether he is often too thoughtless and unwise in their treatment. He strikes right and left, without mercy or discrimination. He shoots the birds because they eat a few cherries. He kills every snake or toad that comes in his way, either from inborn prejudice or because he supposes these creatures to be ugly, entirely forgetting that "handsome is that handsome does." He traps the skunk that hunts and feeds on grubs, etc., because he wants to sell his skin. He scares away or poisons grub-eating crows, traps and shoots owls and hawks that live mostly on mice and insects, and lets city sports hunt, drive away, and kill or maim the quail and partridges that keep his cornfields free from cut worms and root-borers. With equal eagerness he destroys injurious and beneficial insects.

First of all, save and protect the birds. Almost all of them are insect-eaters, and many among them, even English sparrows, are at one time or other helping to clear the farmer's fields and gardens of insects. The young of the English sparrow are raised almost entirely on insect food. So are the young of robin. "Redbreast." Grown birds feast on grasshoppers, cicadas, May beetles, etc., whenever they have a chance, preferring this diet to other food. Crows, owls, and many hawks usually do us more good than harm. Quails, like crows, are great grub-eaters. They need protection, not persecution.

All reptiles, from the alligator down to the smallest lizard, toad, or snake, are the gardener's friends, tried and true, as they wage an unceasing war against his enemies. As the alligator keeps rabbits and coons in check, so the smaller reptiles prevent the over-rapid increase of many species of noxious insects. No reptile, however, can be of greater service to the gardener than the much-despised, homely toad. Place one or more specimens in a hotbed or cold frame, and see the insects disappear. Every crawling thing that comes within sight and reach of the toad, may its smell be ever so disgusting, its flavor ever so rank, its shell ever so hard, falls a prey to the toad's voracious appetite. The toad seems to be always ready for business. Don't kill the toad. Its value as an insect-eater is more generally recognized in England and France than here, for the homely animal has become a regular article of trade in the markets of London and Paris. The demand for the article by English gardeners, in fact, exceeds the home supply, and dealers have begun to look to this country for additional stock. In small gardens we might often employ toads as guards around hills of choice melons, squashes, etc., by providing them with a suitable guard house or hiding place, under a piece of board, a stone, or some rubbish right among the plants.

Insects and Other Foes.—133

Don't extirpate the skunk. Its perfume is not pleasant, and its skin is valuable. All true; but a live skunk in a hop-field or garden is worth more, for its good work in hunting and devouring grubs, than two dead ones any day, even if they are coal black and their skin worth $2 apiece.

Learn to know your friends among insects. The common lady-bug lives largely on plant lice, eggs of potato bugs, etc. The ferocious ground beetle hunts and devours canker worms, army worms, and especially cut worms. Four-winged dragon flies feed upon mosquitoes, etc. The soldier bug and the grand lebia seem to consider the potato bug larva a dainty dish, and destroy great numbers of them. Species of spider, known familiarly as "grand-daddy-long-legs," also make themselves useful by feasting on noxious insects. Blister beetles serve to prevent excessive multiplication of grasshoppers, etc. All these useful insects deserve protection.

CHAPTER XIX.

FUNGOUS DISEASES OF GARDEN PLANTS.

HOW TO PREVENT AND CURE THEM.

"An ounce of prevention is better than a pound of cure."

RECENT investigations have acquainted us pretty well with the true nature, modes of propagation. etc., of most of the fungi which attack and damage our garden crops, and cause the various rots, blights, and mildews. To find a sure cure or sure prevention has been the great problem; unfortunately it must be confessed that in this respect we as yet know far less than is desirable, or required to give us complete control over these diseases. The latter destroy the tissues; and tissues once destroyed, cannot be rebuilt. A cut or burn on a person's flesh will heal up, and skin will grow again and spread over the burnt surface from a near starting point; but a leaf burnt up with scab, or a berry touched by rot, is a leaf or a berry gone beyond the possibility of recovery. The term "cure," therefore, has no application in the treatment of fungous diseases. But we may be able to kill the fungus spores, and thus prevent the spread of the diseases. All our efforts must be exerted in this direction. Here again, as in the case of insects, we must look to change of location—planting at the greatest possible distance from any ground where the same vegetable was grown before, as to the first feasible preventive measure to be adopted. Even this, as in the analogous case of insects, is not an absolute protection, and unfortunately our senses are not acute enough to tell us from what source to expect the infection, and when to expect the attacks.

Heat and moisture favor the development and spread of most of these troublesome plant maladies. Consequently prudence would dictate the use of precautionary measures on hot days after warm rains, or during damp and sultry weather. We should be quick about it, too. While we have means to kill the germs and prevent their starting into life, nothing has as yet been found that will affect the growth of the thread-like mycelium (as the roots of fungi are called) after it has once entered the tissues of the attacked leaf, stalk, or berry. In short, the only way of successfully fighting fungi which attack foliage, consists of covering the yet unattacked leaf or stalk with a coat which the germinating spore is powerless to penetrate, or which kills every spore which tries to get a foothold upon it.

To provide such a coat of mail is the purpose of spraying with fungicides. The safety of the foliage is insured only so long as all its parts are thus protected. This also explains the need of repetitional treatments, especially immediately after heavy or long-continued rains, which are liable to wash the protective armor off, and leave the foliage more or less exposed. Young leaves, usually and fortunately, are less subject to the attacks of fungous diseases than older ones; but in time the new growth of young leaves becomes old, and will also require treatment. Hence we must not only spray early, but also repeatedly, and the oftener, the more favorable the season appears to be to the development of plant diseases.

Spore-Killing Mixtures.—A great number of different solutions and mixtures have been tried and recommended for their fungicidal (spore-killing) properties; but there are only a very few deserving general consideration.

Bordeaux Mixture.—For the purpose of supplying the protective covering spoken of, nothing has as yet been found superior or even equal to the copper and lime compound called "Bordeaux mixture," or "copper mixture of Gironde." The adhesive nature of the lime tends to glue the copper firmly to the foliage. Consequently the mixture will stick longer than any other fungicide yet suggested, and even through moderate rains. Professor Galloway, of the United States Department of Agriculture, recommends the following method of preparation: "In a barrel that will hold forty-five gallons, dissolve six pounds of copper sulphate (blue vitriol, bluestone), using eight or ten gallons of water, or as much as may be necessary for the purpose. In a tub or half barrel slake four pounds of fresh lime. When completely slaked, add enough water to make a creamy whitewash. Pour this slowly into the barrel containing the copper sulphate solution, using a coarse gunny sack stretched over the head of the barrel for a strainer. Finally fill the barrel with water, stir thoroughly, and the mixture is ready for use."

I find it more convenient, however, to make the mixture in a slightly different manner. First get the required ingredients and receptacles, viz.: the copper sulphate (or bluestone); fresh lime; a vial containing a solution of yellow prussiate of potash; a barrel, vat or tank large enough to hold the required quantity of the mixture; a tub or keg in which to slake the lime; some pieces of coarse sacking, and finally a dipper. For every fifty gallons of Bordeaux mixture to be made, use six pounds of copper sulphate. This may be in the ordinary form of coarse crystals, and will dissolve quite readily if you suspend it, in a basket or coarse sack, into the water with which the barrel or vat is partially filled. Slake a quantity of lime, and by adding water prepare a creamy whitewash. Then gradually strain this whitewash into the solution of copper sulphate. Occasionally stir the whole mass together, and test it by adding a drop of the yellow prussiate of potash solution. So long as the latter causes a brownish stain in the bluish mixture, more lime must be added. When the proportions are right, no discoloration will be noticeable after the application of the test liquid. Then add the quantity of water required to give the right proportions, so that there will be fifty gallons of the mixture for every six pounds of copper sulphate.

It is permissible to make a stock solution of copper sulphate, and perhaps also to slake at one time a large enough quantity of lime to last for a number of sprayings; but these materials should be always mixed freshly for every application. I prefer to prepare new solutions and mix them freshly every time when I want to spray with Bordeaux mixture. Always keep the liquid well stirred during the operation of spraying.

BORDEAUX MIXTURE WITH ARSENITES.—The great advantage which Bordeaux mixture has over most other fungicides is that it can be safely combined with Paris green (or perhaps London purple), thus giving us a chance to kill two birds with one stone. In the garden, this compound mixture will be found especially useful in fighting diseases and insects which attack the potato. The proportions usually recommended are four ounces of Paris green to fifty gallons of Bordeaux mixture. I prefer to use a much larger proportion of Paris green, up to one pound to fifty gallons. Be sure that the compound mixture is kept well stirred during the application.

POTASSIUM SULPHIDE.—For some of the plant diseases I have occasionally used a simple solution of potassium sulphide (liver of sulphur). The proportions are one-half ounce dissolved in one gallon of hot water. Allow it to get cold before spraying. This solution has been found to be especially valuable for checking gooseberry mildew.

BICHLORIDE OF MERCURY.—A simple solution of bichloride of mercury (corrosive sublimate, a powerful poison, one part in one thousand parts of water), the well-known and famous disinfectant, is of great service in the treatment of seed potatoes for the prevention of scab in the resulting crop. To prepare the solution, get at the druggist's two ounces of pulverized corrosive sublimate, empty this into two gallons of hot water, and let it stand until it is all dissolved. Into a barrel put thirteen gallons of water, and into this pour the two-gallon solution. After some hours, during which time it should be repeatedly and thoroughly stirred, it will be ready for use. Metallic vessels should not be used to hold the solution.

SPRAYING PUMPS.

THE KNAPSACK SPRAYER.—As a spraying device for general garden purposes, the "knapsack" style has no equal. It is not only a great convenience, but in my estimation an absolute necessity for every gardener of some pretensions. The illustration shows it in its general arrangement. The tank should be of copper. The kerosene attachment, spoken of in preceding chapter, will come handy, although it is not a strictly necessary requisite. As to nozzles, I prefer the improved Vermorel to all others. Certain further improvements on the knapsack sprayer, as for instance in the location of the pump-handle, are yet desirable, and no doubt will come in time.

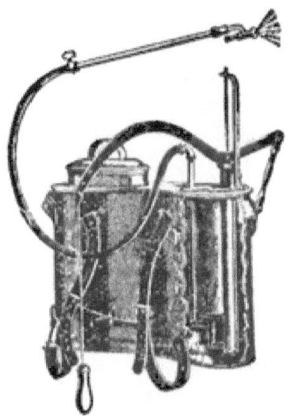

Knapsack Sprayer.

THE BARROW SPRAYER.—This has already been mentioned and illustrated in the chapter on "Insect Foes." It is just the implement for people who grow potatoes, egg-plants, and similar low-growing garden crops by the acre.

OTHER SPRAYING DEVICES.—Many of the cheap hand and bucket pumps which you find advertised in the agricultural papers, will answer in an emergency, but their operation is less convenient and less satisfactory every way. The knapsack is the garden sprayer *par excellence*.

PREVENTIVE TREATMENTS.—First of all, the prudent gardener will take precautionary measures against infection. Strict rotation stands foremost. He will remove his endangered crops to new fields, and as far remote as possible from infected ground. In some cases he may be able to kill the winter spores by direct applications of strong copperas solutions to dormant wood and surrounding soil (as in the instance of grapevines, etc.), by watering the soil with weaker solutions, or by sowing powdered copperas or perhaps flour of sulphur upon ground supposed to be infected with disease germs. Keeping the premises free from weeds and rubbish, and burning wastes and refuse, such as potato tops, old tomato vines, dead weeds, leaves, etc., with all the spores that have found a lodging place on these materials, will close another avenue by which infection so frequently is given a chance to enter.

Another important precautionary measure is the selection of resistant varieties, if any such are known, and the fortification of all plants against the attacks of diseases by good culture and judicious feeding. Strong growing plants are less subject to some diseases than are plants with weakened vitality. Young plants usually have greater power of resistance than older ones. The following notes may serve as a guide in the recognition and in the treatment of the special diseases:

DISEASES OF THE BEAN.—Most common among these, and often very annoying and destructive, is the "*pod spot,*" or *anthracnose,* which appears as small reddish-brown spots on young pods of snap-beans, especially of the wax varieties. The spots gradually increase in size, their centres become blackened, then changing to dirty gray or light brown. The affected pods, of course, are always worthless. The disease can be carried over from year to year by the seed. It also attacks cucurbitaceous plants. Beans and melons (or cucumbers, etc.) should be excluded from direct rotation. Reject infected seed, or disinfect it carefully by washing in the corrosive sublimate solution, or in Bordeaux mixture. The young plants may also be sprayed a few times with the latter mixture. The bean anthracnose has usually been known under the name "bean rust," but the true "*bean rust*" is a different disease, attacking both surfaces of the leaf, and appearing in small round dark-colored spots. Spraying repeatedly with the Bordeaux mixture may prevent its attacks.

The "*bean blight,*" which appears on all the above-ground parts of the plants in small pimples, often having a dull red border, and which apparently is a bacterial disease; and the "*lima bean mildew,*" which attacks and ruins the pods, resembling the downy mildew of the potato, do not seem to have as yet a general or even wide distribution. The preventive measures suggested for the former are the burning of the diseased plants, the selection of healthy seed and crop rotation, while spraying with Bordeaux mixture or other fungicides is supposed to give good results for the other.

DISEASES OF THE BEET.—The "*beet rust*" is little known outside of the sugar-beet fields of California. The attacked plants become dwarfed and discolored. The only treatment thus far recommended is to spray the seed beets with some fungicide (Bordeaux mixture), and thus secure seed that is free from infection. The "*beet leaf-spot disease*" is more generally known, and attacks the leaves of all the ordinary varieties of cultivated beets, mangolds included, appearing in small pale-brown spots, which gradually increase in size and become darker in color. The disease runs its course somewhat similar to the bean anthracnose. Spraying the young plants with the ordinary fungicides is suggested as a preventive. Rotation of crops and the destruction of waste leaves at gathering time, also seem desirable.

DISEASES OF THE CABBAGE FAMILY.—Our cultivated plants of the genus *Brassica* (cabbages, cauliflower, turnips, etc.) are, as a rule, robust and to a remarkable extent exempt from disease. Only a single one, so far as I am aware, the "club root" (club foot, clump foot), has often become a source of real annoyance and loss to the gardener. It attacks the roots of members of the cabbage family, causing swellings and malformations, and ending in the dwarfing or death of the attacked plants. Crops on limestone soil are usually safe from attacks, which fact suggests the free use of lime in seed-beds and cabbage fields. Applications of muriate of potash, kainit, possibly of nitrate of soda and phosphatic fertilizers, to cabbage ground, I believe also counteract the tendency to club root. If we use uninfected plants, and grow any member of this tribe only once in three or four years on the same piece of ground, we will have nothing to fear from the disease.

DISEASES OF CELERY.—Celery is subject to quite a number of fungous diseases, among them two leaf-blights, which are not dissimilar, and quite common and prevalent. The "*celery blight*," sometimes erroneously called celery rust, has become a regular and much-dreaded visitor in our celery patches. A leaflet attacked by this disease is here illustrated. The presence of the blight may be first noticed in small, irregular, yellowish-green spots upon the leaves. These spots soon enlarge and become darker in color. Finally the whole leaf is covered with great blotches, and withers away. The self-blanching varieties seem to be

Celery Leaflet Attacked by Blight.

especially subject to the attacks of this blight. Hot and dry weather favor its development. By providing partial shade and plenty of water, I think we can do much more to keep it in check than by spraying with our common fungicides, although such treatment is recommended, and may be of use.

The other form of *"celery leaf blight"* attacks the leaf, the stalk, and even the seed. The accompanying illustration represents an affected leaflet. The disease is easily recognized by the numerous small black dots which project slightly above the cuticle of the plant, and may be seen with the naked eye, or more plainly with a lens, in the brown spots and blotches on the leaf and other affected parts of the plant. These black dots are the spores of the fungus. The infection is probably carried over by them to the seed-bed. Safe precautions are the rejection of diseased seed, or its disinfection by washing in diluted Bordeaux mixture, in simple solution of copper-sulphate, permanganate of potash, or in similar germicides. Spray plants in the field with Bordeaux mixture. Less prevalent and less dangerous, even where it appears, is the *"celery leaf spot"* and the *"celery rust."*

Leaflet Attacked by Celery Leaf Blight.

The *"soft rot of celery"* is a bacterial disease which especially attacks plants when kept continually wet or damp, and which often causes serious damage. Plants that are kept either entirely dry or entirely under pure water will not be affected. The heart of the plants is most subject to attack, but the leaves are also affected by it. The illustration on next page shows a plant badly struck with this soft rot.

DISEASES OF CUCURBITS.—In recent years we have lost many of our melon, squash, and cucumber vines by a *"bacterial blight."* Suddenly in the heat of the day some of the plants, scatteringly all over the patch, show signs of wilting. At night, or during damp, cloudy weather, they stiffen up again and appear all right, only to repeat the wilting, in an intensified degree, the next hot and dry day, going from bad to worse until the short run of the disease ends in the death of the plant. One vine after another falls a victim to this blight, and sometimes whole patches are entirely ruined. A specially devised rotation which excludes potatoes, tomatoes, egg-plants, and other crops subject to the attacks of the same disease, is recommended as the most feasible method of preventing infection. Fungicides do not seem to possess much virtue in this direction. The "*cucumber mildew*," which attacks the leaves of cucumbers, melons, etc., much in the same manner as the downy mildew affects grape leaves, and the "*melon leaf spot*," which causes light-colored spots in the leaf, and finally holes and openings, and a rather ragged appearance of the foliage, may be fought probably with more success than the bacterial blight by spraying with Bordeaux mixture or other strong fungicides.

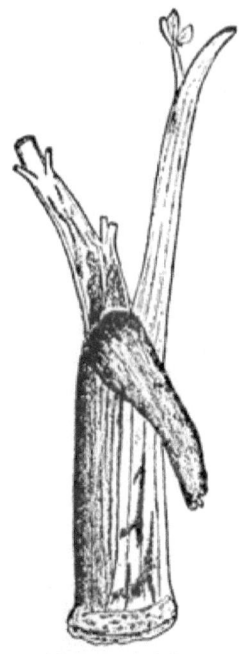

Soft Rot of Celery.

DISEASES AFFECTING LETTUCE.— "*Mildew*" is often very troublesome and destructive on lettuce grown under glass. In the first place we should aim to surround the crop in greenhouse or hot-bed with the same conditions which nature provides in early spring to outdoor lettuce. The temperature should not be much above 40 degrees at night, nor much above 70 degrees during the day. Lettuce needs plenty of moisture, but water from overhead should be withheld on cloudy days. Always water in the morning of bright days.

A sure and easily applied remedy is the one suggested by the Massachusetts Experiment Station (Prof. Maynard), and consists in keeping a kettle or basin of sulphur (brimstone) heated to nearly the boiling point, in the forcing house for three or four hours twice or three times a week. Enough sulphur must be evaporated to fill the room with vapor so that it will be visible, and give a perceptible odor of sulphur. Great caution in the use of sulphur is necessary to avoid its taking fire, for the fumes of burning sulphur will quickly destroy all plant life, and a few minutes of burning might result in the loss of the whole crop in the building. From the testimony of Prof. Thos. B. Meehan we have no reason to doubt that a paint of sulphur and linseed oil, put on the hot water or steam pipes in the greenhouse, will effectively prevent the appearance of lettuce and other mildews. On the whole, however, there is no better or surer method of preventing not only mildew but also the "*soft rot*," which so frequently attacks the hearts of forced lettuces when freely watered from overhead, than the new scheme of applying water by subirrigation, as explained in Chapter XVII.

DISEASES OF THE ONION.—For the "*onion mildew*," which appears upon the tops as a grayish mold, followed by more or less wilting of the affected leaves and the premature collapse of the plant, strict rotation, the destruction by fire of all refuse tops, and spraying with fungicides, where practicable, are recommended as precautionary measures. Hot and dry weather favors the development of the disease. By starting plants under glass in winter and transplanting them to the open ground early in spring, we can usually get the crop pretty much out of the way before the period of danger.

The "*onion smut*," which has become quite destructive in some onion-growing sections of the East, lives in the soil, and from there is transmitted to young seedling plants. It is easily recognized by the appearance of the black, sooty powder (the spores of the fungus). Badly affected plants always die, either by drying up or rotting. Planting on new and as yet uninfected land is the surest method of avoiding injury by onion smut. The new onion culture also offers a way of escape. Healthy seedlings grown in soil free from smut are not liable to take the disease after being planted in open ground. It may be possible to kill the smut in infected soil by watering with weak solutions of copperas, permanganate of potash, or other fungicides, or to protect the seedlings from infection by mixing flour of sulphur and air-slaked lime in equal parts, and sowing with the seed.

The "*onion spot*" disease causes black specks and spots on white varieties of onions after they are housed, especially in a warm and moist room. Onions showing signs of this disease should at once be sprinkled with air-slaked lime, thoroughly cured, and when perfectly dry, stored in dry bins in a cool and dry store-room.

DISEASES OF THE POTATO.—The most malignant of all diseases affecting the potato, is the "*downy mildew*," also called "late blight." Fortunately it is not prevalent to any great extent, except in an occasional season when the atmospheric conditions seem to be especially favorable to its development. Usually it makes its appearance rather late in the season, consequently early varieties always escape. But its attacks are frequently sudden and fatal, the affected plants being killed right down to the ground within a few days. The affected tubers rot-producing the characteristic rank, rotten-potato smell. The disease is easily recognized by the mildew-like growth on the lower leaf surface. All authorities are agreed that spraying repeatedly with Bordeaux mixture will prevent the disease, or at least greatly mitigate its attacks.

Much more to be dreaded, because more regular in its visits, more prevalent, and apparently less understood, is the "*leaf-spot*" disease, "*early blight*," or "*Macrosporium disease*." It attacks the leaf and stem, but never the tuber. The accompanying illustration will give an idea of its general appearance. The attacks may begin at any time after the plants are a few inches high, but usually the first signs of it are noticed at the approach of real hot weather in July. Grayish-brown spots appear on the older leaves, and the affected parts soon become hard and brittle. The disease progresses quite slowly; the spots become gradually larger; the edges of the leaflets curl up, and after a time the larger part of the leaf surface may be brown, withered, and brittle. In a month, more or less according to the weather, all the leaves may have succumbed, and the stalks alone stand—yellowish-green—leafless for awhile, to perish shortly after from starvation. The tubers are checked in growth, and remain undersized. Cool and wet weather usually puts a stop to the further progress of the disease. I have not been able to check it, in a perceptible degree, by even persistent spraying with fungicides.

Potato Leaf Spotted with Early Blight.

The "*bacterial blight*," which is characterized by the sudden wilting and the premature death of the affected plants, and causes the young tubers to decay or their flesh to become discolored, has already been mentioned as a disease of cucumber, melon, and other vines. It also attacks tomato and egg-plants. Its ravages have been more serious in Southern latitudes than at the North. Planting on new and uninfected land is the only precaution that can be recommended.

The "*potato scab*," a disease with which every grower is familiar, can be prevented by the use of clean seed and clean soil. The fungus lives in the humus of the soil, as well as on the tuber. Therefore land which has produced scabby potatoes in previous years, or has been fertilized with manure from stock fed with scabby potatoes, should not be used for potato-growing. The use of commercial (concentrated) fertilizers in place of stable manure can be recommended as a safe precaution. If the soil is free from the scab fungus, clean potatoes may be grown even from scabby seed by soaking the latter in a weak solution of corrosive sublimate. It is advisable to disinfect all seed potatoes in this manner. Prepare the solution as already directed (page 136), wash the seed potatoes, then put as many as you may wish to treat at one time into a coarse sack or basket, and lower this into the solution until the potatoes are entirely submerged. Leave them thus ninety minutes, then take them out, dry, cut, and plant as usual. The same solution may be used over and over again. But the greatest care should be exercised in its use, for it is a powerful poison. All treated potatoes should be planted.

DISEASES AFFECTING SEEDLINGS.—The disease known as "*damping off*" often causes much annoyance and loss to the gardener, as it destroys a large proportion of the young seedlings in flats and beds under glass. The point of attack usually is the root near the surface of the ground. The trouble then extends to the stem; the plant falls over and soon decays. Onion growers who practice the "new onion culture," often complain of serious loss of their seedlings, caused by this fungus. I believe that the soil can be disinfected, and the roots thus protected from attack. The most feasible plan is to water the soil with a solution of permanganate of potash, say an ounce to one hundred gallons of water, or of copper sulphate—say an ounce to fifteen gallons, or with diluted Bordeaux mixture, previous to sowing the seed, or if required perhaps after the plants are up. I believe in the thorough disinfection of all soils in which seedling plants are to be raised, and also in spraying the young plants freely and frequently with fungicides. It is also stated that soil may be disinfected by giving it the conditions (heat and moisture) favorable to the germination of the spores, and then, a few days later, exposing it thoroughly to a very dry, hot atmosphere so as to kill the sprouted spores. Baking soil in a hot oven will also be liable to free it from infection. Still another method of preventing this damping off is to sprinkle flour of sulphur over the surface, and then cover it with an inch of hot sand. Possibly a small quantity of sulphur mixed with the soil may also have a good effect in preventing this disease.

DISEASES OF SPINACH.—The two maladies which attack the leaves of spinach and often destroy whole crops, are "*spinach mildew*" and "*spinach anthracnose.*" Spraying is out of the question, for obvious reasons, and all that can be done is to try to prevent infection by proper modes of culture. The refuse leaves of every crop should be collected and burned, and the location or soil of the spinach bed changed every year. Raking a mixture of equal parts of air-slaked lime and sulphur into the soil, as suggested by Dr. Halsted, may be tried. A spinach leaf spotted with mildew, is shown in accompanying illustration (reproduced from *Gardening*). Other diseases of the crop, the leaf blight, white smut, etc., may be treated in same way.

DISEASES OF SWEET CORN.— "*Corn smut*" is so widely distributed, and so generally known to every soil tiller that a description here will not be required. The fungus can live in the soil from year to year. Infection should be prevented by the early and complete destruction of all smutty plants, and the use of new and uninfected soil. There are still other diseases of the corn plant, but they seldom cause much anxiety or loss to the gardener.

Spinach Leaf Spotted with Mildew.

DISEASES OF THE SWEET POTATO.—Several kinds of rot attack the sweet potato. The "*black rot*" has been found quite prevalent and destructive in the Atlantic coast States, frequently destroying twenty-five per cent. of the crop. Dark, somewhat greenish spots, varying from a quarter inch to four inches in diameter, develop on the tubers, sometimes covering the greater part of the surface, and extending some distance into the tissue. The injury takes place mostly after the potatoes are stored. To prevent it, use only perfectly healthy seed or plants, destroy all infected vines and refuse roots by burning, and practice strict rotation. Commercial fertilizers will be found safer for this crop, in this respect, than large quantities of stable manure. The proper treatment of the tubers in storage is as yet a matter for experiment.

DISEASES OF THE TOMATO.—The "*tomato rot*" is a common and often destructive disease. A small blackish spot appears at the blossom end of the half-grown fruit, increasing in size with the growing tomato, and rendering it entirely worthless. The older (less improved) varieties, like Trophy, the small cherry and plum sorts, etc., are seldom affected by this disease. Training the plants, thus exposing them to air and sun, and spraying with fungicides seem to lessen the tendency to rot.

The "*winter blight*" is a malady of greenhouse tomatoes. When first attacked, the leaves become dwarfed and somewhat faded, with indistinct yellowish spots on the surface. The spots grow larger; the plants dwindle, and the stems become small and hard. Affected plants usually linger along, a constant source of disappointment. All affected plants should at once be destroyed, and the soil of the greenhouse changed every fall.

The "*bacterial tomato blight*" has already been spoken of as affecting cucurbits, potatoes, egg-plants, etc. See page 140.

CHAPTER XX.

SEEDS AND SEED SOWING.

BY MACHINE AND BY HAND.

"Good seed brings a glad harvest."

GOOD seed is one of the essential conditions of success in growing garden stuff, and to secure it is well worth considerable trouble and effort. Compared with the results, particularly with the great difference in the outcome of one kind of seed and of another, the greater expense of a reliable article is not worth taking into consideration. A few cents' difference in cost of seed may make many dollars' difference in the returns. When a whole crop and its quality is at stake, there is no wisdom in running the slightest risk for the sake of a small saving in the expense. Cheap seed is not necessarily poor; but poor seed is always a costly investment. The fact is that seed of really first-class quality cannot be grown profitably at very low figures, and the only judicious course to follow is to buy of a strictly reliable source, and be willing to pay a reasonable price. Would you take a medicine that happens to be on hand, merely for the sake of saving it? It is a no more foolish proceeding than to use seeds because you happen to have them, or can get them at little or no expense. Never plant a seed of the superior character and quality of which you are not reasonably certain. Little difficulty will be experienced if any one is anxious to purchase reliable garden seeds, since there are many firms of established reputation whose goods can be depended upon for quality and purity. All the larger reputable houses send out no seed except that of the purity and reliability of which they are tolerably sure, and only after testing and approving of its vitality.

I cannot warn too emphatically against putting reliance on the seeds sold on commission by grocers and hardware dealers. It is obvious that in buying such seeds you will have to pay for the services of the middleman, while a direct deal with the seedsman will probably insure some saving in the expense. But this is only a minor benefit derived from this direct deal. When only one-third of the packets contained in the commission boxes are sold, it is plain that the dealer cannot afford to throw the two-thirds left over away, but, as a matter of self-preservation, must put the stale stuff on sale again and again until sold. Consequently, you are never sure whether the seeds you buy from such sources are one or five years old, and this also accounts for the frequency of the complaints about "seed that will not grow." While it is true that we run little risk of obtaining stale seeds when dealing directly with our reputable large firms, complaints about the lack of vitality in seeds are by no means uncommon; but I am quite sure that more generally the responsibility rests with the party who sows the seed, rather than with the seed itself, or the man who sold it.

PRINCIPLES OF GERMINATION.—Much stress has recently been laid upon the importance of using the feet in firming the soil over the newly-sown seed. I am inclined to deem the use of the head in seed sowing of still greater consequence. Any one who has a thorough understanding of the principles involved, and follows the dictates of common-sense in their practical application, will have no difficulty in getting live seed to germinate, whether he makes use of his feet in sowing the seed and firming the soil, or not. Yet in a large number of cases the practice is decidedly commendable, and will often insure success where the unskilled would otherwise fail. What are these principles?

Moisture, a certain degree of heat (varying with different seeds), access of air, and absence of light—these are the chief requirements. How can we best supply them?

The warmth generated by the sun rays is our chief reliance for the needed high temperature in open-air culture, without artificial assistance; and only in culture under glass do we resort to various devices to save, augment or supplement this heat, either by the prevention of loss through radiation from the soil, by sash covering alone, or in combination with additional artificial heat from fermenting manures, flues, or pipes.

Constant but moderate supply of moisture is another chief point, and to insure it, the seed should be bedded in mellow soil, and this packed around it just firm enough to bring it in actual contact with it, and facilitate and make sure of capillary action. If left loose over and around the seed, the capillary movement of the soil water would here come to a stop, the pulverized soil dry out in a sunshiny day and, depriving the seed of the needed moisture, prevent its germination, or kill the sprout if this has already started into life. Excess of moisture should also be avoided.

On the other hand, the soil must not be compact enough above the seed to hinder the upward passage of the young sprout. This is a prolific cause of failure with seeds. While having considerable force, yet the tiny plants only too often choke and die because unable to penetrate a hardened crust of soil. This consideration makes it necessary that the ground be well prepared, and thoroughly mellowed before seed is sown, and that the latter be not placed deeper than would correspond with its vital force. Large seeds, of course, have greater life force, and for this reason can be planted deeper than small seeds, from which comparatively weakly sprouts are issuing.

Seeds will not sprout in the absence of air, and if planted very deep, may remain dormant in the soil for years, but when brought nearer the surface, and thereby exposed to the oxidizing influence of the air, will at once start into life. This explains why only the weed seeds near the surface grow, while those lying deeper wait until plow or other implements bring them up within the life-giving influence of air and warmth.

The rule usually given is to plant all seeds as deep as their own diameter, but it is a rule more or less deviated from. Most of the common garden seeds are planted about one inch deep, except such as celery, small herb seeds, etc., that are left very near the surface. Peas may be put from 2 to 4 inches deep, potatoes from 3 to 4 inches, corn from 2 to 3 inches, etc.

PLANTING IN HARD SOIL.—It is comparatively easy to make seeds germinate in sand, sandy loam, muck, or soil rich in vegetable mold. But when the ground is clayey, and it must be feared that it will pack so tight and close, or bake so hard, that the tiny plants will not be able to break through, the shrewd gardener can yet succeed by means of the more liberal use of seed. What a single plant is unable to accomplish, may be but play for the combined efforts of a number of them. The safest way when dealing with soil in this unfavorable condition, is to sow the seed very thickly; and while this involves a greater expense for seed, it insures a full stand, and chances for a full crop without adding other disadvantages, as thinning is needed in either case and requires about the same amount of labor whether you have three plants to the inch or six.

The dried out soil in and after mid-season sometimes proves quite an obstacle to the ready germination of seed sown at that time; but the grower who takes the precaution to sow immediately after the ground is prepared for it, to deposit the seed somewhat deeper than generally done in early spring sowing, and to firm the soil very carefully after sowing, will usually have no difficulty to make good seed come up speedily. *Always sow in freshly stirred ground*—this is a most excellent rule, and deserves to be strictly followed in all cases, and for spring, summer, or autumn sowing. It will seldom fail to insure success, as long as there is life in the seed, and the least moisture in the soil.

SOWING SEED WITH GARDEN DRILL.—When the ground is prepared so thoroughly that the drill works to best advantage, it is usually also in best condition for the germination of seeds. Let the whole surface be mellow and even. This is easily accomplished in a clean loam, sand or muck. Often the only tools required are plow and smoothing harrow. In most cases the roller can be used alternately with the harrow to good advantage, and the surface thus made perfect; but on less friable soil, and if no Meeker disk harrow is at hand, the finishing touch must be given with a good steel rake. On clayey and very lumpy ground the preparation will require more labor, if not a greater variety of tools. The Disk or Cutaway harrow can be used to break up the lumps, and to bring the surface in proper shape for the smoothing harrow. This may be followed with a Meeker (small disk) harrow, and the latter, if properly used, leaves the ground as smooth as if raked over by hand.

Straight rows make the garden attractive, hence it is always preferable to mark off the rows of the desired width, or at least make a perfectly straight mark, or draw a line for the first row, and then use the marker attached to the drill, always trying to correct any deviation from the straight line. The small roller back of the seed coverers firms the soil, when properly prepared, sufficiently to make the use of the feet for this purpose entirely superfluous.

Sowing Seed by Hand, Covering and Firming.

SOWING BY HAND.—For the home garden, and where only small quantities of any one variety are planted, as in test plats for instance, the use of the drill is hardly desirable, and hand sowing is far preferable. A little practice will enable any one of average skill to make a clean job of it. The rows are marked out with the garden marker, and the operator, taking the seed paper in left hand, walks along the row and drops the seed evenly from the right hand held in the position shown in picture. The little finger and its neighbor form a sort of receptacle for a quantity of seed which gradually works down, and is evenly dropped by the

Seeds and Seed Sowing.—151

other three fingers, through a rubbing motion of the thumb against the next two fingers. A person can easily learn to sow in this way nearly as evenly and uniformly as is done by the use of the drill.

The covering is done by simply drawing a steel rake lengthwise over each row, and the firming either by the use of the feet, or by patting with the back of the rake. My favorite practice is to rake in the seed of the first row, then while plying the rake over the second row, to walk on the first row, thus firming it, next, while covering the third row, to walk on the second, etc. Covering and firming all at one time, can also be done without rake, and by the use of the feet alone.

Some of the very fine seeds, like celery, need particularly careful handling. The drill marks are made very shallow, the seed sown rather thickly, and the soil merely firmed by the use of the feet, or back of rake. Special devices are sometimes used for very small seeds, such as covering the soil after seed is sown and lightly covered, with a pane of glass or piece of cloth, etc., and this left on until the young plants appear above ground.

VITALITY OF SEEDS.—In a general way I am by no means opposed to the use of old seeds, when such are at hand, and a thorough test proves that a large per cent. of them will grow readily. This latter is the chief point of importance. Much theoretical matter has recently been written upon the different behavior of plants from new and old seed, as for instance, that new seed tends to produce foliage, and old seed, fruit and seed, etc. This difference in practice, however, is too small to deserve more than passing notice. As a rule, new seeds germinate more promptly than old seeds do, and this is one advantage at least in favor of the former. I have not been able to discover that the new cabbage seeds produce larger heads than seed of the same variety, grown by the same person the year before; nor that old melon seed gives ripe melons a day in advance of new seed of the same variety. The different kinds of seed vary greatly in the time they retain their vitality, and much also depends on the condition in which they are gathered and stored. Onion seed, for instance, is not considered reliable the second season; yet I have known a sample kept over until second season in a tight paper bag in the garret, to contain 85 per cent. live, vigorous seed. Properly ripened and gathered seed, preserved under average favorable conditions, will retain its vitality as follows:

Anise	3 years.	Borage	8 years.
Artichoke, Globe	6 "	Borecole or Kale	5 "
Asparagus	5 "	Broccoli	5 "
Balm	4 "	Brussels Sprouts	5 "
Basil	8 "	Cabbage	5 "
Bean	6 "	Caraway	3 "
Beet	6 "	Cardoon	7 "

VITALITY OF SEEDS.—*Continued.*

Carrot	4 to 5 years.	Mustard	4 years.
Cauliflower	5 "	Nasturtium	5 "
Celery	8 "	Okra	5 "
Chervil	2 to 3 "	Onion	1 to 2 "
Chicory	8 "	Parsley	3 "
Coreander	6 "	Parsnip	1 to 2 "
Corn	2 "	Peas	3 "
Corn Salad	4 "	Peanut	1 "
Cresses	5 "	Pepper	4 "
Cucumbers	10 "	Radish	5 "
Dandelion	2 "	Rhubarb	3 "
Dill	3 "	Rosemary	4 "
Egg Plant	6 "	Rue	2 "
Endive	10 "	Sage	3 "
Fennel	4 "	Salsify	2 "
Hyssop	3 "	Summer Savory	3 "
Kohl Rabi	5 "	Scorzonera	2 "
Lavender	5 "	Sea Kale	1 "
Leek	3 "	Spinach	5 "
Lettuce	5 "	Squash	4 to 5 "
Sweet Marjoram	3 "	Thyme	3 "
Martynia	1 to 2 "	Tomato	4 "
Melon	5 "	Turnip	5 "

Some of these seeds, like melon, pumpkin, etc., often grow readily even after having passed the stated limit of years; but all are liable to fail much sooner if indifferently kept. Such seeds as onions, parsnips, egg plant, for instance, should always be regarded with suspicion except when strictly fresh.

In the matter of quantity of seed to be required for a certain length of drill, it is usually safer to follow common sense than any of the directions found in books, papers and catalogues. The aim must be to insure a full stand in the drill. Fairly heavy seeding will be the means to this end; but a sufficiency may mean more or less, according to conditions of soil and seed itself. The gardener's own good judgment should be the best safeguard against his going to either extreme.

CHAPTER XXI.

NOVELTIES,

AND WHY WE TEST THEM.

"At our gates are all manner of pleasant fruits, new and old."

AN'S mind was not intended to rest content with any thing short of perfection—hence his ardent and never-ceasing desire to better all his surroundings and conditions. Not idle curiosity merely, but the almost divine longing to do away with imperfections wherever we find them, is what makes us take such an interest in promising novelties, and look so kindly upon every effort toward the improvement of fruits and vegetables, and what renders the "testing of new things" so attractive and charming. It is true that the great majority of novelties introduced with high claims of superior merits develop such shortcomings, after thorough test, that they are quickly thrown aside again, and soon forgotten. But the acquisition of a single worthy new thing often pays a royal compensation for all the disappointments caused by a large number of novelties that prove without value. I will cite as one instance, that of the "Prizetaker" onion, introduced by Mr. Wm. Henry Maule, of Philadelphia, in 1888. The little package of seed I got then enabled me to raise about one-half bushel or more of the most beautiful bulbs that it had ever been my pleasure to see growing, and the satisfaction I got out of their possession, and out of the opportunities to show the growing crop to visitors, would have made up very largely for many failures. I think I would not have missed the chance of growing the Prizetaker in 1888, and of planting more largely in 1889, for a number of times the cost of all the novelties I planted that season. It was a similar thing with the Emerald Gem Melon, Dwarf Champion Tomato, etc.

Some of these novelties mark more or less decided steps in advance. Let us look back upon the tomato varieties of 30 or even 25 years ago—small, poor, seedy, irregular, late. Then came novelty upon novelty in quick succession, each better than its predecessor—General Grant, Canada Victor, Trophy, Paragon, Acme, Perfection, Potato Leaf, Dwarf Champion, Lorillard, etc., until now we have reached a state of perfection in tomatoes that leaves room for distrust in our ability to originate anything better than we at present possess.

Verily there is pleasure in testing novelties, and the fact that some turn out good, and others not, only adds interest and spice to the undertaking. We have the satisfaction, also, to know that nobody has better things in vegetables than we have, and that we get the very best just as soon as anybody else has it. It gives us the proud consciousness of belonging to the better-situated and progressive minority.

For the market gardener quite often there is money in testing novelties. If a new radish comes out that is a day or two earlier than any we had before, or a new spinach that will stand the summer heat a few days longer than the older sorts, he may by another season be enabled to turn such knowledge to best account financially. The home gardener, of course, gets only his satisfaction and pleasure for his pay, and the depth of his purse must determine to what extent he can afford to invest in novelties. People who find it extremely difficult to make both ends meet, and are forced to practice strictest economy, should not attempt to test novelties except on a small scale, and in a cautious manner.

CHAPTER XXII.

SYSTEM AND ROTATION OF CROPPING.

"Gardener's, like woman's, work is never done."

N various occasions in this work I have already alluded to the necessity of maintaining a strict system of cropping, changing every year, if possible, or with some crops, like onions, at least at intervals of a reasonable number of years. Rotation is useful in the prevention of fungus diseases of plants, and in rendering it more difficult for insects to discover our patches of just the vegetables they live on, thus in a measure insuring the safety of our crops. For the latter reason we should not plant vegetables in succession which are subject to the attack of the same insect or insects, like radishes, turnips, cabbages, cauliflower, kohl-rabi and onions. All these are attacked both by the flea beetle and the maggot. Egg plants cannot be safely planted where potatoes were grown the year before, etc.

CLOSE CROPPING.—A system of close cropping, advisable even in the home garden for the sake of keeping it in best order and most attractive all through the season, and the weeds in subjection in a very convenient manner, is absolutely necessary for the market gardener who must make the most of his opportunities. High-priced lands cannot be left to lay idle even a small part of the season. The early peas, and lettuce, and radishes, and spinach, and early potatoes and other first early crops can be followed by cucumbers, melons, celery, spinach, summer and winter radishes, late cabbage, sweet corn, turnips, tomatoes, peppers, sweet potatoes, or whatever crop having yet time to come to maturity may be thought to pay best. New Jersey gardeners often plant a late crop of common (Irish) potatoes after strawberries. In fact, the ground can, and should, be kept producing some useful crop from early spring until winter, and then it may be made to carry spinach or kale, further south, onions, lettuce, cabbages, etc., either in actual growing condition, or dormant until spring.

A rotation of crops is also demanded in the interest of strictest economy in feeding them. Different crops need different proportions of the food elements, and the same crop grown to the exclusion of others is liable to exhaust the soil of just the element which it prefers to others; in other words, to disturb the proper balance of soil fertility. A judicious system of rotation prevents all this. The home gardener should also pay attention to this point, and change the location of each particular crop as far as the limited extent of the area will permit, or still better, use a new piece of ground for the garden, if practicable, every few years.

The best scheme which I could devise or recommend, is to have a garden of double the size required, using one-half of it for vegetables, and the other half for clover, changing parts every second or third year. The frequent reference to strict rotation as one of the means of preventing fungous diseases (see Chapter XIX) further emphasizes its importance.

CHAPTER XXIII.

WEEDS AND HOW TO MANAGE THEM.

"*A stroke in time saves nine.*"

CLOSE cropping with thorough culture as practiced by every good market gardener, and worthy of imitation by every home gardener, gives very little chance to weed growth; and where weed seeds are not carelessly scattered over the land, in manure or by other agencies, soon renders the originally tedious and disagreeable task of weed destruction mere child's play. The weeds grow less with every year of thorough cropping and cultivation. On the other hand, they increase in number, and become more and more troublesome with every year of neglectful culture, and with every year of using manures that are full of foul seeds. Such manure is a bad investment at any time, and for any crop, but almost ruinous to some crops, especially onions and strawberries. Rather than use weedy manures I would prefer to operate exclusively with concentrated fertilizers, supplemented by clover manuring, thus avoiding all this serious risk. The old and somewhat stale saying, "One year of seeding makes nine years of weeding," is in no way an exaggeration of the truth.

Weed destruction is not the sole, nor even the principal object of cultivation; but weed growth may often be considered almost a blessing to the more shiftless manager as it reminds him of the necessity to stir the surface, and imperatively demands, at the peril of the whole crop, that this be done.

Where cultivation is given as it should be, namely, as a mere stimulant, not a destroyer of plant growth, and for the purpose of making the surface soil answer for a mulch, and admitting air freely to the roots of plants, this constant stirring will not allow any weed seeds to do more than just germinate and die. To kill all weeds at this early stage, really before any signs of them can be detected above ground except perhaps to an unusually sharp eye and close observer, is the "one stitch in time that saves nine."

Some weeds I refuse to regard as a blessing under any circumstances. One of them is the Canada thistle. This curse of the farmer of which it is next to impossible for him to rid his fields and farm crops, after a neighborhood has once become infested, is easily eradicated in the garden by constant cultivation, and if necessary by the use of hoe and knife, preventing all growth of the weed above ground for a single season. No thistle root—nor any other perennial root—can live long without a chance to breathe. Deprive it of foliage (its lungs), and it must die from asphyxiation. Just for this reason, the larger biennials and perennials, the thistles, the docks, asclepias, etc., give the gardener much less trouble than a number of annuals. Among the latter, we have the purslane as one of the most troublesome; and in July and August, the gardener frequently has hard work to make headway against the immense power of recuperation and multiplication of these weeds. Sometimes there is only one sure way—to gather up every plant in baskets or a wheel-barrow, and remove them from the garden, or dig holes here and there over the patch, fill up with the weeds, and cover with soil. Chickweed is another troublesome thing, and it should be treated in the same way. Wild mustard is abundant in some fields; but it can easily be eradicated by pulling up every plant for a few years, allowing not one to ripen and scatter its seed.

Lang's Hand-weeder in use.

It is a most fortunate thing for the gardener that weeds do not take an early start in spring. Any crop sown in the cool weather of March, April or early May has therefore a good chance to outgrow the weeds. This is one of the reasons, also, that speak in favor of very early sowing of onions, carrots, parsley, parsnips, celery and similar vegetables, which appear somewhat feeble at first. The wheel-hoe will take care of the weeds between the rows of all such crops, and it is only necessary to pull out the weeds in the rows by hand or slash them out

Lang's Hand-weeder.   Hazeltine's Hand-weeder.

with a hand-weeder, such as Lang's, Hazeltine's or Noye's, or with tools similarly constructed.

To learn to use any of them to best advantage requires a little practice, same as the proper use of almost any implement in garden or field. As a substitute for the patented concerns, I have often used (or given to my weeders) common iron spoons, broken case knives properly ground to an edge on both sides and bent in the shape of a curve, etc. In fact, any small sharp-edged tool can be utilized as a hand-weeder, and in very mellow soil the fingers alone will do very well. The process of hand-weeding, of course, has to be repeated as often as weeds re-appear, and if the first weeding was thoroughly done, the subsequent ones do not require so very much time and pains-taking labor. But every weed must be removed; they are no blessing in any sense, and only deprive the crop of moisture (which feature is their worst) and of food.

Many of the annual weeds become very persistent in their efforts toward seed ripening in latter part of summer and early fall. They should not be allowed much rest; for if you give them an inch they will be sure to take an ell.

CHAPTER XXIV.

THINNING AND TRANSPLANTING.

"CROWDED—CRIPPLED!"

THE liberal use of seed gives us the desirable full stand; but also the less desirable feature of a great surplus of plants. Every plant, not required for making the crop, is practically a weed, as it deprives those that are to remain of moisture, food and room. To remove the superfluous, useless eaters and drinkers at an early period of development is just as essential as the early removal of weeds. Uniformity of vegetables—radishes, beets, onions, etc.,—and an even development cannot well be obtained except by giving each plant in the row a uniform and reasonably large amount of space. The annexed figures illustrate the contrast between a section of rows where the crop (onions) was thinned at an early stage of growth, and one where thinning is neglected. The market gardener whose aim is in the direction of an early crop—of beets, radishes, etc., which he can gather all at once, clearing the rows as he goes along, and thus having them ready for a successive crop—has no other way but thin early and thoroughly. The home gardener may do this work gradually with best results. So for instance in case of table beets. Instead of thinning all at once to the generally recommended distance of 4 to 6 inches apart, the plants may at first be

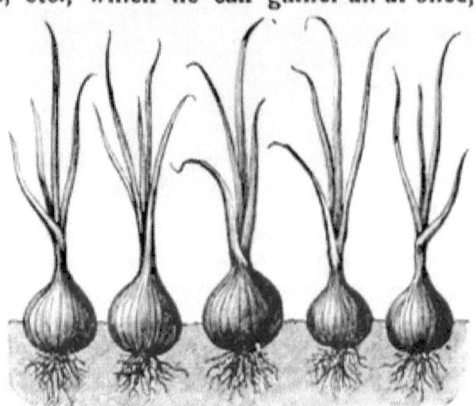

Onions properly thinned.

left 2 or 3 inches apart; and when the roots have grown of some size, and begin to crowd each other in the row, every other one be removed, giving the choicest young and tender table beets, greens, etc. A similar course can be adopted with lettuce, and people who obtain their supply of vegetables in the open market have no idea what luxury the small and tender hearts of half-grown lettuce afford. Try it once by thinning drilled lettuce to three or four inches apart, and when they have nicely begun to head, pulling up every other plant, and preparing just the young hearts for the table. These are some of the pleasures in the garden that mere money cannot buy.

In a general way I have yet to add that the proper distances among thinned plants, when these are yet very small, appear comparatively large; and sometimes people have not the nerve to slash down and throw away thousands of nice plants which as yet, appear to have an abundance of room. But this has to be done. Whatever distance is decided upon as the best for the particular crop, and in any particular case, should be strictly adhered to, and no foolish sentimentality stand in the way of making the distances large enough. It is much safer to err in favor of giving too much space, than in favor of too little.

TRANSPLANTING.— I am not a particular friend of transplanting, and avoid it wherever I can. *In theory*, transplanting, which is a sort of root pruning, induces early fruit production in tomatoes, egg plants, etc., early heading in lettuce, cauliflower, cabbage, and root development, such as is indispensable in good plants for setting outdoors. For this reason, gardeners practice, and writers advocate, repeated shifting, repotting or transplanting of all sorts of vegetable plants, in particular, also, of tomato, egg plant, peppers, cabbage, celery, etc. *In practice*, transplanting, with its unavoidable root mutilation, is a stab at the plant's vitality, and acts as a more or less serious check to its growth, thus invariably dwarfing it in some measure. Sometimes, if the operation was done under favorable circumstances—in a moist atmosphere, and absence of direct sunlight—it is certainly followed by earlier fruit production or earlier heading. At the same time it also and invariably results in reduced size of plant or head, and reduced aggregate yield of fruit. Should less favorable conditions be ruling at the time of the transplanting operation, however, the atmosphere be dry and the sun bright, the plant will receive a set-back which cripples and retards it for a long time, so that the untransplanted plant will come even sooner to maturity.

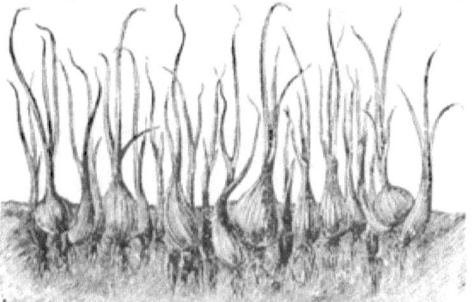

Onions left unthinned.

The great advantage that transplanted plants have over untransplanted ones, is the greater amount of space which people generally allow to the former. Seedlings are grown thickly in the row, and left thickly. In transplanting, the space is given to each plant that properly belongs to it. Let this be done with the seedlings, by early thinning to the proper distance; or, let the seed be planted in a pot or can large enough, leaving only a single plant to grow; and we can thus produce plants with a well-developed root system, and fully the equal to transplanted plants in every respect. This comparison, of course, refers to plants started from seed at the same time. Much higher rates are always asked for "transplanted" cabbage and celery plants, than for common seedlings. The former, it is true, are usually fine plants, with large roots and stocky tops, and well worth their price. I obtain just as good plants by growing seedlings thinly in drills. All seems to depend chiefly on the amount of space given to each plant, as may be seen in illustrations of celery plants. Well grown, untransplanted plants appear to be as hardy and as liable to take hold of the soil in their new quarters, as those that have been transplanted once or oftener, and they certainly can be grown much more cheaply and more conveniently. Strong, stocky seedling plants are good enough in any case, and preferable to poorly-grown transplanted plants. In determining the fruiting time of tomatoes, peppers, egg plants, etc., rapid growth of the seedling, favored by proper allowance of space, however, is not the only, and perhaps not even the chief factor. Age of the plant is certainly of equal, if not superior, influence. For this reason, the plants must be

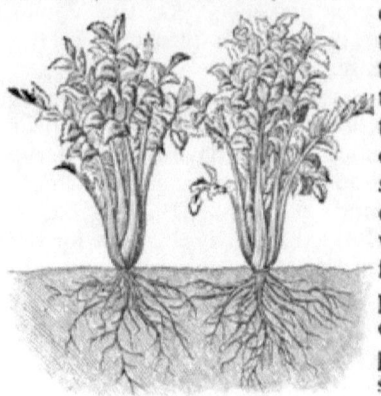

Celery plants thinned to two inches apart.

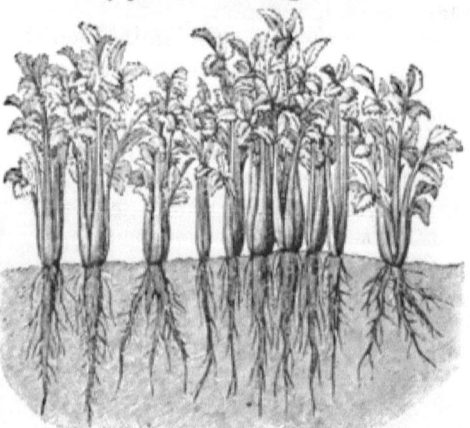

Celery plants irregularly thinned.

started early, and as the production of seedlings is more difficult, and requires so much longer time than that of cabbage plants, they must properly be started in "flats" or hot-bed, thickly together, and planted out at an early age, giving the space required for the production of good plants. Even in this operation it is always safest to select the most favorable conditions—moist atmosphere and least root disturbance—and thus to limit the unavoidable check to plant growth to the smallest amount practicable.

CONDITIONS OF SUCCESS IN TRANSPLANTING.—In a wet season, or during a wet spell, setting out plants in the open ground is an easy enough operation, and anybody, no matter how unskilled, can succeed without effort. During a prolonged spell of heat and drought—and we are apt to have such at the season for setting celery and late cabbages—the gardener often finds his skill and experience put to a severe test by the task. A supply of first-class plants, *i. e.*, such as were grown with proper allowance of space to each plant, and consequently possess a fully-developed root system and a short, stocky top, makes success reasonably certain even under otherwise unfavorable conditions, especially if some soil be left adhering to the roots in lifting and shifting. The most essential requirement, however, in any case is that the soil be moist, not wet or sticky, but so that it will easily crumble between the hands. If the soil be dry, it must be freshened and moistened by artificial watering, or failure will be the sure result. Planting in dry soil is usually fatal, even if water be applied afterwards. *Always plant in freshly-stirred soil*, is as good a rule as the similar one relating to seed sowing.

PUDDLING.—Simply dipping the roots of plants in water just before setting them, is fully as effective as the famous manipulation known as "puddling" (dipping in thin mud), and it is much cleaner, more convenient, and generally preferable. I, myself, have no use for "puddling," neither for vegetable, nor small fruit plants and trees; but dipping the roots in clear water, just before setting the plants, is a precaution which I, or any other gardener, can not afford to neglect.

FIRMING THE ROOTS.—Another indispensable requisite in successful transplanting is the thorough firming of the soil around the roots. It should be packed so tightly and closely that parts of the plant would sooner tear off than allow the plant to be pulled up by them. It is advisable, however, to draw a little loose soil as a kind of protection and mulch up over the firmed soil and around the plant, and in very dry weather the latter may be well-nigh covered up with loose soil to prevent rapid evaporation.

SHORTENING TOPS AND ROOTS.—Another sensible precaution in dry weather is the trimming or shortening in of the tops of cabbage, celery and other plants when getting them ready for setting out. It is done in the most convenient manner by taking a bundle of plants in the left hand, and removing about half of the tops by a twisting motion of the right hand. Celery plants with excessively long roots should have the tips cut off with a sharp knife. Plants treated in this way, after being planted out, appear as here illustrated.

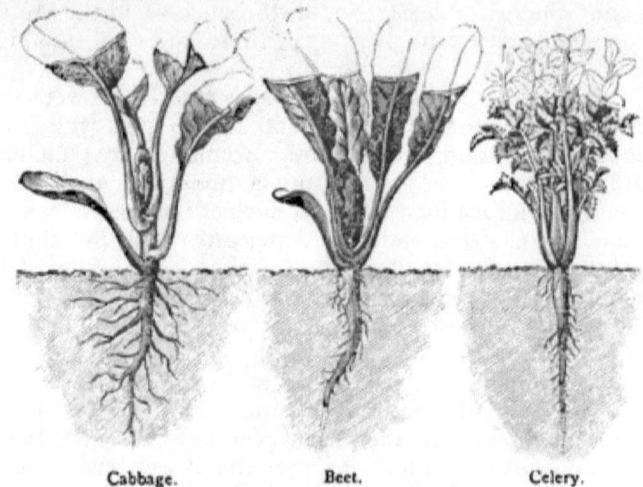

Plants properly trimmed.

TIME OF DAY.—Cloudy weather permits of setting out plants safely and with equally satisfactory success at any time of day or night; but when the sun shines hot and bright, and the soil is somewhat dry, the proverbial "after 4 p. m." is the right and proper time, and better than earlier in the day. If a little shade can be provided for newly-set plants, it is certainly worth some trouble to do so—soiled and discarded berry boxes, broken pots, etc., answer a good purpose, and leaves of large weeds, burdock, for instance, will be much better than nothing. Good celery plants are quite sure to survive the fiercest heat, on first being transplanted, if shaded for some days with a line of boards resting upon blocks or little stakes, and held there a few inches above ground. Bottomless plant pots (5 inch) which I had made for the purpose of bleaching celery, make first-class plant protectors, and plants thus covered for a few days, as appearing in picture, generally pass safely over the critical period. Tomatoes,

Plant Protectors and Celery Bleachers.

Thinning and Transplanting.—165

egg plants and sweet potatoes, all of which rather enjoy heat, and are somewhat indifferent to drought, require less care in the selection of cloudy weather, or moist soil when planting out, and may often be set safely when cabbage and celery plants could not be transferred to the open ground without suffering considerable loss.

SPINDLING PLANTS.—Even the most ill-looking, spindling, almost rootless plants of tomatoes, cabbages, cauliflowers, etc., can be transplanted with entire success under average conditions of soil and season. All that is needed is to insert the plants into the ground up to their very hearts. Overgrown tomato plants may be laid down in slanting position, care being taken to bring the moist earth in firm contact with the soil where underground.

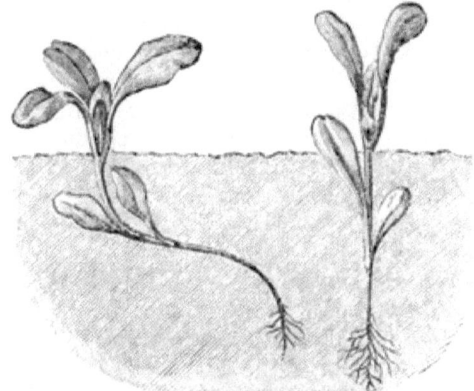

Planting Spindling Cabbage Plants.

Cabbages may be set either straight down or slanting, according to depth of surface soil and length of stalk. In either case roots will form all along the stems, and the heads will grow closely above the ground, instead of being held high up as if on stilts.

TRANSPLANTING DEVICES.—A number of transplanting machines, both for hand use and for horse power, have recently been put on the market. The most elaborate of these are rather expensive, but are said to do the work well, and not only set the plants, but water them, and apply fertilizers at the same time.

CHAPTER XXV.

MEANS OF PROTECTION AGAINST DROUGHT AND FROST.

SIMPLE AND PRACTICAL DEVICES.

"Saving is Earning."

IN most localities of the United States the gardener rarely passes through a season without encountering one or more longer or shorter periods of dry weather. Sometimes these periods assume the aspects of a serious drought, and the average crops of vegetables and fruits are often greatly reduced by these periodically repeated occurrences. Irrigation is the expedient most naturally thought of for meeting such emergencies; but as we have seen in the chapter treating on that subject, artificial applications of water—irrigation or sprinkling, etc.—are useful only under rare conditions, and mere sprinkling can never supplant the rains from the skies, in fact, is often more hurtful than of benefit. But we are not left without means of passing safely over any period of drought of reasonable duration.

PRECAUTIONS AGAINST DROUGHT.—During the colder part of the season, when the evaporation from the soil is slow, and the supply of moisture from the clouds abundant, the movement of the soil water is chiefly downward, while during the summer evaporation is usually much faster than rainfall, and necessarily the soil water in the main moves upwards. In other words, the soil forms a sort of reservoir that is filled every winter, and gives off its supply for the use of vegetation (and by evaporation) during the growing season. If this reservoir is shallow, as in case of soils resting upon an impervious clay stratum, the surplus is carried off by surface wash, or in the drains, and the supply is liable to give out when most needed; but if deep, as in the case of a naturally porous subsoil, or one loosened by subsoiling, the available water supply is large, and not liable to become soon exhausted. It is true that capillary action is also going on in the clay hard-pan, but it is far too slow to satisfy the combined demands of surface evaporation, and absorption by plant roots in a dry time. Hence our first aim must be to secure depth of reservoir. It is essential to supply the conditions which favor a free movement of the soil water up and down, and especially capillary action between surface soil and subsoil, namely, perfect drainage, and subsoiling wherever this action is stopped by an impervious character of the subsoil.

Having once secured these conditions as a foundation, the task before us is rendered comparatively easy, and we can now pay attention to the mechanical structure of the surface layer. Some soils absorb more moisture, and part with it more reluctantly, than others. The following table will make this plain:

Each 100 lbs. of clear Sand is able to absorb and retain 25 lbs. of water.
Limestone and Sand " " " 29 " "
Sandy Loam " " " 40 " "
Clay and Limestone Soil " " " 45 " "
Clay Loam Soil " " " 50 " "
Clear Clay Soil " " " 70 " "
Rich Garden Soil " " " 85 " "
Peat Soil " " " 175 " "

Soils, therefore, suffer most from dry weather in the order given. Peat never suffers from an ordinary drought, but gorging itself with moisture, which fills all its pores, is much more liable to suffer for want of air. The addition of sand, limestone soil, and even clay, will correct it in this direction. The absorptive and retentive character of sand can be improved by the addition of clay, peat, or more naturally, as in the legitimate way of crop feeding, by the incorporation of coarse manure, or plowing under of green crops. The beneficial agent in the latter cases is vegetable mold. Soils filled with humus absorb and hold water well; a rich soil consequently stands drought better than a poor one. Judicious selection of soil, or improvement of its composition by the addition of clay, manure, peat, etc., are among the most effective precautionary measures against drought.

Applications of wood ashes, (carbonates of potash and lime) also serve to make soils more retentive, and to counteract the evil consequences of a prolonged drought. Some of our best gardeners use them very largely, at the rate of 100 bushels or more per acre, as much with this object in view, as for their fertilizing qualities. I believe that nitrate of soda, and the potash salts also, serve to attract moisture, and to retain it for the use of the crops. Suppose we have paid proper attention to all the points before mentioned. We then find ourselves in first-class shape at the beginning of the season. The subterranean reservoir is well filled, and all we will have to do, to defy even a protracted drought, is to use the supply economically, and prevent its undue waste.

Our aim now is, and should be, to retard evaporation from the surface, and reduce it to the smallest possible amount. This might be done by a mulch of hay, straw or other litter; but the most convenient material at hand for the purpose is the soil itself. We simply pulverize the surface, for an inch or two in depth, by stirring it freely with cultivator, harrow, hoe, or whatever implement of tillage we may find most convenient and most effective. This covering of pulverized soil we must try to keep on top all through the season. The capillary action from below stops when it meets this loose material with its large interstices; and moisture cannot pass through and beyond it except by the method of slow evaporation; so that our supply is held for the use of plants below the stirred portion of the soil.

Hard rains, of course, again pack the soil tightly, and when this happens, capillary action is at once resumed, and moisture brought up by it clear to the surface. Therefore it is of the greatest urgency that we begin work again with the cultivator and hoe, as soon after each rain as practicable, to replace the important mulch of loose soil. When this point is properly attended to, and with the fundamental conditions spoken of in our favor, we will have little to fear from any drouth of average duration; and even an unusually severe one will not be likely to cripple us. Our yields may be reduced, but thoroughness and promptness in cultivation on judiciously selected and wisely managed land will not admit entire failure on account of drought.

PRECAUTIONS AGAINST FROST.—Quite frequently spring begins with a long mild spell, lulling the gardener into a sense of security, and inducing him to plant all sorts of tender things in the open ground. Suddenly a cold rain sets in, and on clearing, is followed by a night frost or two that make a clean sweep among all unprotected tender vegetation. In an early warm spring the gardener must take some risk, for there is no gain without. So we may plant some sweet corn, and set a few tomato plants, but never more of the latter than we will be able to protect by covering, or replace, should a late frost occur. If the plants were well-grown and properly hardened, they will often pass through the ordeal of a cold spell or a very light frost without suffering injury, where plants not so hardened would succumb at once.

The main crop of tender plants, however, should not be transferred to the open ground until the soil has become thoroughly warm, and all danger of late frost is past. This for the latitude of Philadelphia will be about May 15th, and further north not until June 1st. Tender plants up to that time are generally much better off in a protected place, frame or greenhouse, where with proper allowance of space they continue to grow uninterruptedly, than when exposed to the comparative hardships of cool soil and occasional chilly days and nights of early spring, conditions which will not permit much growth, and more generally keep the plants at almost a perfect standstill,

Means of Protection against Drought and Frost.—169

retarding them to such a degree that the plants set at a more congenial time often overtake the coddled things set two or three weeks earlier.

Should an unusually early and warm spring induce you to plant more largely before the usual time, one precaution must never be lost sight of, namely, to hold a supply of good plants in reserve for the very possible emergency of a mishap to those set out first. Here is just where so many growers come to grief annually, and almost every year we see people, after having lost their plants by a late frost, anxiously hunting the country over in June, for a new supply, and finally being compelled to take up with a poor lot of late-grown plants, or go without.

DEVICES OF PROTECTION.—Some afternoon in early spring the weather reports announce the rapid approach of a cold wave, and all the indications point to a coming freeze. Then comes the anxious inquiry: How can we save our nice tomato plants, our sweet corn, potatoes and beans, all of which were growing so finely? It will not do to stand by with folded arms, complaining of the weather, and bad luck. Our only safety lies in covering the plants. This may be done by sheets of cloth or paper, litter, or by boxes, large flower pots, etc. The number of boxes and pots on hand in average gardens may not go very far, and I would advise to make use of common manilla paper bags (the two or three pound sacks of grocers) for placing over tomato, and egg plants, etc. Smaller sizes will answer for pepper and smaller plants generally. Round off the corners at the open end slightly, and fasten the bag to the ground by a little wooden pin thrust through each of the two flaps and into the ground, or by a small chunk of soil or a stone placed upon each flap, as may be seen in the accompanying figure.

Devices of Protecting Plants.

Another mode of giving protection to tomato plants in an emergency, and one which I have seen practised with excellent success on a larger scale, consists of covering the bent-over plant with earth. Sweet corn can also be treated in same way, although it is much less liable to suffer serious damage, even if left unprotected. The soil must be carefully removed next morning, and the plants again straightened up. Early potatoes can be protected by simply hilling up, entirely hiding the plants from sight.

When you have marsh hay, or coarse litter of any kind on hand, a much better material for covering strawberry patches, and exposed vegetation of a tender nature generally, need not be looked for. Spread the litter thinly over the rows, and remove again next morning. It may be left as a mulch between the rows, or gathered up and drawn off for other uses if desired.

Smoke has often been mentioned as a safeguard against frost, and writers often give the advice to burn rubbish heaps, or heaps of a mixture of coal tar and moist sawdust, placed at intervals over the area to be protected. But this is another case where theory is better than practice, and I do not recommend it either for spring or fall.

Covering with hay, straw, paper, muslin, etc., is about the only feasible plan of protecting crops against the first early fall frosts. The home gardener can often save a few tomato and pepper plants, melon and cucumber vines, etc., by such means, and thus prolong his season of fresh fruits of these tender garden plants for several weeks, for a warm spell usually follows closely upon the first, and (often only) early fall frost. A few tomato and pepper plants may also be lifted with all the soil that will adhere to the roots, and placed in tubs or boxes in the cellar, or under a shed; or they may be simply pulled up and hung up somewhere out of the reach of frost. They will then ripen all the larger fruit that is on them, and give a full supply some time after all the plants left in the open ground are killed by frost.

The crops of winter squashes, late melons, and all others which even the slightest touch of frost would render worthless for keeping, should of course be gathered and stored in a safe place before such mishap can befall them. Full-grown green melons, if properly stored, may be kept for some time, and yet come to full maturity.

CHAPTER XXVI.

HIRED HELP.

EMPLOYMENT AND TREATMENT OF LABOR.

"The laborer is worthy of his hire."

THE finer quality of garden work, with its many somewhat delicate operations, calls for greater mechanical skill, wider experience and riper intelligence than required for the performance of the simpler and more primitive manipulations of average farm management.

Really first-class help is scarce even on the farm. If we watch the average plowman in the field, or the hired man as he wields the hoe, we will soon find that there is a wonderful difference in the quality of such work, and that the man who does a perfect job, like a true friend, is a *rara avis* indeed. More than in any other respect is it a truism of the labor market, that the "best is always the cheapest." The simplest manipulations in the garden are more than doubled in value and lasting benefit when directed by a fair amount of intelligence. One thorough hoeing, for instance, will keep the ground in better condition and free from weed-growth for a longer time than two or three of the average kind of so-called hoeing. The former (thorough hoeing) may require more "elbow grease," but very little more time. The same with other operations.

Years ago I had my onion-weeding done by young boys, picked up wherever they could be found willing to work for 50 cents a day. The poor quality of the work done by the great majority of them, the unceasing and close supervision and discipline they required, the damage caused by the careless destruction of many of the finest plants, the general inclination to slight the work, and the frequency of hand-weeding rendered necessary thereby —all these drawbacks made boy-labor at 50 cents a day come pretty high. Grown persons might have been employed at the same time at $1.00 a day, and they would probably have done the work 25 per cent. faster and 50 per cent. better, and that without damage to the crop, consequently at a large saving of expense, of supervision and of considerable annoyance. Verily, the good laborer is worthy of his hire: but the poor one certainly is not.

The gardener everywhere has to face this difficulty of getting intelligent labor—labor which alone is worth having, and worth paying for. It is well worth the trouble—perhaps an absolute necessity—for the market gardener to educate his workhands, and then try to keep those permanently that suit his requirements. In the first place he must plan to have work all through the year, summer and winter, and to engage his men by the year, and year after year. We can better afford to give a good price to thoroughly skilled workmen, than to employ careless and unintelligent raw hands at a one-third rate.

To make our good hands still more contented to stay, and willing scholars, good books and treatises on gardening, and the better class of horticultural periodicals should be freely provided for them, and the employer should not neglect to acquaint them with his plans of operation, and the reasons for the adoption of the various courses in garden management.

Everything, in short, must be done to make them feel as if it were their own work they are engaged in, and to make them do it with an object in view other than the mere passing away the time, and getting their pay for "time." If this latter is the only consideration for which their work is given, it will most surely be of inferior quality, and not worth its price.

CHAPTER XXVII.

MONTHLY MEMORANDA.

A CHRONOLOGICAL SUMMARY OF THE YEAR'S WORK.

"Doing the right thing at the right time—that is success."

IT would be a futile attempt to give specified chronological directions strictly applicable to all the gardens over the different sections of the United States with their varied climatic and atmospheric conditions. In the following chronological schedule of garden operations, the latitude and general climate of Philadelphia (Southern Pennsylvania, South Jersey, etc.), is taken as a basis. The growing season of the greater part of New York and the New England States, etc., is several weeks shorter at each end, with a month or two more of hot-house and cold frame management, comparative leisure and opportunity for planning, studying books, papers, catalogues, etc., during the winter. Gardeners must govern themselves accordingly, and make every effort to do the right thing just at the right time.

JANUARY.

Attend to cold frames, hot-beds and greenhouses, giving all the fresh air possible during pleasant hours of the day, closing again as a change of temperature occurs. Some days the sashes may have to be opened and closed several times. Cold-frame wintered plants need all the light that can be given, unless the plants are frozen, when they may remain covered with shutters or snow for two weeks without injury.

Market celery or any other vegetable that you may have on hand from last year's crop.

Draw manure to the compost heap, and compost to the fields. Order fertilizers.

During a thaw secure soil for your beds, protecting well with litter or coarse manure, to have it ready for use in making hot-beds.

Plan the season's work, aiming to have the ground occupied all the time, embracing crops that are most profitable, yet do not encroach upon each other.

174—How to Make the Garden Pay.

Order seed catalogues of leading dealers, and study them carefully; then make your selection of seeds, providing for all possible wants, and send in your order without unnecessary delay.

Select and engage the required hired help. Now you have choice—later you will have to take what others have refused.

FEBRUARY.

Attend to frames, and greenhouses, as in January. Ventilate freely in fine weather.

Test the vitality of seeds on hand, and order a new supply if necessary.

Inspect all implements, harnesses, wagons. Repair where needed.

First of month sow cabbage, cauliflower and lettuce in well protected cold frame or hot-bed for earliest planting, if no wintered plants are on hand.

Latter part of month sow tomatoes, egg-plant and pepper in a strong hot-bed, or in greenhouse.

Continue drawing manure. Fork over the compost heaps.

Last of month, if season is favorable, begin setting wintered plants of cabbage and lettuce in open ground.

MARCH.

Attend to frames, greenhouses, etc., as in February.

Cart and spread manure on the fields to be planted. Plow, harrow.

Sow seeds of radish, lettuce, onion, spinach, early beets, turnips, carrots, celery, hardy peas, parsley.

Dig around the rhubarb plants, and apply fine compost, liquid manure, or nitrate of soda.

Pulverize the asparagus patch, hilling up the rows. Apply nitrate of soda at the rate of 200 to 300 lbs. per acre.

Continue setting cold frame plants of cabbage, cauliflower, lettuce.

Plant onion sets and first early potatoes.

Prick out tomato seedlings in flats or on greenhouse benches three or four inches apart each way.

APRIL.

First of month sow seed of all hardy vegetables—radishes beets, carrots, peas, spinach, celery; the last of the month the first planting of the tender kinds, beans, sweet corn, etc., can be made.

Sow onion seed for sets.

Thin all the drilled crops planted last month.

Cultivate freely between rows.

Continue "spotting" (transplanting) tomato seedlings.
Apply nitrate of soda to the early crops.
Sow peppers in hot-bed.
Whitewash sashes of greenhouses, etc., to protect plants from excess of light and heat. Begin hardening off the earliest tomato plants.
Market earliest crops — spinach, bunch onions, radishes, lettuce.

MAY.

For succession sow radishes, beets, peas; also cabbages and cauliflowers for late crop. By middle of month sow mangels for stock, carrots and salsify for main crop.

After first week of month sow seed of beans, cucumbers, melons, corn and lima beans.

After middle of month set tomatoes, peppers and sweet potatoes in open ground.

Plant common potatoes.

Mellow the soil around plants set last month, to keep them growing vigorously.

Keep celery bed well cultivated and free from weeds.

Market early crops—onions from sets, lettuce, radishes, spinach, beets, cabbages, earliest peas.

JUNE.

Plant peppers, tomatoes, egg-plants, sweet and white potatoes, winter beets, late cauliflowers and cabbages.

Clear ground of early spring crops—onions, radishes, lettuce, spinach, etc.—and prepare it for second crops.

Keep celery plants growing vigorously by frequent cultivation. Thin plants as needed.

Thin carrots, beets, onions from seed, parsnips, salsify.

Stir the surface of soil frequently among all crops.

Poison the potato beetles and slugs.

Plant cucumbers for pickles.

Set celery plants for early crop.

Market radishes, lettuce, onions, celery, cabbage and other vegetable plants, peas, string-beans, cauliflower, etc

JULY.

Finish marketing early crops, clearing and preparing the land for succeeding crops.

Plant out late cauliflowers, cabbages, peppers.

Plant tomatoes on the discarded strawberry patch.

Set celery for main and late crops.

Sow seed of winter radish, early beet for winter, ruta-bagas, turnips; last of month kale, spinach.

Harvest onion sets.

Market early potatoes.

Keep the ground among all crops well stirred to guard against drought.

AUGUST.

Early this month finish setting celery.

Sow for late crop spinach, radish, turnip, kale.

Keep ground well cultivated and hoed.

Pull the late weeds before they mature and shed their seed.

Hoe cabbages frequently, also apply pyrethrum (buhach) wherever worms are troublesome.

Dig and market potatoes. Market cucumbers, melons, tomatoes, peppers, etc.

SEPTEMBER.

Stimulate growth of celery by cultivation, hoeing and applications of nitrate of soda.

Handle celery for early use.

By middle of month sow seed of spinach, and kale for spring.

By twentieth of month sow in drills, cabbage and cauliflower for plants to be wintered in cold frames.

Harvest onions, and sell them at the earliest possible date.

Clean up the hot-beds and cold frames, and get them ready for use.

Watch turnips and drive off flea beetles by application of proper remedies.

Market tomatoes, peppers, lima-beans, egg-plants, melons, cucumbers, pickles, etc.

OCTOBER.

Market the second crops planted in July: radishes, cabbages, endives, string-beans, beets, carrots, cauliflowers, sweet corn, celery.

Handle late celery, earth up gradually.

During middle of month sow lettuce for plants to go in cold frames.

Before frost pick green and half-ripe tomatoes, peppers, etc.

House squash. Harvest sweet potatoes before vines are injured by frost.

Harvest root crops and store in cool, moist cellar, or pit.

Set cabbage plants in cold frames, leaving beds open until hard freezing or snowy weather.

NOVEMBER.

Finish gathering and storing late crops.

Set cabbage and cauliflower plants in cold frame, and harden them by exposure.

Mulch spinach for spring lightly.

Protect parsley from snow and extreme cold by a board cap or inverted trough.

Celery not well protected is to be gathered early and trenched in, or stored in root cellar.

Market the bleached celery.

Harvest and store root crops. Gather salsify and leeks for winter use, and store like celery.

Top dress rhubarb with manure, bone meal, muriate of potash.

Clear up the garden generally, and get ready for spring crops.

Draw manure to compost heap or to the field.

DECEMBER.

Look to frames and forcing houses.

Keep cold frame plants dormant. Too much protection is worse than exposure.

Mulch spinach. Draw soil lightly over the tops of salsify.

Market celery, cabbage, onions, beets, hot-house lettuce.

Draw material for the compost heaps from city or town.

Look over the credits and debits of each crop. Figure which are the profitable and which are the unprofitable ones, and study the causes of failure wherever it occurred, to learn how to avoid it in future.

Part II.
Growing Special Crops.

CHAPTER XXVIII.

CULTURAL DIRECTIONS.

HOW THE VARIOUS CROPS OF OUR GARDENS ARE GROWN MOST EASILY AND PROFITABLY—THEIR LEADING VARIETIES.

"Care brings crops."

IN the following pages I have attempted to describe the best methods of growing the various vegetables, as practised by myself and good gardeners generally. Of varieties, I can only mention the leading or typical ones, and of the newer sorts those that have passed examination creditably, or at least give promise of value. Concerning untried novelties, I must refer the reader to the annual catalogues of our progressive seedsmen.

ANISE.

Pimpinella Anisum. German, *Anis.* French, *Anis.* Spanish, *Anis.*—Anise is one of the half-hardy "sweet herbs," and almost as easily grown as a weed. Sow seed in April or May where it is to remain, in warm and well drained soil, drills to be 12 or 15 inches apart. It is but little grown in American gardens.

The seed has a delicate flavor and perfume, and is prized for its medical properties. Germans use it quite commonly for flavoring apple-sauce.

ARTICHOKE—GLOBE.

Cynara Scolymus. German, *Artichoke.* French, *Artichaut.* Spanish, *Alcachofa.*—The Globe Artichoke is propagated from seed, division of roots, or from suckers. In order to obtain a stock of plants, seed may be sown early in hot-beds, and plants transferred to open ground in May, setting in rows three feet apart, with two feet distance between plants. The rich black soil of river bottoms, moist but well-drained, answers the requirements of this crop best. A bed once established will remain in bearing for a number of years, but needs protection in the northern states; and for this reason leaves or coarse manure should be applied between the plants from three to six inches deep, according to the usual severity of the winters.

The part used, generally in the raw state, is the base of the scales of the flower. Sometimes they are boiled and served as a salad. The term "Artichoke Salad," however, is more frequently applied to the side shoots, which are loosely tied and bleached somewhat after the fashion of endive. The vegetable is rarely found in American home gardens.

European seedsmen catalogue a number of varieties. The **Green**, or **Green Globe**, is probably as good as any other, and the one offered by American seedsmen.

ARTICHOKE—JERUSALEM.

Helianthus Tuberosus. German, *Erdapfel.* French, *Topinambour.* Spanish, *Namara.*—The Jerusalem artichoke or Tuberous-rooted sunflower is easily grown from the tuber, and where the latter has once taken possession of a field, is hard to eradicate. Poor, gravelly soil, too dry for most any other crop, suits this artichoke very well, and will soon be filled with tubers. Plant in open ground in April or May, in rows three feet apart, placing the seed tubers 12 or 15 inches apart in the rows. They require no especial attention until dug, and are not affected by frost if left in the ground. The varieties only differ in the color of their tubers, and are named accordingly, Red-skinned, White-skinned, etc.

Green Globe Artichoke.

USES.—The tubers, like potatoes, can serve as food for man or beast. Sometimes they are eaten in the raw state, as pickles or salad; sometimes they are boiled like potatoes; but however served, they can by no means be considered a great delicacy for the average American taste. Flesh sweet and watery. Hogs are very fond of the tuber. I think that on a piece of land having little value otherwise, the crop would be quite a profitable one for turning into pork, especially since we can leave the job of harvesting entirely to the pigs themselves. Hog snouts are also the most convenient tool with which to rid a piece of land of the Jerusalem artichoke, when this becomes a nuisance, which it is liable to do.

ASPARAGUS.

Asparagus Officinalis. German, *Spargel.* French, *Asperge.* Spanish, *Asparrago.*—Asparagus not only gives us a most excellent, wholesome and palatable vegetable, but also a great quantity from a comparatively small area, and this at a time when other fresh succulent vegetables are scarce, and the average person's appetite sharp for just that kind of food after a long period of "much meat and little vegetable." No wonder the demand for the crop, in spite of heavy annual plantings, and a steadily increasing area, has until now been larger than the supply. Very little of it has thus far found its way to the canning establishments, and it seems that these would be glad to work up quantities of it, if a steady supply at reasonable rates were available. The crop, in short, is, and probably will continue to be, a paying one, both for the home gardener, whose little patch supplies his table bountifully from April or May to July, for eight or ten weeks, and for the market gardener near town or city whose crop nets him from $200 to $400 per acre, and under very favorable circumstances even more, and all this with comparatively little labor and expense, and year after year when a bed or patch has once been established, and reached bearing age. Yet many home growers, especially among the farmers, have not yet learned to appreciate this crop as they should for their own and their family's good, and thus far fail to grasp the opportunities that it offers.

GROWING THE PLANTS.—In order to grow a supply of first-class plants, it is only necessary to sow seed thinly in drills one foot apart, giving to each plant about two or three inches space in the row. Of course, the soil should be well enriched, and thoroughly prepared, and after sowing, well stirred between the plants by means of hand wheel-hoe, hoe, rake, hand-weeder, etc. Weeds must not be tolerated. In this way on rich, moist, mucky or sandy soil I have often grown plants as large, and fully as good, as the average two-year-old plants purchased of nurserymen. A surplus of good plants can in most cases be disposed of to neighbors or towns-people at a good price, say from 40 to 100 cents per 100 plants.

STARTING THE BED.—The price depends largely on earliness and especially on size and general appearance. The earliest "grass" brings the highest price, and market quotations taper off gradually as the season advances. Large first-class stuff always brings almost double what is paid for an inferior article. These considerations should guide us in the selection of soil and site, manuring, planting, etc. No factor that might have a tendency to promote earliness, and size and quality of the "grass," can be safely ignored. On the other hand we give the cold shoulder to the old style of digging deep trenches, and filling the whole soil with manure to a considerable depth as formerly practiced—as a waste of labor and manure. Neither do we consider it necessary to apply a great deal of manure when first setting the plants in the permanent bed.

In the selection of soil and site, however, we will be apt to exercise the greatest care. Our first choice will be a deep, warm,

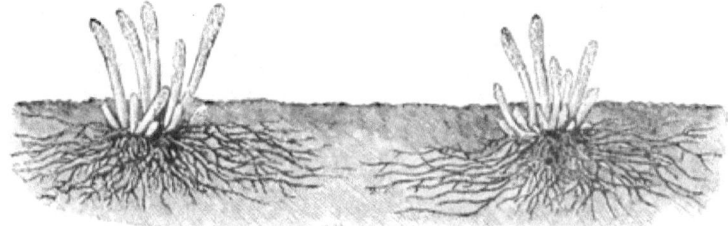

Asparagus Grown Above Ground.

sandy loam, preferably slightly sloping to south or southeast, our next choice a light clay loam. Porous subsoil is almost a necessity, and the use of subsoil plow will be a great advantage where this condition is not perfect. Prepare the ground thorougly by plowing, harrowing, rolling.

The two ways of growing the crop, both for market and home use, are illustrated in the accompanying figures. In the first, the plants are set shallow, perhaps three or four inches deep, and the stalks broken or cut off near the surface of ground,

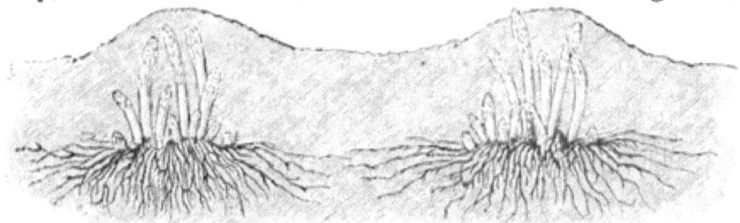

Asparagus Grown for City Markets.

when six or eight inches high. This gives us green "grass," always tender, but of a somewhat pronounced flavor. It is a favorite way with the home grower, and in some particular markets.

For most larger markets, especially that of New York city, the stalks are grown under ground, as above illustrated, and thus naturally blanched. It is true that the lower end of each stalk is apt to be somewhat tough, and needs peeling and perhaps shortening, but the flavor is decidedly milder, and of a more refined character than that of the stronger-flavored green stalks.

The market gardener, of course, has to comply with the demands of his available market; the home grower may consult his own individual taste and preference. I will only add that the bleached "grass," when poorly grown in hard, starved soil, is poor indeed; but under good culture, in warm, mellow soil, it is a superior article.

The preparation of the ground, setting the plants, and after-culture, are much the same for both methods, except that the plants are placed only three or four inches deep in one case, against six or eight inches deep in the other.

DISTANCE OF PLANTS.—The size and consequent market value of the stalks is influenced more by the amount of space allotted to each plant, than by any other single circumstance, and for this reason I consider wide planting the only sensible and safe course for the market grower. Some of our most successful gardeners make the rows six feet apart, with three or four feet distance between the plants. Even then the roots completely fill the soil, and interlock between the wide rows. Planting at this distance admits of cultivation both ways. The least distance that should be given in a bed expected to yield fine large stalks for many years is five feet by two, requiring between 4000 and 5000 plants to the acre; and nothing can be gained by planting closer. Fifty plants thus set in good soil will furnish an abundant supply of "grass" for a large family.

PLANTING.—Plow out furrows in well-prepared soil, at least five feet apart, and 10 or 12 inches deep, or if less, at least as deep as depth of surface soil will allow. Then scatter a few inches of rich, well-rotted compost into the furrows, fill in about as much soil, mixing this well with the manure, and set the plants, good, strong, one-year-old to be preferred, at least two feet apart, each upon a little mound of soil and with roots nicely and evenly spread, in the manner shown in picture, and at such a depth that the crowns will be about 7 inches below the ground level. Then cover with two inches of soil, and another dressing of fine rich compost. As the plants grow, and in the due process of cultivation by horse, the furrows are gradually filled up level with the surface.

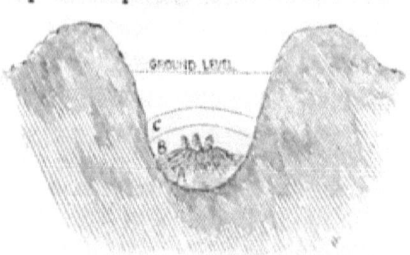

Planting Asparagus in Furrow.

AFTER CULTURE.—The bed should be kept well cultivated, and free from weeds. The first season some hoed crop, like potatoes, cabbages, radishes, turnips, etc., might be grown between the rows, but in that case the application of the fertilizer required to make up for the removed plant food must not be neglected. In the fall, and every fall afterwards, the tops are to be cut before they shed their seed, taken off the field, or piled up and burned. The young plants, that spring up from seed carelessly left to drop, are sometimes worse than weeds. Winter protection by covering with coarse litter or otherwise is not needed except at the extreme north. The stalks should all be left to grow the next (second) season, and same thorough cultivation and general treatment given as in the first. In the spring apply a top dressing of good compost.

With careful planting in the way described, and strong plants to begin with, the bed will yield a fair crop the third season, and a full one every year afterwards. The wise grower will cut sparingly the first cropping season, and always and every season stop cutting at the first indication of weakness of the plants. Long-continued cutting is a great strain on the roots, and some rest is absolutely needed to keep them in health and strength. Some kind of manure is to be given every spring, according to the needs of the soil. Compost may be alternated with commercial fertilizers. A good practice followed by growers in New Jersey and elsewhere, is to open a furrow with a one-horse plow between each two rows, fill this with compost, and turn the soil back upon it. Excessive manuring will hardly ever be required. Salt may be beneficial in some cases, but generally has little or no effect. Being a salt-water plant, asparagus can stand almost any quantity of salt without injury, but it does not show any partiality for it. All manures should be applied in the spring, and an annual top-dressing of nitrate of soda, at the time that the first shoots begin to start (in March or April), and at the rate of 200 or 300 pounds per acre, is one of the surest-paying investments.

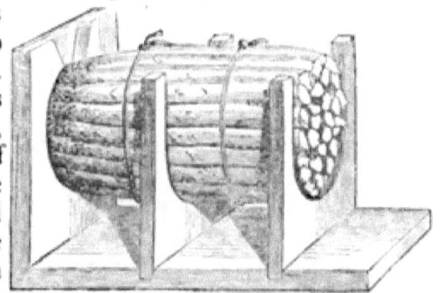

Home-made Asparagus Buncher.

When the time of cutting the stalks draws nigh, the rows are nicely rounded off, as was shown on page 143, and the crop is gathered every morning. Cutting has to be done with a careful hand in order to avoid injury to the tops of other stalks that have not yet reached the surface.

MARKETING.—Reject all the ill-shaped and under-sized stalks, and using one of the modern asparagus bunchers now on sale in every hardware store, make neat, firm bunches, which should be about eight or nine inches long, and four or five in diameter, holding two or three pounds of "grass". Rubber bands are now coming in use in place of raffia or other tying materials; they save time and make a neat, salable package. The butt ends of each bundle are squared by a smooth, clean cut. People who have only a comparatively small area in asparagus, may, if they prefer, bunch their stalks by means of a home-made buncher, such as, for instance, is illustrated on page 185. It needs no further description.

If the product is to be shipped to market, the bunches, to insure their arrival in market in best condition, are packed in some soft material, and pressed firmly and tightly into the package to prevent injury by jarring or shaking about. Knives for cutting

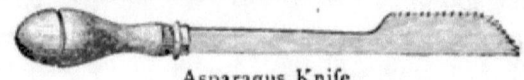

Asparagus Knife.

the crop are kept on sale by hardware dealers, seedsmen, etc. One of the various shapes is illustrated above. In an emergency a common sharp kitchen knife will answer.

SUPERIOR METHOD FOR AMATEURS.—The home grower who is after extra quality, can well afford to take a little extra pains in the preparation of his bed. Instead of filling the furrows with soil simply, he may prepare a very light, very porous compost of fresh horse droppings, muck, wood, or chip dirt, chaff, fine sawdust, rotten forest leaves, etc. This material lies very loosely over the crowns of the plants, and is warmed through very easily by the sun rays, at the same time affording a good protection from cold. Instead of cutting the stalks with a knife, the hand can be easily pushed down along them into the loose soil, and the stalks snapped off at the base with a pressure of the finger. Asparagus grown in this way is very superior, and it may even be profitable when thus grown on a larger scale for market. I have been well pleased with the results of one trial.

VARIETIES.

Conover's Colossal is the variety now generally grown by both market and home growers. **Philadelphia Mammoth**, recently introduced as an extra large and prolific sort, **Palmetto**, and a few other newer varieties, have not been generally tested, but deserve further trial.

BALM.

Melissa Officinalis. German, *Citronen Melisse;* French, *Melisse Citronelle;* Spanish, *Toronjil Citronella.*—Although a perennial, balm is usually cultivated as an annual. Sow seed in finely prepared soil, in April or May, having drills one foot apart, and thin or transplant to six or eight inches. It can also be grown by division of the root. In that case plant in spring one foot apart each way. All the green parts of the plant have a most agreeable aromatic odor, especially when bruised. The leaves are used for seasoning.

BASIL—SWEET.

Sweet Basil.

Ocymum Basilicum. German, *Basilienkraut;* French, *Basilic;* Spanish, *Albaca.*—Select light, warm, rich soil, and sow in May, in drills one foot apart, thinning or transplanting to 6 or 8 inches apart. The leaves have an agreeable perfume and flavor and are used for seasoning.

BEANS.

Phaseolus. German, *Bohne;* French, *Haricot;* Spanish, *Judia.*—Horticulturally we divide the varieties of this important vegetable in two great sections—the Bush and the Pole varieties. In the former we include all those usually grown as a field crop for dry shelled beans, as also the various green-podded snaps, and the yellow-podded wax beans. A more practical classification could hardly be adopted, since the cultivation of all the varieties of each section is pretty much the same.

BUSH BEANS.

The modest requirements of the crop are proverbial, and so it is nothing uncommon to hear farmers speak of land "too poor to raise white beans." Yet the fact which this suggests, is true only in a very limited sense. Their cultivation is decidedly easy and simple, and a crop can be grown on soils of most widely-differing character; but a crop worth growing cannot be produced on soils exhausted of available mineral elements of plant food, especially of potash. Wood ashes and other potash fertilizers are generally of especial benefit to this crop.

All beans are somewhat tender, and should not be planted until danger of late spring frosts is past, or until the time farmers usually plant corn. For a field crop, on a large scale, seed is best sown with a one or two-horse drill; but it can also be done with the garden drill. I prefer to lay off the land in furrows, three feet or so apart, made with a common field marker, and to follow with the drill in these marks. This deposits the seed just about right, two or three inches deep, and if any of the beans remain uncovered in the rows, I follow, cover and firm them with the feet. In the garden I simply open furrows, either with a hand plow, or with the hoe, or in any other convenient way, scatter the seed an inch or two apart in the furrow, and immediately cover the soil in over the seed with the feet, firming the soil as I go, in one operation. For the first crop we may select land just cleared from early radishes or spinach, and for successive crops, any ground as it becomes vacant, continuing the planting every two weeks until July or August. The width of rows may be varied between one and one-half and three feet, according to the gardener's convenience and the fertility of the soil. For it is a very general rule, applicable to all crops, that for best results we must plant the closer the poorer the ground, and the wider the richer it is.

After-culture consists in simply keeping the ground well stirred, either with horse or hand cultivator, and free from weeds and in drawing up the soil slightly to the rows when the plants have attained some size. An old precept warns against hoeing or working among beans when the leaves are wet with rain or dew, as rendering them liable to become affected with rust under this treatment. The statement is periodically passed around in the agricultural press. Professional writers, who are not always practical gardeners, love to repeat it. I am not afraid to hoe my bean vines any time that it is convenient for me to do so; and I have never yet noticed the bad results prophesied.

Round Pod Valentine.

HARVESTING DRY SHELLED BEANS.—The field varieties, or any of the garden sorts grown for seed on a large scale, are harvested as soon as ripe, best by means of one of the modern devices constructed for the purpose, and operated by one or two horses, or the plants are pulled up by hand, laid in rows on the ground, and when sufficiently cured, put in small stooks, or taken to the barn and in due time thrashed out and cleaned. Beans intended for market must be picked over by hand—a somewhat tedious operation, which, however, can be performed during the winter and winter evenings at leisure, and by cheap labor.

Along the coast, near the principal shipping places, from Virginia to Florida, string or snap beans are quite extensively grown for northern markets; and there they generally pay quite well.

VARIETIES.

Early Round Pod Valentine resembles the older Early Red Valentine in every way, but is somewhat earlier. In this we have probably the best variety for market garden purposes.

Early Valentine. The pods are fleshy, tender, succulent, and remain on the vines in condition for table use longer than those of most other varieties. Seeds speckled.

Yellow Six Weeks.—Very early, with straight flat pods.

Early Mohawk. A hardy, early sort, and of old-established reputation. Color of seeds, a kind of drab, spotted with purple.

Refugee. (Thousand-to-one.)—Somewhat later than the preceding two, but very productive; pods tender; seed speckled. Largely grown for pickling.

Nonpareil Green Pod.—About the very last bean to mature; a wonderfully vigorous grower; vines being always full of numbers of long dark green pods.

Best of All. A medium early, thrifty and productive variety. Pods are long, stringless and of good quality.

The leading sorts grown in field culture as dry shelled beans are **White Marrowfat, Navy or Pea Bean, Prolific Tree Bean, Red and White Kidney Bean.** The newly introduced **Burlingame Mediums** is claimed to be the earliest, hardiest and most productive field bean in America. The wax sorts, with their tender, delicate yellowish pods, are especially suited for culture in the home garden. The list of varieties has been swelled very largely by recent introductions. We may choose among a large number and hardly make a miss.

Maule's Butter Wax.

Black Wax is one of the older standard sorts, with tender, waxy, yellow pods. Seed black.

White Wax differs from the preceding chiefly in color of the seed, which is white.

Yosemite.—No other dwarf bush bean approaches Yosemite in size; the pods being often eight to ten inches long, and as thick as a man's finger. The pods are nearly all solid meat, and stringless, always cooking tender and delicious. It is enormously prolific.

New Prolific German Wax.—A decided improvement on the old German Butter Wax, and more than twice as prolific. The very handsome, golden yellow pods, entirely stringless, are borne in immense quantities on every plant.

Golden Wax, one of the newer introductions, is early, prolific, and altogether reliable both for market and home use.

Maule's Butter Wax.—A very early wax bean of superior quality; full of solid meat, as a pithy or hollow pod can seldom be found.

Perfection or Flageolet Wax resembles the preceding, but is characterized by remarkable vigor of plant and productiveness.

Ivory Pod Wax. A moderate grower only, but producing tender, exquisitely delicate, white, waxy pods in great profusion, and during a longer period than most other bush sorts. Especially valuable for the home garden.

POLE OR RUNNING BEANS.

The running or pole varieties are still tenderer than the bush sorts, and should not be planted until the weather has become thoroughly settled, and the ground warm in spring. Seed, when planted in cold, wet ground, is much more liable to rot than to germinate. All, especially that king of beans, the Lima, need high culture, and succeed best in rich, sandy loam, but can be grown in any rich, warm soil. The Limas are one of those crops that find ready sale in almost any larger market, and in suitable localities are grown with fair profit.

The usual way of proceeding is to set poles four feet apart each way. These poles, as used by most growers, are from eight to ten feet high, which I think is from two to four feet more than is really necessary, or even of advantage. The height of pole should correspond with the length of the season in any given locality, five or six feet being fully sufficient, and better than more, for the short northern season. At the south they might be a foot or two longer, as this will have a tendency to lengthen the bearing period.

The hills, previous to setting the poles, should be made rich and porous, by mixing a shovelful or two of well-rotted compost with the soil. Five or six seeds are then to be planted in a circle around each pole. Press each one firmly into the soil, nearly or fully two inches deep. All our old precepts agree in recommending to place the seed eye downward. Prof. Halstead, upsetting this old theory, proves that the seeds should always be planted flat on their side. In practice, however, it seems to make little, if any difference, and in drill planting I simply scatter the seed in the furrow and cover them up with feet or hoe.

Thorough cultivation and frequent hoeing will make the young plants grow rapidly and vigorously, and soon the vines will require tying to the poles. The pods are gathered as the seeds in them get large, and shelled for market or the table. In some localities the beans are sold in the pod. The ripe beans also find a willing market at from $4.00 upwards per bushel, and the crop is generally a profitable one in either case.

In my own practice I prefer to grow the Limas and other running sorts on a trellis instead of poles. The illustration on next page shows a small section of what

I am tempted to call a model trellis for this purpose. Heavy posts are set firmly and deeply into the ground at the ends of each row, and smaller or stout stakes at intervals of 18 or 20 feet between them. The upper end of posts and stakes is sawed off square at a height of five feet, and in line, so that a perfectly straight wire (10 or 12 size) can be run from end to end over the tops, where it is held by simple wire staples, but firmly fastened to the end posts, which, for safety's sake, should be firmly braced. A lighter wire or twine is run from post to post at a height of about 6 inches from the ground, and common white cotton yarn wound zig-zag around the two wires (or the wire and twine). Usually I have a row of Limas, etc., in this shape on one side of my kitchen garden, running its entire length, and fully four feet away from other vegetables, in order to give a fair chance for thorough horse work. I also aim to set the posts straight and uniform, to stretch the wires reasonably tight, and to adjust the yarn regularly ; and I can assure you that this trellis is not only useful, but when vine-clad, also quite an

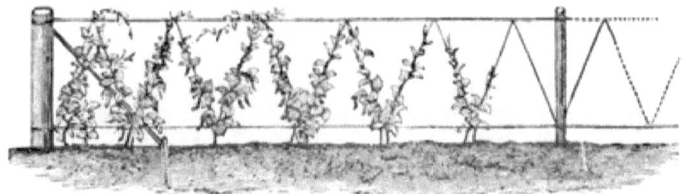

Trellis for Lima Beans.

ornament to the garden. With such a trellis the vines require very little attention in the way of fastening to the strings. The latter are so temptingly near, that the runners take hold without much coaxing.

One of the most important advantages of this trellis style over the pole method, I find is the opportunity which it affords us to plant the Limas in a continuous row. Here I use plenty of seed, for I am anxious to secure a full stand, and prefer pulling up plants rather than have vacant spots that spoil the looks of the whole, and materially diminish the yield. Should a bare space occur after all, it is easy enough to fill it with plants taken up from where they stand pretty thickly. Lima beans transplant quite readily, especially if lifted after a rain. Carefully take up a clump of soil with a few plants on it, on a spade or trowel, and set where needed to fill a gap.

The royal Lima requires a pretty long season. Many gardeners pinch the ends of the runners after they have made five or six feet of growth, for the purpose of hastening the crop. This treatment is not needed, especially with short poles or **the** five-foot trellis, since the forced downward course of the vines, after they have reached the highest point of the comparatively low support, gives us practically the same effect as pinching back.

The great fault of the Limas in the northern states is their lateness. We often only get a small part of the crop to reach table size, not to mention the difficulty of getting them to mature on the vines. To make the crop earlier by a week or two, the seed can be planted in a cold frame or hot-bed, either in pots or on pieces of inverted sod, about two or three weeks before it could be safely planted in the open ground. At the proper time, the sods, or the plants turned out of the pots, are then set 4 feet each way for poles, or 2 feet in the row if for trellis. Three or four good plants are left to grow in each hill in the former case, and two plants only in the latter. When seed is planted in drills, as described for my trellis method, the plants, of course have to be properly thinned, one to every 9 or 12 inches.

VARIETIES.

I have tested about a dozen different varieties of the Lima bean, but found next to no difference in time of giving earliest picking.

Large Lima.—This is the old standard sort, reliable and productive. Salem Improved is introduced as a selected and superior strain of this.

Extra Early, Early Jersey, or Extra Early Jersey.—Proves to be slightly earlier than the Large Lima, and is claimed to be the earliest of this class. Pods are quite long, and well filled. I have picked pods containing seven and eight seeds each in New Jersey.

Dreer's Lima gives quite short, but closely-filled pods. The seeds are rounder and plumper than those of any other Lima, and of superior quality. A fine variety for the home grower, and profitable for the market gardener who sells the shelled bean, or for the consumer who buys in the pod.

King of the Garden.—Pods of enormous size, beans large. The reverse of Dreer's—profitable to sell in the pod, and to buy shelled.

Red and Speckled Lima are newer introductions of strong and vigorous growth, about as early as the earliest, and decidedly prolific. Seed of fine, rich flavor, but objectionable in color, and consequently not wanted for market.

Small Lima or Sieva.—I cannot see that this makes up in earliness for what it lacks in size, productiveness and flavor. So I have no use for it in my garden.

Henderson's Bush Lima might be included in this list. It appears to be a dwarf sport of the Small Lima or Sieva, resembling it in every respect except habit of growth. Its bush

Cultural Directions.—193

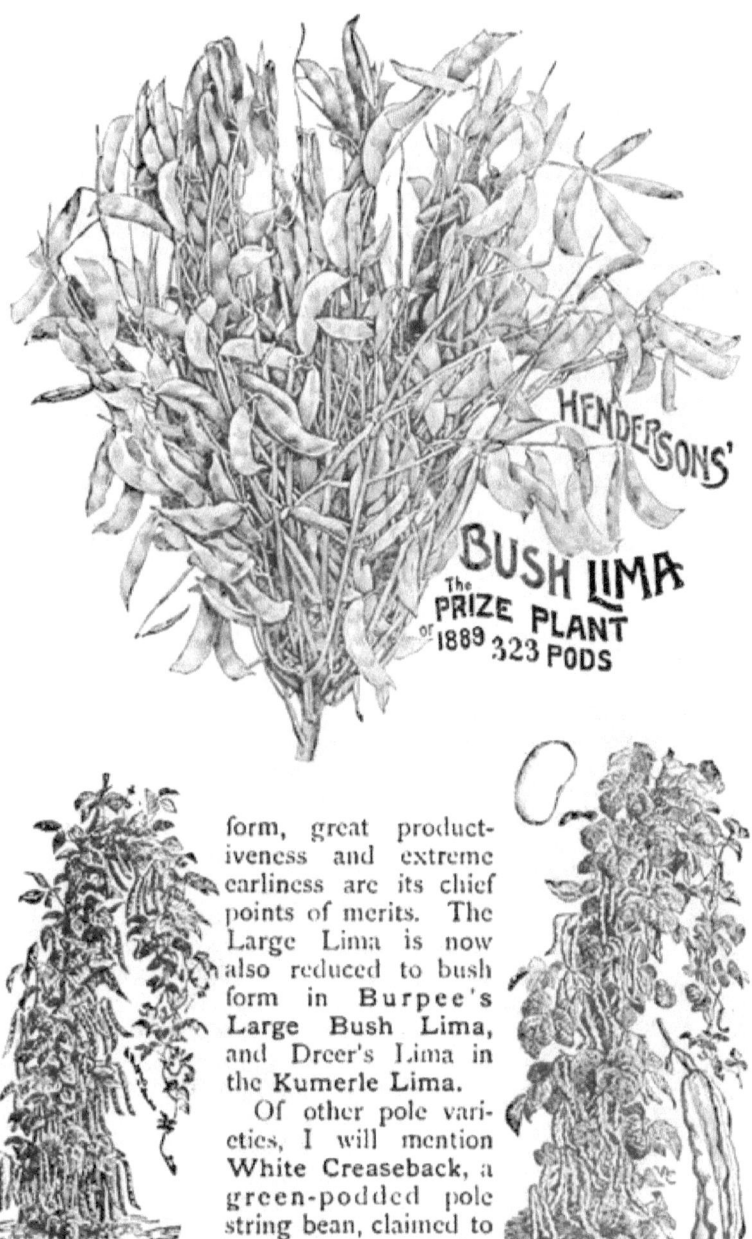

form, great productiveness and extreme earliness are its chief points of merits. The Large Lima is now also reduced to bush form in Burpee's Large Bush Lima, and Dreer's Lima in the Kumerle Lima.

Of other pole varieties, I will mention White Creaseback, a green-podded pole string bean, claimed to be the earliest of that class.

Lazy Wives.   Golden Cluster.

German Wax, Golden Wax and Golden Cluster are yellow-podded running sorts for both string and shell beans.

Lazy Wives.—Pods are wonderfully broad, thick, fleshy, and above all entirely stringless, retaining their stringless and tender qualities until they are almost ripe. The vines cling remarkably well to the poles. Pods are rather flattish, oval shape, and when fully grown are from four to six inches long.

Horticultural, Speckled Cranberry or Quail Track, much esteemed for the home garden. Seeds oval, speckled.

Improved Dutch Runner has many of the characteristics of the Lima in growth, and is very productive. Beans clear white and of largest size. Next to the Lima, the best for market.

Scarlet Runner.—A strong grower; flowers of beautiful scarlet, and produced in great abundance. Probably more ornamental, than useful for the table.

BEETS.

Beta Vulgaris. German, *Rothe Rübe;* French, *Betterave.* Beets for early bunching are a leading crop of the market garden, and generally quite a profitable one. I have already in a former chapter alluded to their cultivation under glass, in cold frames, and cold houses. In open air they are grown in a similar way, only more space is usually given, and no radishes are grown between them as a secondary crop. Rich warm soil (sandy loam) is the chief requisite. It is well-manured with rotted compost, and prepared as for other small vegetables, that is to say, plowed well, harrowed well, and made thoroughly smooth, if necessary with steel rake. In early spring when soil conditions and weather will permit, the seed is sown in drills from 12 to 18 inches apart, and clean and thorough cultivation given from the start. The crop is especially grateful for one or more applications of nitrate of soda, and can be largely increased or made earlier by this means. The market gardener's aim is to get a uniform lot of roots, bunch them for market while small (two to three inches in diameter), clear the land at the earliest possible date, and replant to some other crop. From this standpoint he must thin to a uniform distance of three or four inches soon after the plants have made a few leaves; and since he does not intend to let the plants grow to large size in the bed, he can make the rows as close as he may desire, 12 inches distance between them being ample. In the kitchen garden we usually have the rows 15 or

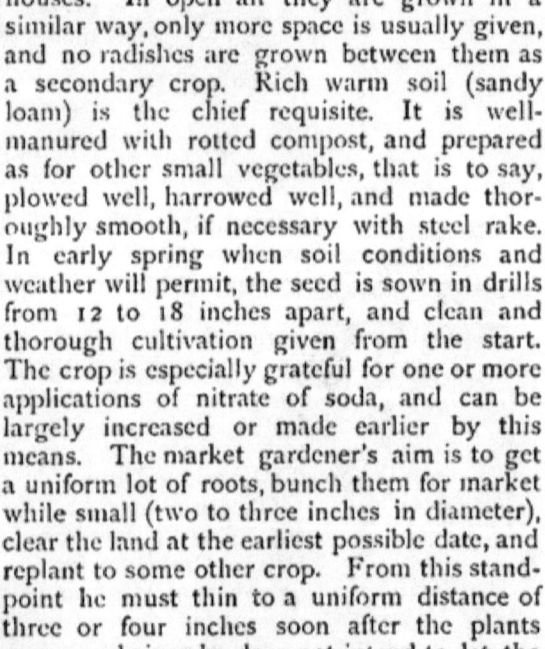

Cultural Directions.—195

18 inches apart, since we prefer to use up the crop gradually, perhaps thinning at first for greens, then beginning to pull the roots when yet small, and continue using them as we desire for the table, thinning all the time, and perhaps leaving the last of the crop to attain quite a respectable size. For a succession, seed can be sown every two weeks until midsummer, if desired. A supply for winter use may be stored in boxes, barrels or heaps in the cellar, but should always be kept covered with sand, soil, sods, etc., to prevent evaporation, and consequent wilting, and shrivelling of the roots. The pitting method, as hereafter described

for mangel wurzels, can hardly be improved upon for keeping beets fresh, crisp, and in best table condition generally, until spring.

VARIETIES.

Extra Early Egyptian, Early Egyptian or Egyptian Turnip.—This and the Eclipse are now almost the only kinds grown for early market in many localities. Tops small. Roots of a uniform deep blood color, and of rapid growth. Best for forcing.

Improved Blood Turnip.

Eclipse.—This is now preferred to the Egyptian by many gardeners. Flesh much lighter in color. About as early, and decidedly a good variety.

Bastian's Early Turnip,
Philadelphia Lentz Early Turnip,
Blood Turnip,
Improved Blood Turnip,

Early Bassano,
Edmand's Turnip, etc.

All these belong to the class of "Blood Turnip Beets," and are good early or intermediate sorts for the home garden everywhere, and for market in many places. All are so reliable, it would not be easy to choose the best among them.

New Market Gardeners, is very symmetrical, with small tap-root, and but few fibrous roots. One sowing only is necessary to produce early beets for market and main crop for

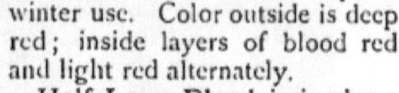

winter use. Color outside is deep red; inside layers of blood red and light red alternately.

Half Long Blood is in shape what the name indicates. Good for second early, late fall or winter. **(Long or) Improved Long Blood** still remains a standard late and winter variety, excellent for the kitchen garden. Color of root a dark crimson.

Swiss Chard forms no edible root, and is cultivated mainly for its leaves, which make very fair greens, like spinach. The coarse midribs of the leaves are sometimes served like asparagus, and by some pronounced a good substitute for it. There are also varieties having variegated and quite ornamental foliage, and we sometimes meet them in flower gardens and borders.

BEET.—Mangel-Wurzel and Sugar.

Root crops for stock (horses, cattle, sheep, swine), chief among them the mangels, sugar beets and carrots, are not yet appreciated as a farm crop by our people as they deserve to be. I have grown such crops for many years, to a greater or smaller extent, and can assure my friends that they are exceedingly profitable. Such immense amounts of succulent food for winter and spring feeding, in the shape of mangels, can be produced on comparatively small areas, when well managed, that I am convinced any farmer who keeps stock, but makes no use of the silo method, will never again omit planting mangels, carrots or both, after having once made a thorough trial *in the right way*. This latter is the important point; for if mismanaged, the first trial is apt to result in utter disgust. Begin cautiously; plant a small area, and never more than you are sure you can give

Cultural Directions.—197

prompt attention when needed. This will show the novice how to proceed, and insure his success, even on an enlarged scale.

PLANTING MANGELS.—The safest way, especially for the beginner or when cultivating a somewhat large area, is to plant wide enough for easy cultivation by horse power—say in drills three feet apart. Select any piece of good, clean farm land, but giving a young clover sod the preference. Cart on plenty of good fine manure; 40 loads to the acre is not too much, and even more will pay. This is plowed in; or composted poultry manure, in smaller quantity, may be applied after plowing, and harrowed in. Get the land in good condition for sowing the seed, by the use of roller, smoothing harrow, or, if you have it, of the small disk (Meeker) harrow. The surface should be smooth and fine. A good way of sowing seed is with a grain drill, with part of the discharge tubes thrown out of gear, so that those in operation will leave the drills somewhere near three feet apart.

Or the field may be marked off in shallow furrows, of distance mentioned, with a common field marker, and seed sown with the garden drill, following in the marks and sowing about four pounds of seed to the acre. If you have no drill, you can simply drop a pinch of seed (three or four) every 12 inches apart in furrows made same as for planting corn, preferably one and a half inches deep. Then cover with the hoe or foot, and firm by stepping upon it, or pressing soil upon it with the back of hoe. A few radish seeds might also be scattered along the rows with the beet seed. The radishes will better indicate the rows, so that we can begin to cultivate a few days after sowing. The radishes may be pulled up when of table or marketable size.

CULTIVATION.—Prompt action is the all important point. Weeds should never be allowed to crowd. Cultivate with a narrow-bladed horse-hoe or cultivator; hoe as often as needed, and while the plants are young, run the hand wheel-hoe astraddle the rows, to keep them as near as possible free from weeds without much hand hoeing or hand weeding. Thinning should be attended to before the plants begin to crowd one another. Most of this work can be done with a hoe, and since we desire but one good plant to 10 or 12 inches of drill, we can easily strike out the plants and weeds growing on the spaces between. Of course there may be a number of plants left on each clump near the plant we wish to save, especially where the seed was sowed like corn (in pinches). We then have to pull up the surplus plants by hand.

GATHERING AND STORING.—Thorough cultivation and timely attention on good and well-manured land is pretty apt to bring a crop that will astonish the novice, as a yield of 40, 60, and even more tons to the acre is not uncommon under favorable circumstances. Before frost, in autumn, the beets are pulled by hand and thrown in heaps to be topped (*i. e.*, foliage cut off with a sickle or corn cutter) and drawn to the cellar or pit. The best storage place, undoubtedly, is a regular root cellar in the basement of the barn. A separate root or potato cellar, such as a dug-out in a hill-side, or the root cellar described for the winter storage of celery, also makes a very good place for beets, carrots, etc., to be fed out during winter and spring. If we have neither of these conveniences, we must store what we want to use during winter in the cellar we have at our command, although it is not a wise nor safe practice to store many vegetables and fruits under the rooms in which we live, and rear a family.

No difficulty will be experienced in carrying root crops over until spring in pits outdoors, in same way as farmers frequently winter apples and potatoes. Select a dry spot or one for which drainage can easily be provided, and dig an excavation about a foot or 18 inches deep, 6 feet wide, and of the length required to hold the quantity of roots to be wintered over. They are placed in a conical heap, as shown in illustration on page 160, covered with six, eight, ten or twelve inches of straw, according to the severity of the winters in the particular locality, and with a foot of soil upon the straw. A whisk of straw or a section of common tile drain, reaching from the straw covering through the soil to the outside, should be adjusted in the centre of every eight or ten foot section to provide the required ventilation. If such a pit is opened before the cold weather has entirely passed, the roots remaining in it need careful covering to guard against freezing.

VARIETIES.

Long Red.—This with its various strains and improvements, Prize Long Red, Jumbo, etc., is the variety for rich, deep soil, where it grows to enormous size.

Yellow Tankard, Golden Tankard.—A beautiful, solid and prolific variety. Flesh rich, deep yellow all through.

Yellow Globe and its various strains, **Champion Yellow Globe, Kinver Globe,** etc., are preferable for shallower soil, and reliable for all. Roundish in shape, beautiful, solid, and altogether desirable. When young they make very fine table beets; by many people even preferred to the Blood varieties.

Giant Yellow Intermediate.—This new variety has a magnificent root, which is easily lifted from the ground. Produces very large crops, and has proven itself to be a most excellent keeper. Has a fine neck, large leaves with green stems, and very smooth skin; flesh firm and sweet.

Gatepost.—One of the very finest mangels. The roots are heavy, handsome and clean, with single tap-root. Very rich and nutritious. With good cultivation crops at the rate of 2500 bushels per acre have been grown.

Imperial Sugar, like all other sugar beet varieties, does not yield quite as handsomely as the mangels, but makes up in richness what it lacks in yield. Especially profitable for cows.

Pit for Wintering Potatoes, Root Crops, etc.

BORECOLE (See Kale).

BORAGE.

Borago Officinalis. German, *Borretsch;* French, *Bourrache;* Spanish, *Boraja.*—This annual, which is of free-flowering habit and grows to a height of a foot or 18 inches, is rarely found in American gardens. It can be grown as easily as a weed, by sowing the seed in any corner or waste place in spring or summer. Some uses, not known to me, are made of it in cookery, and also in medical science.

BROCCOLI.

Brassica Oleracea (Botrytis).—German, *Spargel Kohl;* French, *Chou-fleur d'Hiver;* Spanish, *Broculi.*—In broccoli we have little more than a cauliflower under another name. It thrives under the same conditions of culture, namely, moist, fertile soil and cool atmosphere, and is always grown for fall and winter use. Seed is sown in seed bed in May, or later further south; and plants may be set in July (August or September in southern latitudes) in well-manured and well-prepared soil, 2½ to 3 feet by 1½ feet apart. Cultivate and hoe frequently. Heat and drought are the great enemies of the crop, and often prove fatal. A good crop, like that of the cauliflower, however, hardly ever fails to be very profitable.

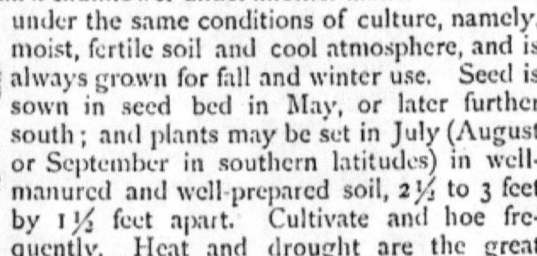

Broccoli.

VARIETIES.

White Cape and Purple Cape are the varieties generally grown in America. More than forty different forms or varieties of broccoli are known to English gardeners.

BRUSSELS SPROUTS.

Brassica Oleracea.—German, *Brüsseler Sprossen Kohl ;* French, *Chou de Bruxelles.*—The " head " of this cabbage variety consists of a few loose, crumpled leaves borne on a tall stalk, and no culinary use is made of it. The stalk itself, however, is surrounded and often completely covered by the "sprouts," which are miniature cabbage heads, seldom much larger than a walnut, and of choicest quality, not inferior to cauliflower. While it is as easily grown as a cabbage, it is seldom found in American gardens. There seems to be a good demand for it in city markets, and the crop can be made as remunerative as cauliflower. Sow seed in April or May, and in July set the plants about two feet apart in soil prepared as for late cabbages, giving about the same cultivation. The sprouts will be ready for use in autumn, and until severe freezing. Where, as in the south, the plants endure the winters in open ground uninjured, a supply of sprouts can be had until spring. In gathering, they should not be broken off, but cut off the stems with a sharp knife, leaving as much of the spur as possible, in order to induce the formation of successive sprouts.

Brussels Sprouts.

VARIETIES

Dwarf Brussels Sprouts.—This is the variety generally catalogued by American seedsmen. It is of low, compact growth, and produces the little heads closely all around the stalk.

Tall Improved.—The stem of this is much taller, and the heads grow more scatteringly around it.

CABBAGE.

Brassica Oleracea. German, *Kopfkohl ;* French, *Chou ;* Spanish, *Col Repollo.*

GROWING FOR EARLY MARKET.—Early cabbages are one of the foremost crops of the market garden, and usually yield a fair profit. The plants are started in September, and wintered over as directed in chapter on " cold frames," or grown in hot-houses or hot-beds during the second half of winter. When grown in the latter way, great pains should be taken to have the plants thoroughly hardened off, for they are to be set as soon as the ground can be put in working order, and in all probability will have to endure considerable cold and uncomfortable weather.

Selection of soil for the crop is also of utmost importance. Nothing can be better than a rich calcareous or sandy loam, naturally drained, and manured with at least 40 tons of good compost to the acre, or in the place of it a proportionate quantity of wood ashes (a most excellent fertilizer for cabbages, by the way), complete concentrated (commercial) fertilizers, etc. Fall plowing, throwing up the soil in ridges to better expose it to freezing and thawing, always tends to improve the mechanical condition of the soil, and to get it in planting condition much earlier in spring than could be expected otherwise. Mark off rows from 2 to 2½ feet apart, and set the plants 16 or 18 inches apart in the rows, and down into the ground to the heart. Cultivate and hoe frequently to keep the ground mellow, moist, and free from weeds. Occasional dressings of nitrate of soda, at the rate of 250 to 300 pounds in the aggregate, will seldom fail to pay exceedingly well. It is not necessary, either, as is often recommended, that these applications should be made during or just before a rain. When the ground is reasonably moist, the effect is sure, and all the more lasting; even if it should not rain for a week or longer after applying it. Look out for the maggot, and if necessary resort to the remedies found in the chapter on "insects."

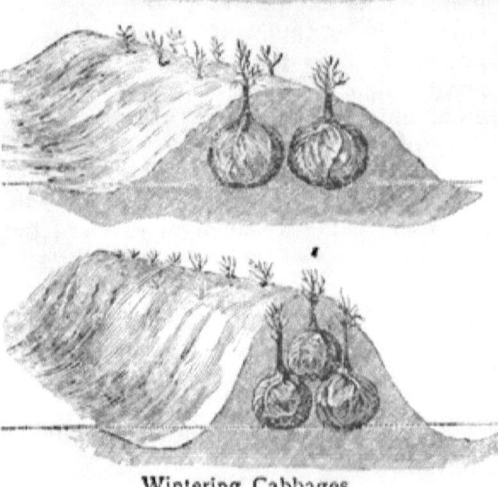

Wintering Cabbages.

This is the market gardener's method. The home gardener is less anxious to get cabbages for the table in May or June. If he is content to wait until nearly July for a really superior article, he may adopt my method of sowing early in the spring (March or April) in open ground, in drills 2 or 2½ feet apart, and thinning to 15 or 18 inches in the drills, leaving the best plants. For a second early crop the market gardener can also sow seed in April, and transplant in May to the permanent patch, or thin to the proper distance apart.

LATE CABBAGES.—These are much more a farm than a market garden crop, and as a farm crop are often quite profitable. A possible surplus, as well as the waste and all the unmarketable part of the crop can generally be put to good use in the cattle yard. Sow seed during May in seed bed, and transplant during June in well-prepared and liberally-manured soil, making rows

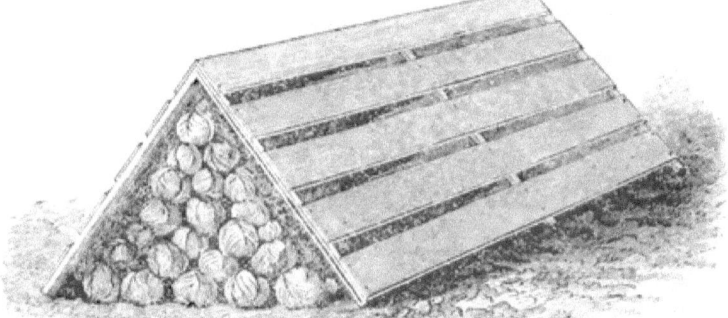

Wintering Cabbages in Pit.

three feet apart, and plants from 1½ to 3 feet apart in the row, according to vigor of variety, and strength of ground; or sow thinly during June in drills three feet apart, and afterwards thin to the proper distance. In either case thorough cultivation and frequent hoeing are conditions of best success. The intermediate varieties, such as Winningstadt, Fottler's, etc., will often give good heads for winter, at least in a moist season, even if sown as late as July. A handful of good fertilizer, bone-dust, potash, etc., (according to the needs of the soil) or a somewhat larger quantity of wood-ashes or composted hen manure, scattered around the plant after it has become well established after transplanting, as also light dressings of nitrate of soda, are always a great help. All of our hard-heading cabbages, when they are approaching maturity, and are not soon gathered, are liable to burst open or crack, which spoils them for market if not for use. Heads show-

Express.

ing this inclination may be pushed or pulled over to one side. This breaks or loosens part of their roots, and for some reason appears to counteract the undesirable tendency. I still have to add that cabbages should not be grown soon after cabbages on the same land. Club-root—a disease which attacks the root, and hinders the full development of the plants—is the usual penalty of a violation of this rule.

METHODS OF WINTERING.—There are numerous ways in which cabbages can be kept successfully for home use, or the often good market during latter part of winter or early spring. A general rule is applicable to all methods. It is this, to pull the crop on a dry day, and pack it only when perfectly dry. Also put off the final covering, or storing in buildings, cellars, etc., as long in the fall as can be safely done. One of the most commonly practised methods is to wrap the outer leaves of each plant firmly around the head, and stand root side up closely together, either in single line or in a close double row, with or without another layer on top; then plow a furrow from each side to the ridge of cabbages thus formed, and finish covering up with soil, using shovel or spade, leaving only the extremities of the roots sticking out. The illustration on page 162 represents a cross section of each of the three arrangements. Another good way to store cabbages is to put them in pits, like root crops. The excavation is made 6 or 8 inches deep, 4 feet wide, and as long as needed to make room for the quantity of cabbages desired to store. Here the heads are packed in a conical heap, roots inward, and covered with 8 or 10 inches of soil, packed firmly. In case we should want to use all or part of them during the winter, it will be a good precaution to cover the south side of pit with straw or other dry litter deep enough to keep the soil from freezing, and thus secure easy access to the cabbages whenever wanted. An improvement on this method was recently published in the *Rural New Yorker*. Boards or slabs are placed on bottom of pit. The cabbages, well trimmed

Early Wakefield.

Etampes.

and dry, are packed in, as was illustrated on page 163. Triangular frames of 2 by 4 scantling are then set upright into the pit, one at each end only if pit is less than 8 or 9 feet long, one additional in the centre for a pit of from 9 to 15 feet in length; and common fence boards are nailed to them, thus forming something like a large three-cornered crate around the cabbages. This is lightly covered with straw, and 4 to 6 inches of soil upon that. The ends need only be stuffed with dry straw, which will give free access to the contents of pit at any time. I know of no simpler or better method than this. For wintering a few dozen heads only, a barrel may be sunk into the ground to the brim, filled with trimmed heads, covered with dry forest leaves, chaff, etc., and a simple roof to exclude

Midsummer.

rain and snow. The cellar under the dwelling house is, for sanitary reasons, hardly a place for storing cabbages; but a very few after removal of the coarse outside leaves, may each be wrapped in several thicknesses of common newspaper, so that only the

206—How to Make the Garden Pay.

roots are showing outside, and hung up in a convenient place in the cellar. Farmers might put a load of cabbages in some corner of the barn, on the floor, hay-mow, etc., and keep them lightly covered with loose straw, and thus have them ready for use at any time during the winter that they may desire them. The regular root cellar is also a good storing place for cabbages.

VARIETIES.

Of these we have an endless number, and among them quite a good many that are very good. In fact, we have so much choice that the selection often puzzles us. Of many varieties again, we have almost as many strains or selections as we have leading seedsmen. Often the difference between many

of these strains and the original type are decidedly "strained," and too nice for us clumsy observers; again, they are often so strikingly distinct that they give us the difference between very indifferent and quite complete success, and this, I repeat, merely from different selections—strains—of one and the same variety.

A serious fault of many of the cabbage seeds that I have bought of various sources during recent years, is their somewhat "mixed" condition. We often get too many sorts in one and the same lot, and the consequence is a mixture of all sorts. The evil seems to be on the increase, too. In justice to the publisher of my work—Mr. Maule—I have to say that I have been much pleased with both the high quality, and the purity of all the cabbage seeds I have had of him. I cannot agree with him and other leading seedsmen, however, in regard to the wisdom and propriety of their nomenclature, especially their methods of multiplying names by adding their own for the sake of distinguishing strains.

EARLY VARIETIES.

Early Wakefield. In this we have yet the leading early market variety, making solid, conical heads, with few loose outer leaves. For both home and market garden it has no superior as an early sort. Seed of this is grown quite extensively on Long Island, and I have always had excellent success with it.

Earliest Etampes. Much spoken of as a good market variety, earlier than the preceding, while it is decidedly reliable. I have never been able to discover

Flat Dutch.

Surehead.

more than a slight difference in earliness between the two kinds (in favor of the Etampes), nor other points of merit above those of the best strains of Wakefield.

Early Express. Another early variety of the Wakefield type, introduced as considerably earlier than that variety, and profitable for early market. Said to produce heads in 70 to 75 days from time of sowing seed.

Early York, and **Early French Oxheart**, being extremely early, were formerly the leading sorts for market; but since their heads are little more than loose bunches of leaves, they have deservedly lost favor with the growers.

INTERMEDIATE VARIETIES.

Early Winningstadt should be planted by all who have usually but indifferent success with other varieties. As a sure header, even under adverse circumstances, it has no peer; and in spite of its earliness, it forms large cone-shaped heads, which are of good quality. It is emphatically the home grower's and the novice's sort, and can be planted for early, intermediate and late, by planting at different times, sometimes as late as July, even at the north.

Early Summer comes a week or two after Wakefield, is much larger with round, flat heads, of excellent quality, and altogether one of the best and most reliable second early market sorts, and desirable in the home garden also.

Midsummer.—Very nearly as early as the Early Summer, and at the same time producing very much larger heads, which for solidity and compactness cannot be surpassed. It is a remarkably sure header and for a market crop is one of the most profitable varieties.

Fottler's Improved, or Improved Brunswick.—This large, hard-heading and reliable sort can be grown alike for summer, fall or winter use, and is the earliest of the large Drumheads.

Early Bleichfield Giant also makes large, solid heads, with dark green leaves, and is reliable for second early.

Early Flat Dutch is a good early sort of the Flat Dutch class, with good-sized heads, and can be recommended especially for the south, as it seems to stand heat better than many other varieties.

Blood-Red Erfurt makes extremely solid heads of a deep red color. Used for pickling. May be planted for both early and late.

LATE VARIETIES.

Prize Flat Dutch, Large Flat Dutch, Excelsior Flat Dutch, etc., is a thoroughly reliable short-stemmed late variety, forming large flat heads. Good for both market and home use, and deservedly popular.

Surehead is introduced as an improved sort of the Flat Dutch type, and I find it pretty much what its name indicates. Can be planted with entire confidence.

Red Dutch is the best late pickling sort, with round and extremely hard heads, and dark red in color.

Mammoth Red Rock. This is the largest and hardest heading red cabbage in cultivation. Successful Long Island market gardeners will raise no other kind of red cabbage, for they consider this the best of all. The heads frequently average 12 pounds each, and it is a very sure cropper.

Stone Mason, much grown in New England States, makes very solid heads, and is quite popular at the north.

Large Late American Drumhead, with its various strains (Louisville Drumhead, Short-Stemmed Drumhead, etc.), is a late sort with very solid heads of good quality. Decidedly a good variety, both for market and home use.

Felderkraut.—A German variety, especially desirable in making krout; heads large, hard and solid.

Drumhead Savoy.—Few cabbages have given us as much satisfaction in the home garden as the Savoys. In quality they are far ahead of the common varieties, and not so very inferior even to the cauliflowers. The Drumhead Savoy, in addition, can be depended upon to yield large, solid heads under fairly favorable conditions, and also stands high as a winter keeper. It deserves to be more generally planted.

Marblehead Mammoth is undoubtedly the largest of all our cabbages, and makes firm heads of good quality; but needs high culture and the entire season to come to perfection. It is especially recommended for warmer latitudes.

CARDOON.

Cynara Cardunculus. German, *Spanische Artischoke;* French, *Cardon;* Spanish, *Cardo.* Cardoon is one of the many vegetables quite commonly grown on the Continent of Europe, especially in France, yet almost entirely unknown to American cultivators. Neither is there any prospect for its coming in general use. I confess I have not yet seen it in a single American kitchen garden. It belongs to the same species as the Artichoke. Its leafstalks, blanched like celery, are used for salads, in soups, etc. Sow seed in early spring, in very rich, and moist soil, having rows 3 feet apart; then thin the plants to 1½ or 2 feet apart in the rows. Give good cultivation, and in autumn tie up the leaves with matting or bands of straw or hay, covering them up entirely almost to the tips of leaves, then earth up like celery. In four or five weeks the hearts will be blanched enough for use. Take up before frost and store like celery.

Cardoon.

CARAWAY.

Carum Carui. German, *Kümmel;* French, *Carvi Cumin;* Spanish, *Carvi.* A common European biennial meadow weed. Seeds used in flavoring bread, cheese, pastry and sauces. Seed may be sown in spring or fall, in drills. Little or no cultivation is required except to thin, and keep reasonably free from weeds.

CARROTS.

Daucus Carota. German, *Möhre, Mohrrübe;* French, *Carotte;* Spanish, *Zanahoria.* I have already referred to the carrot as a vegetable grown in cold frames, etc., for early

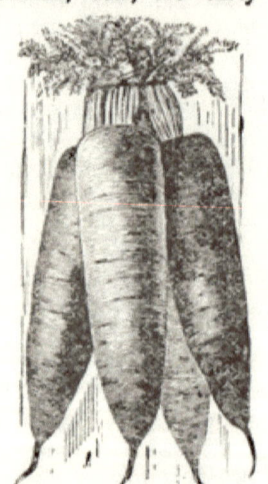

market. See Chapter on "Cold Frames." As a market vegetable, carrots are tied up in bunches, in same fashion as early

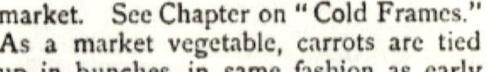

Danvers.

beets, bunch onions, etc., and generally prove profitable. When grown as an early outdoor crop for market or family use, seed is sown as soon in spring as the ground is in proper working order, in rows 12 to 15 inches apart, and the plants thinned to 2 or 3 inches apart in the rows. The ground need not be as heavily manured as required for most other garden crops; but early attention must be given, for the plants have a small beginning, and start somewhat feebly, and if neglected are liable to get crowded out by weeds or lost among them. Keep the wheel-hoe going from the very first, and pull up every weed.

Except in the limited way of bunch carrots, the vegetable is more of a farm than a garden crop. Carrots, although good culinary material in the hands of skilled cooks, are not used so extensively for a kitchen vegetable here as they are in Europe; but we are learning to appreciate them more and more as a root crop for stock, especially for horses and milch cows. In many places, especially near larger cities, carrots for stock feeding are one of the best paying farm garden crops, being in ready demand at $1.00 to $1.50 per barrel; and since 300 barrels and upwards can be produced per acre with good culture, the reader may draw his own conclusions concerning the profits.

The crop can be grown as a second one after spinach, radishes, early beets, and even strawberries, early cabbages, etc., without further manuring. One of the best selections of soil

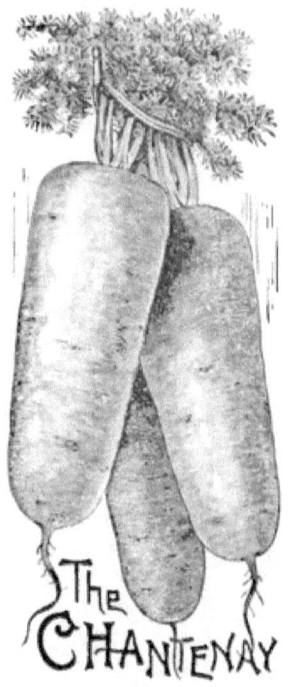

on the farm is a piece of good, strong, well-drained, clean clover sod, manured with twenty-five or thirty tons of compost or 1000 to 1500 pounds of fertilizer, or a ton or two of wood ashes per acre. The cultivation which carrots require will also fit such land admirably for a succeeding crop of onions, or vegetables of that class. The ground should be deeply worked and thoroughly prepared. For home feeding I prefer the White Belgian. For market sale the Long and Half Long Orange sorts must be grown. Mix a few radish seeds with the carrot seed, and sow in drills 18 to 24 inches apart, using about six pounds of seed per acre. The radishes come up quickly, and the wheel-hoe or cultivator should at once be brought in use. When the radishes are of fair eating size, they have fulfilled their mission, and may be used, or thrown away. Again let me emphasize the necessity of timely weeding and early thinning. Weeding on weedy soil will require a great deal of labor; hence weedy soil and weedy manure should be carefully avoided. The large late varieties need three, and on rich soil perhaps even four inches space in the row to each plant. After once having taken a good start they grow fast, and do not need so very much attention. Gather the crop before severe freezing. This is best done by running a one-horse plow close to each row on one side, thus almost laying the roots bare on that side, and then prying them out with a spade, or simply pulling them up by hand. Top, and store in same way as described for mangel wurzels. The roots should be perfectly dry when put away, or when packed for sale.

VARIETIES.

Early Scarlet Horn.—This is most generally used for forcing for early market. Deep orange with small tops, and of good quality. Adapted for shallow soils.

Oxheart.—An intermediate between the Early Horn and Half Long varieties. In quality it is extra good, and will prove

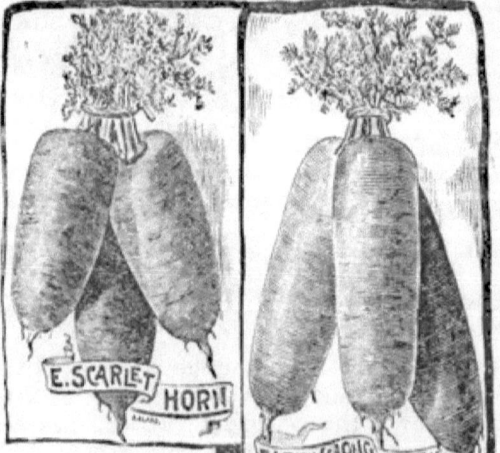

profitable in both the home and market garden. Where other sorts require digging, Oxheart can be pulled.

Early Half Long Scarlet.—A stump-rooted sort, well adapted for shallow soils, and good for table use.

New Chantenay is an improvement on the Half-Long Scarlet, of same general characteristics, and rich orange color.

Danvers.—A Half Long variety of large size, is deservedly popular for general uses—a sort of all-purpose carrot. I have grown it for years and still consider it one of the best. It gives greatest bulk with smallest length of root of any of the orange sorts. Roots handsome, smooth, easily gathered, and of rich dark orange color.

Cultural Directions.—213

Long Orange, Improved Long Orange, is another good sort for general purposes, and especially adapted to deep soils. Very productive; roots smooth and handsome.

Saint Vallery.—Very straight roots, broad at the top. Of superior quality for table use. Of deep orange color.

White Belgian.—In this we have a somewhat coarse, but excellent variety for stock, attaining largest size, and for this reason the most productive of all sorts. Grows partly above ground and can be gathered by hand.

Yellow Belgian, another fine variety for stock, resembles the White Belgian, but is perhaps richer, and less productive.

White Vosges is introduced as an enormously productive field carrot, adapted for shallow soils. Can be pulled up without the use of tools. Not recommended for the table.

CATNIP.

Nepeta cataria. German, *Katzminze;* French, *Menthe de Chat.* This perennial weed is quite common here, and more generally considered a nuisance than fit for cultivation. The leaves and young shoots are sometimes used for seasoning, and the plant has valuable medical properties. It is also appreciated as a honey-bearing plant, and cultivated on that account. It grows easily from seed sown in drills 18 or 20 inches apart, in almost any soil, and will need little or no attention.

CAULIFLOWER.

Brassica Oleracea (Botrytis). German, *Blumenkohl;* French, *Chou-fleur;* Spanish, *Coliflor.* High culture, deep, rich, moist soil plentifully provided with humus, and cool atmosphere, are the chief requisites for best success with this crop. Nice heads cannot be grown in hot, dry weather and soil; hence gardeners always aim to have the plants head up either in early summer or in late autumn. For early crop the plants are wintered over in cold frames, or grown in greenhouses or hot-beds during the winter, in the same way as already described for early cabbages; but being less hardy, they need more protection, by mats, shutters, etc.

Good cauliflowers always find ready sale at paying prices, $15.00 to $25.00 per one hundred not being an unusual figure; and for this reason it would be very unwise to attempt economizing in the manure account. Fifty tons or more of good stable compost per acre, besides liberal dressings of fertilizers, wood ashes, nitrate of soda, etc., are no more than can be applied with profit. Plow deeply and pulverize the ground thoroughly. In early spring, as soon as the ground is ready (March or April, earlier at the south) the plants are set 30 by 15 or 18 inches apart, and cultivated and hoed frequently. This is the crop of all crops with which irrigation, by any of the natural methods, if it can be adopted without unreasonable expense, will pay. A plentiful supply of moisture, either by such means, or in consequence of frequent rains during the time of heading, insures a good crop.

Prize Earliest.

When the heads begin to form, be sure to clear out the worms that may be on the plants, by the prompt use of buhach, tar water, or thymo-cresol, and then gather up some of the large leaves over the head, and tie loosely to exclude the direct sun rays. This treatment keeps the heads clean, white and delicate. For late crop, seed is sown in May or June, the plants set out at same time as late cabbages, 3 by 2 or 3 feet apart, according to variety. Same general treatment as for cabbages is required, but soil should be richer.

VARIETIES.

Until now seed of all sorts had to be imported from abroad, very little being grown near the Atlantic coast. An effort is now being made to grow it on the Pacific coast, and it seems with entire success. The American-grown seed is remarkably large and plump, and gives strong plants. The heads I had from such seed were not inferior to any from foreign seed. I have no doubt that American seedsmen will soon offer only the home-grown especially since this promises to be the cheaper of the two. The best foreign seed has always been excessively high-priced.

Early Snowball, now recognized as the leading sort for early use, probably is good for late also. A very reliable header.

Prize Earliest has recently been introduced as earlier even than Snowball or Early Erfurt; desirable alike for forcing and open-air culture.

Earliest Dwarf Erfurt.—One of the old stand-bys, and a sure header.

(Extra) Early Paris.—Popular for forcing.

Autumn Giant, Veitch's Autumn Giant.—A large, late, vigorous growing sort, with large firm heads, well covered by the inner leaves.

CELERY.

Apium Graveolens. German, *Sellerie;* French, *Céleri;* Spanish, *Apio.*—Celery fits so admirably into the crop rotation of market as well as home gardens, that it has become indispensable in both. It affords an opportunity, after early crops are taken off, to make profitable use of the ground from mid-season until winter, and brings money to the market grower, and a daily relish of unsurpassed deliciousness for fall and winter to the home gardener. The newer methods and newer varieties have now greatly simplified its culture, and rendered quite easy what formerly was an awkward and laborious task.

GROWING THE PLANTS.—A supply of good plants is the very foundation—an indispensable requisite of success. It is true, plants are freely advertised for sale by good growers at very reasonable rates; but my experience with such plants, after they have been packed for shipment, and gone through the hands of express companies, is far from satisfactory. I find that they come pretty high in the end, and often they cost more than the crop is worth after it is grown. The average quality of celery plants sold by growers, in my estimation, is rather poor. I grow annually a few thousand plants above what I need for my own use, and usually sell the surplus. After the best plants are picked out for planting, I consider those I sell of no more than fairly passable quality; yet the buyers hardly ever failed to compliment me upon the fine plants that I furnished them. This shows that they are not accustomed to buy really first-class plants, and for this reason I am sure that the wisest, in fact the only safe, course for celery growers is to raise their own plants. If my instructions are followed to the letter, it is a comparatively easy thing to do.

For the summer crop sow seed of the self-blanching sorts, White Plume, Golden Self-Blanching, etc., in flats in the greenhouse, during February, and prick the young seedlings out when an inch high, in other flats or directly in a hot-bed with moderate bottom heat (or in simple cold frame), giving each plant half an inch space in the row, with rows three inches apart. The soil should be made very rich, and be watered and ventilated freely, so that the plants will grow rapidly, and be large enough to go out in open ground sometime in May.

They may be set out in single rows in same manner as will be directed for the late crop, and bleached with boards, straw mulch, or earthing up, boards being preferred by most growers; or they may be planted closely in a piece of ground that is made excessively rich and if possible arranged for irrigation, ten inches apart one way, and five inches the other, thus forcing them to grow upright, and to blanch in the shade of their own foliage.

THE NEW CELERY CULTURE.—The latter method has been called "The new celery culture," and I confess that I think highly of it, both for the early and the late crops. With the former (the summer crop), you can seldom succeed except when you apply liquids freely, for the immense mass of foliage that grows on a comparatively small spot of ground, needs immense quantities of water, and the rains of heaven, during the period of rankest growth, are seldom half sufficient to support it. In the home garden, where we have only a few hundred plants, or a thousand at most, we may turn the washing suds and similar liquids from the kitchen to good use by emptying them, and barrels of water besides, into a line or lines of small tile laid six or eight inches below the surface in the celery patch, or by letting these liquids run along between the rows on the surface, gradually soaking into the ground, and always causing a rapid and rank growth. Such a growth, say at least two feet high, is absolutely necessary in order to blanch the plants well, and make them salable, without further manipulation. Usually, however, I set boards up all around the patch, in order to blanch the outside plants all the better. An excellent plan, for the early crop especially, is to provide a sort of half shade over the patch, by setting posts at reasonable distances, over which to string poles, or lattice work, or anything that will give the desired half shade.

If the season be hot and dry, and water is not given in the required quantities, the blight (should it once get into the patch) will have a chance to do a great deal of damage, and perhaps utterly ruin the crop unless checked by timely spraying.

For the late crop, shading as well as watering may often (partially or entirely) be dispensed with.

GROWING PLANTS FOR THE LATE CROP.—As early in spring as practicable prepare a rich, but clean, moist, and somewhat protected patch of ground. Put on plenty of fine compost, which should be free from weed seeds; and fork, spade or plow it into the soil. A top-dressing of composted poultry manure (wood-ashes, fertilizer, or whatever is on hand and thought of benefit to the land) may then be applied and mixed with the surface soil, using harrow or steel rake. In short make an extremely rich and perfectly mellow seed-bed. Now mark out shallow drills one foot apart, and in these sow the seed, at the rate of one ounce to about 200 feet of row, firming it afterwards thoroughly with the feet. Next smooth the surface by drawing the back of rake lengthwise over each row, or, holding the rake perpendicularly, handle upwards, pat the ground by pressing or striking the teeth flat and firmly upon the row. Rolling, although not strictly necessary, is, however, a good precaution. A small patch may be kept supplied with moisture by occasional watering, by covering with a slatted screen, providing half-shade, or by spreading a piece of cloth directly upon the soil until the seeds have germinated. Water, when required, may in the latter case be given upon the cloth, and soaking through it will provide the soil with moisture. The cloth must be removed as soon as the plants begin to show themselves above ground.

My own practice differs from this in so far as I grow the plants in my regular vegetable patch. The ground is prepared in the usual way and as required for sowing onions, radishes, lettuce, and similar crops; marked out with the common garden marker and in same distance as for the other crops. I walk upon the rows to firm the seed, and otherwise treat as above described; but without shading and rarely watering. The wheel-hoe is promptly and persistently brought into use, and the ground kept loose and free from weeds from the very start. Early thinning is of the utmost importance, and I refer the reader to what is said on this subject in the chapter on "Transplanting and Thinning." Give the plants room enough if you want them to grow large, stocky, and to make strong roots. Narrow the row down with the blades of the wheel-hoe, or slash into them with a hand weeder, until not more than 40 or 50 plants are left standing to the running foot. An occasional light top-dressing of nitrate of soda (in its absence perhaps of saltpetre, preferably in solution) will do wonders in giving you rapid growth of the plants. Once or twice the tops may be cut back with a sharp sickle or knife, to induce still increased stockiness, and by the time the plants are wanted for setting out, you will have a stock that for its excellence must astonish people accustomed only to see and handle the average plants of the professional plant grower. I have not yet seen a place so far back that a few thousand good celery plants could not find ready sale amongst neighbors and towns-people at 50 cents per 100, or $4 per 1,000. I can grow them profitably even at a lower figure.

Southern people who need their plants so much later, namely, in September or October, generally depend on northern-grown plants. To supply this demand the seed should be sown toward the end of May. A somewhat shady, moist piece of land will be best, and shading may be required in most cases. But it seems to me that southern people, if they take these same precautions in the selection and treatment of a patch, could grow their own supply of plants without much difficulty.

In the foregoing I have given you one of the "secrets" in horticulture that are of money value to those who make a proper use of it. The knowledge of "how to grow celery plants" brings me at least a little money every season.

PLANTING.—Now we have the plants, and good ones, too. The next thing is to set them so they will make a good crop. The soil selected is usually such as is cleared from an early crop, or, in the home garden, any available spot in composition between sand and clay. If the first crop, as is very likely the case, was well supplied with feed in the shape of compost, there will be enough left of it to carry the celery crop through all right. In practice, I prefer to apply additional manures or fertilizers even then, and I do this in various ways, according to the particular circumstances of the case. To plant a patch, even if not larger than for a few hundred plants, furrows are opened with a one-horse plow, going twice in same furrow to get the desired depth. These furrows are made three feet apart for the self-bleaching sorts, and somewhat more (from 4 to 5 feet) for the common sorts that have to be bleached by "banking" or earthing-up. They are partly filled with fine, thoroughly-rotted compost— preferably of cow manure—, fine barn-yard scrapings, etc., and some soil mixed all through it. More soil is then filled in, and the rows made nearly level with the surface.

If only a single row of celery, and a short one at that, is to be planted, as sometimes happens when a small strip of the vegetable garden becomes available, I merely apply the compost along the row to the width of about a foot, and fork or spade this nicely in. A little fertilizer or wood-ashes is scattered on top, and the soil raked smooth and even. After the ground has been prepared by either method, the garden line is tightly stretched along the row, and the plants set six inches apart.

At the north our usual time of setting celery plants is early in July, and for winter use up to August. Gardeners in the middle and southern states plant correspondingly later. The plants should be lifted from the seed row when the ground is wet, or at least moist. In a dry spell I always give the plant rows a thorough soaking an hour or two previous to pulling plants. The ground where plants are to be set should also be moist. Let me again call attention to the general rule (which especially is not to be disregarded during a dry time): Always sow and plant in *freshly-stirred soil;* then firm thoroughly. The plants after being pulled are properly trimmed or clipped at both ends, the roots dipped in water and planted with a dibber, which is also used to press the soil firmly against the roots, so that a leaf would tear off quicker than allow the plant to be pulled up by it. To apply a half pint of water to each plant after setting is a good precaution.

AFTER-CULTURE.—The ground must be kept clean and mellow, and the plants in growing condition by the frequent use of wheel-hoe, horse-hoe, steel-rake, and hoe. Next comes what is called "handling." When the plants have made a good growth, and the nights begin to get cool, late in August, the ground near the plants receives a thorough loosening, either by plowing a shallow furrow towards the row from each side, or by drawing soil up to it with the hoe. The gardener now gets down on his knees, straddling the row, and gathering up all the stalks of one plant after another in his left hand, packs the soil firmly around with his right, to retain them in this compact and erect position. More soil is then drawn up, or hoed up, to them.

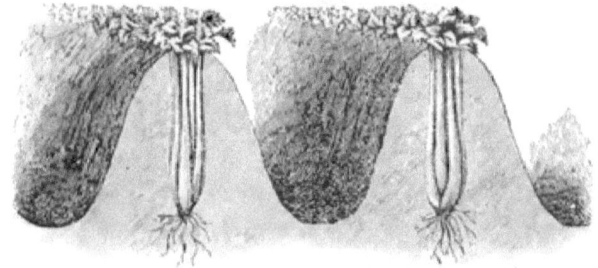

Celery after Earthing-up.

BLANCHING.—No further treatment is necessary for the self-blanching sorts to blanch them for market; yet we can greatly improve their flavor by earthing them up like the common varieties. Various methods are employed to blanch the crop. The one, though old, but yet commonly used, is by earthing up or "banking." This had best be done gradually, in two or three operations. Soil is dug up from between the rows, and banked up against the plants from each side, at the last operation almost to the tips of the leaves, as shown in above illustration.

Blanching by means of boards is coming more and more into favor with market gardeners, and well deserves recommendation. The plants are first "handled" in the usual way, and boards 10 inches wide are then set on edge against the rows from each side, as illustrated on next page, and held in that position by tying a string around each set of two at each end, by pegs driven into the ground, by clamps, or in any other convenient way.

Common drain tile, 4 or 5 inches in the clear, are sometimes used and recommended for bleaching celery; but this method does not always give satisfaction. I have thought to improve on it, and had some "bleachers" made, 5 or 6 inches high, with 5 inches inside diameter, in shape like bottomless flower-pots. These are placed over the plants, one only for each plant of the self-blanching kinds, and two, or even three—one above the other—for each plant of the common sorts. This

Blanching by Boards.

method in its different phases is illustrated on next page. I have had good success with it, and grown some fine blanched celery; but it seems to me that the expense connected with the purchase and breakage of the pots, and the labor required for storing and taking to and off the field, must prevent the more extensive or general use of this method.

Early in the season, and while the plants are yet growing rapidly, celery bleaches beautifully in from 2 to 3 weeks after banking or boarding up, and is then in first-class condition for use or market. Later it will take 4 or 5 weeks, perhaps even more, to bring the plants out in marketable shape.

PREPARING FOR MARKET.—When the crop is ready for market, draw the soil away from the plants desired, take hold of the top with one hand and pull, at same time prying under the root with a spade. Thus one plant after another is easily lifted out without breaking a stalk. Shake the soil off the roots, and take the plants to the vegetable house, to be properly prepared for sale. Trim the main root smoothly with three or four sloping cuts; remove the coarse outer leaves, and on one side open the stalks sufficiently to expose the heart in its tempting whiteness. From three to five, or even six of such plants, according to size, are then tied in a neat flat bunch, the exposed hearts all showing on one of the flat sides. The price depends very much on the tempting appearance of the bunches, on neat trimming and skillful tying. Such a bunch, properly put up is shown on page 222. Of course the plants when dug should be guarded from freezing; and in cold weather the boxes in which the crop is taken to market, must be provided or lined with matting, coarse cloth, etc.

When speaking of cold frame management, I have already alluded to celery as a crop grown for early marketing as "soup celery," in same way as parsley is handled. During fall and winter, the better outer leaves of the regular crop, and the plants too small for market otherwise, are bunched and sold for soup celery in the same manner. The thinnings from the seed-bed, as well as tops shorn off to induce stockiness, are often similarly utilized during summer.

STORING FOR MARKET.—Celery intended for winter use or winter market only requires handling, but no earthing up, since it blanches perfectly, and with no extra labor, in winter store. Necessary precautions that must be observed are to lift the plant

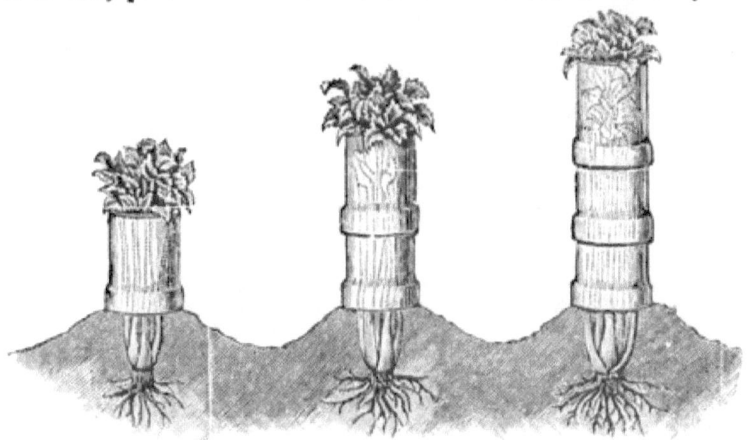

Celery Bleachers.

on dry days only, and never touch a frozen plant. If these rules are violated, speedy decay will usually follow. The method of winter storage in general use in the market gardens of New Jersey and vicinity is as follows:

On a well-drained spot a trench is dug as narrow as possible, and deep enough that the tops of the plants standing in it will just about reach to the level of the surface. The crop is then taken up, the soil shaken off, and the plants placed perpendicularly, and as closely crowded together as possible in the bottom of the trench. Here they are left until there is danger of severe freezing. Light frosts will do no hurt. The plants thus trenched in early (middle or end of October) may be used directly from the trenches, as wanted, during December. Except at the extreme north, no covering will be needed for them until this time. Roots trenched in during November, which will not be ready for use before January, need protection. During forepart of December boards a foot wide are laid in single line directly upon the trench, resting with an inch or two on the sides, and in the centre perhaps directly upon the foliage. When a cold night is expected a few inches of soil are drawn or shovelled upon the boards and allowed to freeze. Afterwards (early in the morning) litter of some sort is put over this crust *to keep the frost in;* and this covering, during severe weather, must be increased to perhaps a foot in thickness.

Celery kept in such trenches generally comes out beautifully bleached, crisp and tender. The chief point is thorough drainage, for if water is allowed to stand in the trench, celery is sure to rot. The trench method is probably the best, simplest and safest for a mild climate like that of New Jersey; but in colder localities I would give a genuine root cellar the preference. This gives us easy access to the crop at any time when wanted, and when it would not be safe to open a trench or expose the plants even for the shortest period outdoors. A dug-out in a hill-side, covered over with a substantial roofing of rails, poles, litter and a foot of soil, will answer quite well. Celery houses similarly constructed on the level are used quite extensively by the large growers near Rochester, N. Y., and elsewhere.

Bunch of Celery ready for Market.

Mr. Theo. F. Baker, of South Jersey makes use of a structure of this kind, and says it proves a great convenience, keeping the celery in perfect condition almost any length of time, and saving him a large amount of labor. The stock can be inspected at any time, taken out in cold and rainy weather, or at night, at pleasure, cleaned, washed and packed all under the same roof. Celery once handled can there be bleached in three weeks, and be free from rust or earthy flavor.

The cellar is 40 feet long, 16 feet wide, and 3 feet deep. The walls, which are 18 inches thick, rise 1 foot above ground. The rafters reach clear to the ground, where they rest on plates placed there to keep the roof from spreading. The ends are weather-boarded on both sides of six-inch studs, and filled in with sawdust. The roof is also double with a sawdust filling. A number of partitions well-lined with paper, and forming two or three, perhaps even four dead-air spaces of two inches each in width, would probably be still more effective and convenient. The height of the house inside is 4 feet at the eaves, and 11 at the peak. A ventilator at the peak admits air when needed, and gives a chance for the escape of heat that may be generated by the mass of celery. A door at each end, a small window over each to admit light, and steps to get down, complete the house.

"In storing the celery," writes Mr. Baker, " posts are set in the ground about 16 inches apart, beginning at each side on one end of the house, and coming toward the centre, giving seven posts or alleys to a side, and leaving a passage-way two feet wide the entire length of the building. Three sets of posts on one side of the passage-way, and four on the other will suit 16 feet boards, two and a half lengths on one side, and two lengths on the other. This leaves a space 8 feet square for washing tank, and room to prepare the stuff for market."

"Beginning next to the wall, we nail a board a foot wide to the post, so that the top of the celery will be even with the top of the board, leaving a space of four to six inches between the bottom of the board and the ground, through which one hand can be thrust to pack the roots firmly while the other holds the tops of the celery over the board. Some loose rich soil is thrown over the roots after the box or trench is filled from end to end. With a hose from the hydrant the soil is given a thorough wetting, and settled around the roots, causing them to throw out new fibres in a few days, when a new growth of the heart commences. Considerable heat will at first be generated by the mass of celery thus stored, and proper ventilation must be given, else rot will surely follow. After the one heating we have no further trouble from this cause."

STORING FOR HOME USE.—A few hundred plants may be stored in a common cellar, standing them upright on a couple of inches of moist soil or sand upon the floor, and dividing them in narrow sections between upright boards, in a similar way as described for celery-house storage. Instead of placing directly upon the cellar bottom, we can make use of narrow boxes (shoe boxes, for instance) putting in a little moist soil or sand, and standing the plants upon this. An improvement on this plan is, to bore inch holes at the ends and sides of the box, four inches

224—How to Make the Garden Pay.

from the bottom, and in packing the plants cover their roots with sand or soil. Keep this moist by watering occasionally through the holes near the bottom.

Unquestionably the simplest, and I find quite a safe method of storing a supply for home use is by packing the plants, already trimmed, almost as closely as for market, in boxes between layers of moist moss, and keeping the latter moist by occasional

A Southern Celery Bed.

sprinkling. This plan permits of packing celery in the smallest possible space for keeping, and it does keep well even until spring. As a further precaution, however, I would advise to moisten the moss before packing with a weak solution of salicylic acid (a teaspoonful dissolved in a gallon of hot water).

Whatever method of storage is adopted, attention must be paid to two points, namely, *to keep the foliage dry*, to prevent rotting, *and the soil moist*, to prevent wilting.

A SOUTHERN WAY OF GROWING CELERY.—The method which I found in general use from Maryland south, is almost entirely unknown to the northern cultivator; yet its many decided ad-

Southern Method of Handling and Banking Celery.

vantages strongly recommend its adoption, at least for trial, in every northern kitchen garden. I is especially suited for growing the self-blanching sorts.

The ground is laid off in beds 5 or 6 feet wide, with alleys of the same width between them. These beds are usually lowered 3 or 4 inches by shovelling the soil off the surface and throwing it in the alleys.

An outline of such bed is shown on the preceding page. Fine compost is then applied to the depth of several inches, and spaded or forked into the soil, after which the plants are set in rows one foot wide across the bed, and 6 inches apart in the rows. This is crowding the plants so closely together that they will grow pretty nearly upright without handling. They will need hoeing once or twice, and in a dry time can easily be watered, or provided with half shade, since the area is so ridiculously small for the number of plants. For convenience in earthing-up, two boards each 10 inches wide, and 7 or 8 feet long, with ends tapering for a handle, are set up on edge between two rows of plants, one to each side, as shown to the right of illustration. Pegs driven into the ground on the

Crawford's Half-Dwarf.

outside at each end hold the boards in position. The space between them is then filled up with soil from the alleys. This work—and earthing-up celery generally—can be done to best advantage by two men, one standing at each side of the bed. When the space is shovelled level full, each man grasps the boards by the handles on his side and presses the upper ends together with a few smart raps, then proceeds to take the boards out, and to insert them in the next row. Thus the soil is left in a sort of ridge between each two rows of plants, and the handling is done afterwards by hand in the usual manner. The boards are then again brought into use in same way, and the process of earthing-up continued as needed. For winter protection the whole bed is covered up with a thick and well-rounded layer of earth, and further protected with leaves or litter of some sort. Northern growers who wish to adopt this method, may have to vary it in some respects to suit the circumstances.

VARIETIES.

There is more difference in quality between different lots of the same variety when grown under different conditions and differently managed, than there is between different varieties grown exactly alike and at the same time. As I grow it year after year, forcing rapid succulent growth by the free use of nitrogenous fertilizers, especially of composted hen manure and nitrate of soda. I have celery in perfection—white as snow or yellow as gold, brittle as glass, and sweet as a nut. But it is always at its best when freshly dug from the bed. Early celery after it has been shipped long distances, and lying about exposed to the air on the sidewalk in front of grocery stores, is not to my taste. The self-bleaching celeries need higher culture than the common sorts, otherwise they are liable to be more dwarf than desirable. Their flavor and appearance may be improved by board or earth blanching same as other celeries, but they can be made fit for the table by mere

Golden Heart.

Golden Self-Blanching.

"handling," hence are sometimes, and justly so, called "the busy (or lazy) man's celery." The red or pink celeries are characterized not only by greater vigor of growth than the other classes, but also by very superior flavor, hence deserve to be much more largely grown than they actually are.

The tall sorts formerly grown for market to the exclusion of all others, are now almost gone out of cultivation, and the dwarf sorts have taken their places— very deservedly so, too.

White Plume.—The general favorite among the self-blanching varieties, and especially valuable for early use, both as a table sort and for market. It is quite dwarf, but compact, and decidedly attractive. No grower for any

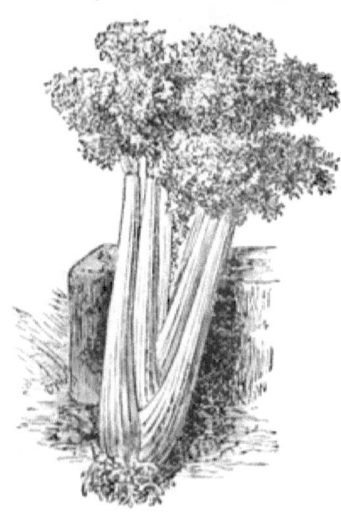

Fern-Leaved.

purpose should neglect to make the acquaintance of White Plume.

Golden Self-Blanching, of beautiful golden color, but of too dwarfish habit of growth except under highest culture.

Crawford's Half-Dwarf, Henderson's Half-Dwarf, until recently the most popular sort among market gardeners; yellowish white when blanched, of compact habit of growth, and fine quality; very solid.

Giant Pascal.—This variety is an offspring of the Golden Self Blanching, most carefully selected. It partakes of its nutty flavor, and has no bitter taste at all. The stalks are very large, solid, and not stringy, in fact it is the largest celery yet known as to width of stalks. It blanches very easily.

Golden Heart is constantly gaining in popularity, both as a market variety and for the family garden, and well deserves it. Of beautiful golden color when bleached, and fully the equal of Crawford's Half-Dwarf in every other respect. Can be planted with entire confidence. **Kalamazoo** is probably identical with Golden Heart.

Large White Solid.—Popular among growers who plant the taller kinds.

Boston Market.—A somewhat branching or suckering sort of rich, nutty flavor. Very popular among the gardeners near Boston. Stalks solid.

Dwarf Large Ribbed.—Very solid, of crisp nutty flavor; pearly white and an extra good keeper. Largely grown in the Kalamazoo celery districts.

Fern-Leaved, Bouquet.—Very attractive during growth on account of finely-serrated leaves; apparently a strong grower.

New Rose.—Beautiful; vigorous in growth; superior in flavor. Decidedly desirable for the home garden.

CELERIAC OR TURNIP-ROOTED CELERY.

Apium Graveoleus; German, *Knollen Sellerie;* French, *Celeri Rave;* Spanish, *Apio nabo.*—Celeriac is merely a variety of the common celery with abnormal root development, and like others, requires good, rich, mellow soil. It is sown in seed-bed in early spring, and planted out in rows 18 inches apart and 6 inches apart in the rows. Keep free from weeds and well cultivated, neither handling nor earthing-up being required. The tuberous root is the part used, especially for flavoring soups, etc. Boiled, sliced, and served with oil and vinegar, etc., it forms the celebrated dish known as "Celery Salad." Of the various varieties the newer **Apple-Shaped** deserves to be mentioned as one of the best.

Chervil.

Celeriac.

CHERVIL—TURNIP-ROOTED.

Chærophyllum bulbosum. German, *Kerbel;* French, *Cerfeuil Tubereux;* Spanish, *Perifollo.*

The root of this hardy vegetable resembles a short carrot or parsnip; somewhat smaller, of dark gray color, and with yellowish white flesh, which is sweet and mealy, reminding of sweet potato. Chervil, if fresh seed is sown, either in autumn or early spring, is of easy culture, being managed and used in same way as parsnips. It succeeds everywhere, and is improved by frost. The stalks grow tall and vigorous, and die down early in the season, indicating that the tubers have reached maturity.

CHICORY.

Cichorium Intybus; German, *Cichorie;* French, *Chicorée;* Spanish, *Achicoria.*—Chicory is generally known as a substitute for coffee. For this purpose the root is roasted and ground. The vegetable is easily grown, somewhat like carrots. Seed should be sown in spring, in drills a foot apart, and plants thinned to about 4 inches distance in the drills. The leaves are sometimes blanched and used as salad. The blanching is done in the cellar. The plants should be taken up at the beginning of cold weather, the leaves cut off ½-inch or so above the root crown, and placed horizontally in layers, alternating with layers of sand or soil, the root crowns all pointing outward of the sloping heaps, to give them a chance for free growth. If the soil is rather dry, a slight watering may be given. In a few weeks, if the temperature of the cellar is high enough, the leaves will have made considerable growth, and may be used.

Chicory.

Collard.

CHIVES.

Allium Schoenoprasum; German, *Schnittlauch;* French *Civette;* Spanish, *Cibellino.*
A plant of the onion family, growing in large tufts, perfectly hardy, and requiring no attention after being once planted. Bulbs, oval and small, forming a compact mass. Leaves numerous and slender, and generally used in the raw state as a relish, with bread and butter, etc. Propagated by division of the root. Planted in permanent border, 6 or 8 inches apart.

COLLARD OR COLEWORT.

Brassica Oleracea. Nothing more nor less than common cabbage used while young. It seems to me that one might be satisfied with the good American name "cabbage greens," and as such they are known and used quite commonly in the southern states. Cabbage seed is sown thickly in rows a foot apart, cultivated as if grown for plants, and cut and used when about 8 inches high. English gardeners cultivate a distinct variety under the name of '"Green Rosette Colewort" or Collard.

CORIANDER.

Coriandrum Sativum. German, *Coriander;* French, *Coriandre;* Spanish, *Culantro.*—An annual herb of easy culture, with branching stems, grown for its aromatic seed. It likes light and warm soils. Sow seed in spring, in rows a foot apart, and keep free from weeds.

CORN SALAD OR FETTICUS.

Valerianella Olitoria. German, *Acker Salat, Lämmersalat;* French, *Maché;* Spanish, *Canonigos.*—This hardy plant is much grown and used for salads, and freely offered in large city markets. For summer use, sow early in spring, in rows one foot apart, and keep the ground well cultivated and free from weeds. For early spring use, seed is sown in September, and same treatment and protection given as for spinach. Several varieties are quoted in English catalogues, of which Large Round-Leaved is as good as any.

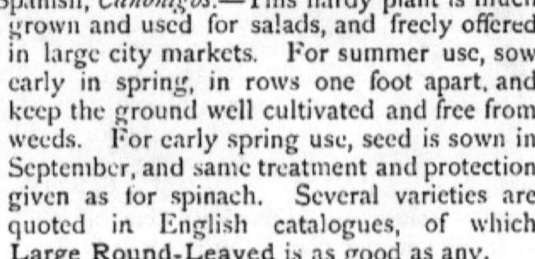

Corn Salad.

CORN.

Sweet Corn. *Zea Mays.* German, *Mais;* French, *Mais Sucré;* Spanish, *Maiz.*—Sweet corn for market is emphatically a farm garden crop, but rarely grown in the market garden, since the area required for its culture is by far too large to fit into the market gardener's limited space. On the other hand, really good sweet corn furnishes such a delicious and wholesome dish, one that graces our table, and gratifies our palates for several months every year, that a large part of the kitchen garden (if it be a large one) may be profitably devoted to this crop. In that case it should be our aim to have an unbroken succession all during the season; and we can easily have it by planting the early, intermediate, and late kinds at one time, and then continue to plant a patch of the latest every two weeks until middle of July. Farmers, who usually have but a small garden (certainly much smaller generally than they ought to have), had better plant it with garden crops requiring less room, and devote a quarter or half acre of the regular cornfield to the production of sweet corn for the table. I know there is considerable prejudice in the minds of most people against the free use of "green" corn. I consider it decidedly wholesome, almost in the light of a natural and needed medicine, and consequently we indulge in it to the fullest limit of our natural appetites, without ever experiencing the ill effects so dreaded by the masses.

As a farm or farm garden crop, I place it far ahead in profitableness to common field corn or potatoes. There are few localities in which a reasonable quantity of good boiling ears could not find ready sale at 75 cents or $1 per hundred. Where grown for canning or evaporating, of course, the ruling price has to be accepted. I find that I can plant sweet corn closer, and grow at least one-half as many more ears to the acre than I can of field corn, and this even with less labor and risk, and with no greater amount of manure. Consequently the grower easily realizes two or three times the profits on sweet corn that he would on the other.

Sometimes I have wondered why farmers living in a locality where there is a steady and sure annual demand for "roasting" ears at the prices mentioned, go on planting their whole available ground with field corn, which they have to sell at 25 cents per bushel ears, or 50 cents shelled, while so much better opportunities are offered to them in the cultivation of sweet corn.

SOIL AND CULTURE.—Corn delights in warm, well-drained soil; and none is better for it than a rich clover sod. The plant is a quick grower and a powerful eater, and not in the least particular as to the kind of food. Anything in the shape of plant food comes acceptable, even fresh, coarse stable manure. Good crops can be grown in thin soils, if dressed broadcast with from 400 to 800 lbs. of some high grade complete fertilizer per acre, harrowed or plowed in. Sometimes we may plant corn on unmanured land, in the supposition that it is rich enough for the crop; only to find out our mistake afterwards, by seeing the plants at almost a complete stand-still. Even at this late period the matter can be easily remedied in most cases, and a fair crop obtained, by applying a few hundred pounds of the fertilizer per acre as a top-dressing between the rows.

Planting in hills for the purpose of cultivating both ways may be admissible on rough, stony, or gravelly farm land, and for farm crops; but we want none of it in the garden, provided it is such as it should be—long and narrow in shape, and of clean, well-tilled soil. The drill method with corn, and most other crops, gives us an increased yield at no increase of labor; for with skillful management of the narrow-toothed cultivator or wheel-hoe, going twice (back and forth) between each two rows, each time close to the one at the right, the entire surface of a reasonably level and smooth piece of land can be so thoroughly and effectively stirred, that the field will appear as if it had been harrowed all over. While the plants are yet young, in good

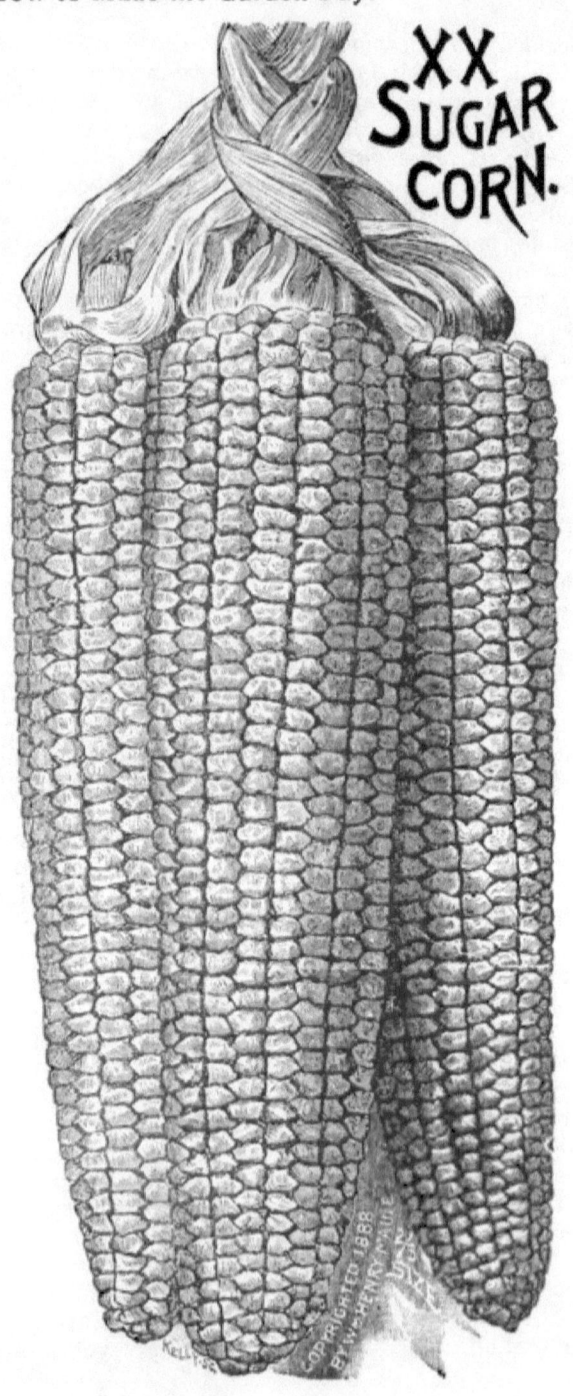

mellow soil, there will be absolutely nothing left to be done with the hand hoe, nor will there be, or at least only very little, later on, if skillful cultivator work is persistently and timely done.

The early dwarf sorts may be planted in drills 2½ or 3 feet apart, one stalk every 6 or 8 inches, or two to three plants every 12 to 18 inches; the intermediate varieties need a little more space; and the late tall sorts should have the rows 3½ or 4 feet apart, one stalk every 8 or 10 inches, or two to three stalks every 18 inches. The ears are of best table quality when freshly broken off the plants, and greatly lose in this respect by standing about and becoming wilted.

VARIETIES.

Cory Sweet.—I have grown this for a number of years, and consider it by far the best of the earlies, and the earliest of all that are worth growing. Stalk remarkably dwarf, and ear remarkably large for such a small sort. Easily grown and always satisfactory. Tender and sweet.

Early Minnesota, Early Marblehead, and Crosby's Extra Early, are early sorts with small ears, but largely grown for earliest market and home use.

Mexican Sweet, Black Mexican, Blue Mexican.—A second early sort with fair-sized ears. Kernels extremely sweet and tender, and of a dark bluish purple when ripe. Good only for the home garden.

Perry's Early, of vigorous growth, fair-sized ear, and good quality.

Maule's XX Sugar.—Fit for the table in 9 to 10 weeks from planting, and of a most delicious sweet and sugary flavor. It is of comparatively dwarf habit, stalks seldom growing more than 4 to 5 feet high. Remains long in an edible condition, and matures in a comparatively short time for such a large-eared sort.

Everbearing.—Ears are of good size, and covered with kernels clear to end of the cob. Ripening a few days after the Amber Cream, each stalk will produce one to two, and at times four to five, well-developed ears.

Amber Cream.—Medium early, of strong growth. Ears of good size. Kernels amber colored when ripe. Held in high esteem wherever grown.

Evergreen, Stowell's Evergreen.—This is probably the most popular late variety, both for market and home use, of strong vigorous growth, and with large tender ears, that remain in condition for table use for a long time. Also much grown for fodder purposes.

Egyptian, in all its valuable characteristics somewhat similar to Evergreen. Ears very large, tender and sweet. Much grown for canning purposes.

Gold Coin.—A recently-introduced variety, with as large an ear as Evergreen, but maturing a few days earlier.

Mammoth Sugar is very late, and produces the largest ears of any variety. Of good quality and superior for canning. Remains long in the green state.

POP CORN.

VARIETIES.

Pop Corn is emphatically a crop for the children, and they would hardly consider the garden complete without a row or two. It is as easily grown as field corn, and while the ears are not very large, their number, especially with somewhat close planting, will go far to make up for lack of size.

White Rice is more generally grown than any other. Ears quite large, a number of them growing on one stalk. Kernels sharply pointed. Superior for popping.

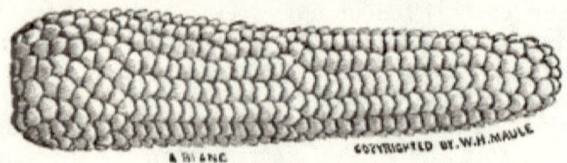

Queen's Golden Pop Corn.

Golden Pop, Queen's Golden Pop. Handsome, prolific and reliable.

Marblehead Prolific.—This new variety is claimed to be the most productive pop corn in cultivation. Ears are eight to ten inches long, filled out to the end with bright handsome white grains.

CRESS OR PEPPERGRASS.

Lepidium Sativum. German, *Kresse;* French, *Cresson;* Spanish, *Mastuerzo.* No vegetable starts quicker from seed, or is easier to grow if the flea beetle is kept off. The leaves have a very pungent taste, and are much used as a salad, usually as a condiment with lettuce and other salad materials. Sow seed thickly in drills one foot apart, guard against flea beetle depredations while the plants are small, and cut as desired. The plants run to seed quickly, and frequent successive sowings must be made, if a constant supply is wanted.

Of the several varieties, the **Curled or Normandy Garden Cress** and the **Extra Curled Dwarf** are generally grown in America.

Water Cress.—*Nasturtium officinale.* German, *Brunnenkresse;* French, *Cresson de Fontaine;* Spanish, *Berro.* This hardy perennial aquatic plant roots readily both in water, and wet or moist soil, and after once being introduced, will thrive in almost any small stream of clear, cold water, ditch or pond, without care or culture. On account of the pleasant pungency and hygienic properties of the leaves, it is highly esteemed as a table delicacy, and extensively grown for market near all the larger cities. It makes a superior salad, and fine material for garnishing. To introduce it in any stream or body of water, sow seed or a few cuttings or pieces of root in the mud, along the margin, and it will increase rapidly, often entirely overrunning ditches and small brooks. Flooding is the best winter protection. Gather and market in spring. It also grows well on a moist greenhouse bench, and on any upland that can be kept continuously moist.

Water Cress.

Upland Cress, American Cress.—*Barbarea praecox;* German, *Amerikanische Winter Kresse;* French, *Cresson de terre.* —Native biennial of Europe, resembling Water Cress in taste, and used for seasoning and garnishing. Easily grown from seed. I have no high opinion of it, and do not recommend it

Upland Cress.

CUCUMBER.

Cucumis Sativus. German, *Gurke;* French, *Concombre;* Spanish, *Cohombro.* Under heading of "Cold Forcing Houses" (Chapter XIII) I have already alluded to cucumbers as a profitable crop for culture under glass. Otherwise the bulk of cucumbers and pickles grown for market is produced in the farm garden rather than the market garden, simply because the market gardener has not sufficient space. Almost any kind of well-drained soil will produce cucumbers, provided it is rich enough, or made so. Young clover sod is good. The selection of new ground—wide crop rotation—is always a good precautionary measure, and liable to lessen the dangers from insect and disease attacks.

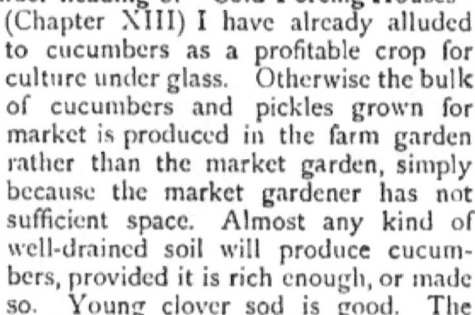

236—How to Make the Garden Pay.

Plow deep and thoroughly, and mellow the surface in the usual manner. Then mark out the ground four feet apart, both ways; put a large shovelful of good compost in each intersection, and mix it thoroughly with the soil. When danger from

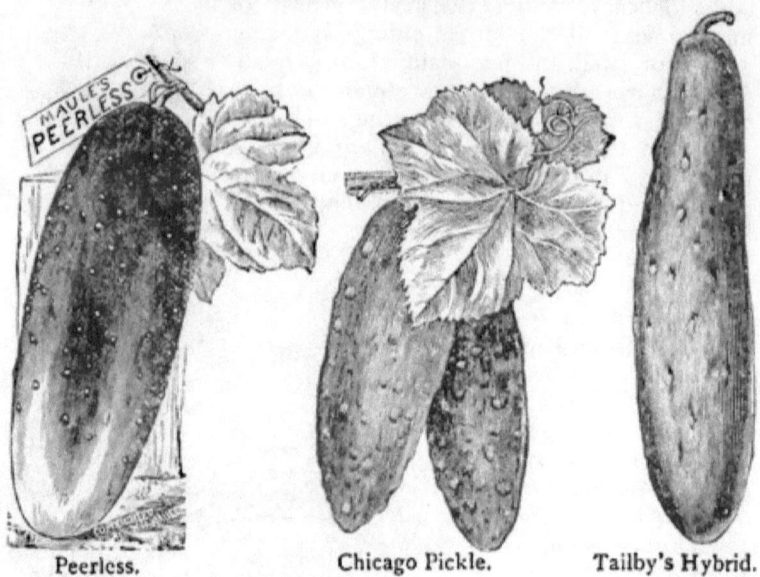

Peerless.   Chicago Pickle.   Tailby's Hybrid.

late frosts is past, plant into the hills thus made, using plenty of seed to make allowance for injury by insects, etc., and when the plants begin to run, thin to the best three or four in each hill. From the time they begin to come up until several leaves are made, they should be kept dusted with plaster or a poisoned plaster mixture, as a preventive for insects. Occasional watering with washing suds during dry weather is of great benefit. Keep the ground well cultivated and free from weeds. It is not desirable to plant or hill up in great mounds, since cucumbers

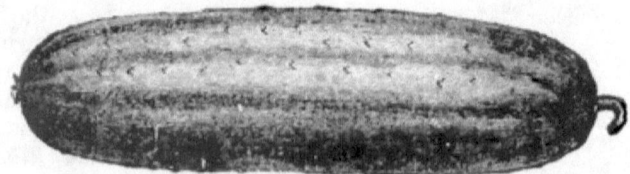

Evergreen Cucumber.

need considerable moisture to do well. Gather the fruit regularly, without leaving any specimens to ripen, or the vines will stop bearing. For early market, and as a safeguard against insect depredations, the plants may be started on inverted sods **under**

Cultural Directions.—237

glass in same way as mentioned for Lima beans, and also practised with melons and squashes. This is done two or three weeks before the usual period for outdoor planting.

The demand for pickles is largest in the fall, and the planting for pickles is usually postponed until latter part of June or fore-part of July.

VARIETIES.

Maule's Extra Early.—A cross between the Early Russian and Green Prolific; as early as the former, while it combines the fine pickling qualities of the latter.

Early Russian.—The earliest variety. Fruit small, growing in pairs, and produced in great number. Good for small pickles.

Early Cluster, Green Cluster,

Early Russian.

**Green Prolific,
Early Frame,
Short Green,
White Japan,
Jersey Pickle,
Chicago Pickle,**
all these are intermediate sorts, reliable for pickling purposes.

**Peerless White Spine,
Evergreen,
Long White Spine,
Improved Long Green,**
are popular varieties for table use and large pickles.

Nichol's Medium Green, recently introduced, is a good all-purpose cucumber.

Nichols' Medium Green.

Tailby's Hybrid.—A hybrid of White Spine with one of the large English Frame varieties. Very large and solid, containing but few seeds. A really fine and handsome sort, but not as prolific as I would wish.

Snake Cucumber (*C. Flexuosus*).—More of a curiosity than of practical usefulness. Several feet in length, and always growing in a coil.

Giant Pera.—A newly introduced sort of great length and solidity, having but few seeds.

Small Gherkin, Prickly Gherkin, West India Gherkin, Burr (*C. Anguria*).—A strong-growing plant bearing its small, prickly fruit in great abundance. It is largely used for pickles. Should be planted in hills not less than 5 feet apart each way, with two or three plants to the hill.

Snake Cucumber.

DANDELION.

Leontodon Taraxacum. German, *Löwenzahn;* French, *Dent-de-lion.*—This common weed of our fields and meadows is often gathered and prepared for "greens." Esteemed especially for its hygienic properties. Careful selection of seed has resulted in a number of improved varieties, which are cultivated in European gardens, both for spring greens and salad.

Americans are only just beginning to introduce its cultivation into their gardens. I have a mammoth variety from Pennsylvania under trial.

The cultivation is simple. Sow seed in early spring in hills one foot apart, and thin or transplant to from 10 to 12 inches. Keep free from weeds. Leaves may be cut for use in fall; and the plantation will continue to yield during the spring of next year. European gardeners often improve the flavor of this vegetable by blanching the leaves, either by covering the bed with a layer of sand or by putting a large flower pot, inverted, over each plant.

Dandelion.

DILL.

Anethum graveolens. German, *Dill;* French, *Aneth;* Spanish, *Eneldo.*—An annual herb of easiest culture, much used by Germans as a condiment, or flavoring for pickled cucumbers, beans, etc. Sow seed in spring or summer, in drills one foot apart, and keep free from weeds. Where seed was left to ripen plants will spring up in great abundance the season following Little attention in the way of manuring or cultivation is required.

EGG PLANT.

Solanum melongena. German, *Eierpflanze;* French, *Aubergine;* Spanish, *Berengena.*—In the cultivation of the egg-plant we have to face several serious difficulties, among them chiefly its half tropical nature, which calls for the display of especial skill in raising good plants, and the great fondness of the potato bug for this particular food.

Long Purple.

GROWING THE PLANTS.—First of all we need strong plants. To start the seed and cause thrifty plant growth, a higher degree of heat and that of longer duration is required than for tomatoes or peppers. A good greenhouse, with heat under full control, is a great convenience in this emergency. The temperature should not be allowed to fall below 70 degrees Fahr. during any of the stages of development. Sow seed during March or early April, and when plants are about an inch high, prick them out in pots or old tomato cans, in good rich potting soil. Where no warm greenhouse is at hand, a fresh hot-bed will have to answer for sowing seed; but the young plants as soon as potted off should be transferred to another, freshly-made hot-bed. Better plants are usually grown in tomato cans, or in large boxes, than in ordinary flower pots.

New York Purple.

PLANTING AND CULTIVATION.—Well-drained, warm, rich soil is an indispensable condition of success with this crop. Good compost, or other good fertilizer, should not be spared. When the ground has become thoroughly warmed through, *and not before*, set the plants 2 or 3 feet apart each way —the latter distance in rich soil—and keep well cultivated and free from weeds. Dusting the plants frequently with plaster, especially if a little carbolic acid is mixed with it, has a decided tendency toward making bug visits less frequent; but where these are very troublesome, applications of the Paris green mixtures will be necessary. For a number of years, while in New Jersey, I have tried in vain to save a few plants from utter destruction by bugs in early autumn. When the tops of the late potatoes have died down (in August) it becomes a matter of life and death to the hordes of hard-shell beetles to find a little food. So they all at once pounce in full force upon the egg-plants in the neighborhood, and will devour them even to the stalks, in spite of all the applications we might make. In such cases the only hope for success lies in extensive planting and close watching. If any one can tell me a practical method of protecting a few plants I shall be glad to hear.

VARIETIES.

New York Improved, New York Improved Purple.—This is more generally grown for market than any other; and on account of its mammoth size, handsome shape and color, a great favorite. A selection of this naturally very prickly sort, much grown among New Jersey market gardeners, is entirely free from spines.

Earliest Dwarf Purple.—Too small for market, otherwise resembling the New York Improved, only considerably earlier, and for this reason valuable for home gardens at the extreme north. Here I have little use for it.

Early Long Purple.—Two or three times as long as it is broad. Color varies somewhat. Not much grown for market, but good for the home garden, as it is early and comparatively of easy culture.

Black Pekin.—Almost round in shape, and very dark in color. Quite early for so large a variety.

Japanese Varieties.—Of these I have two under test. They appear to be much hardier and easier to grow than other egg-plants, but fruit is small and only valuable for the home garden.

ENDIVE.

Cichorium Endivia. German, *Endivien;* French, *Chicorée Endive;* Spanish, *Endivia.*—Endive, one of the best of fall and winter salads, is not yet appreciated in America as is deserves. Practically unknown in the average home garden, it is found only in larger markets, and often there in but limited quantity. If my readers will once try it, and bring it on the table well bleached, crisp and tender, as a salad, in late fall or winter, I think they will continue to grow it, thus adding to the luxuries of their table.

Its culture is simple; its requirements as to manure and soil are modest. For summer use sow seed in April or May; for fall and winter use in June, July, and early August. Have drills one foot apart, and thin or transplant to same distance in the drill. Hoe occasionally to keep free from weeds; and when the plants have made about their full growth, gather up the leaves and lightly tie at their tips. In from one to three weeks the hearts will then bleach beautifully, when the crop should at once be marketed or used. Do not tie faster than the crop can be disposed of; for if left after blanching, the hearts will soon begin to decay.

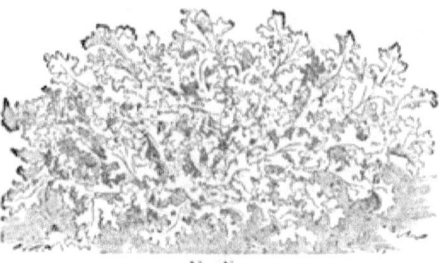
Endive.

I have succeeded in bleaching endive in less than a week's time, and much more beautifully than usually seen, by simply placing one of my celery bleachers (largest size) over each plant.

VARIETIES.

Green Curled.—Generally grown for market and home use, and good for salad, greens or garnishing. European catalogues list and describe nearly a score of other varieties, among them the Moss-curled, Rouen or Stag's Horn, Green Curled Upright, Broad Leaved or Batavian, etc.; but the Green Curled will do me.

FENNEL; LONG SWEET FENNEL.

Anethum Fœniculum. German, *Fenchel;* French, *Fenouil Doux;* Spanish, *Hinojo.*—The seeds of this easily-grown herb are used in the manufacture of liquors, and the leaves for various culinary purposes. Sow in drills one foot apart, like Dill, and keep free from weeds.

GARLIC.

Allium Sativum. German, *Knoblauch;* French, *Ail Ordinaire;* Spanish, *Ago vulgar.*—A well-known bulbous perennial of peculiar strong taste, mostly used by the foreign part of our population, and valued more in southern countries than at the cold north, for the simple reason that it has much less of the biting flavor when grown in a warm than in a cold climate.

This vegetable—if it deserves that name—is only propagated by means of its sets or "cloves," of which each full-grown plant has about ten. In early spring plant them in shallow one-foot drills, about 5 or 6 inches apart in the drills, one clove in a place, and cover lightly. The crop ripens about the same time as onions, and is harvested in a similar manner.

Garlic Sets.

GOURDS. Fancy Gourds.

None of these are grown or used here for culinary purposes. Fruit of various shapes and sizes, often quite ornamental, and unique. Plant in hills, and train on trellis.

Nest Egg Gourd (*Cucumis colocynthis oviformis*).—Plant strong growing. Fruit white and resembling a hen's egg in size and shape. Often used as a nest-egg, and answering this purpose admirably.

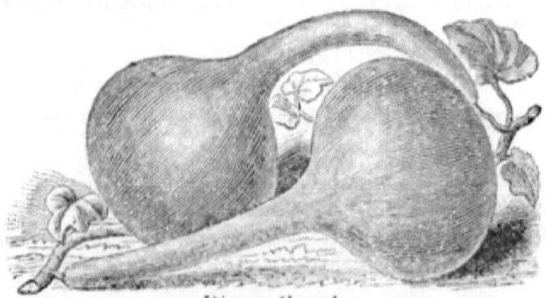

Dipper Gourd.

Dipper Gourd (*Cucurbita lagenaria*),
Sugar Trough (*Cucurbita lagenaria*),
Dish Cloth (*Cucurbita lagenaria*),

The fruit of all these is sometimes used for the purpose indicated by their respective names. When bruised, all the green parts of the plant emit a strong odor which is far from agreeable, while the flowers are quite fragrant. All are of rapid growth, and valuable for covering trellises, arbors, and unsightly places of any description, but of no use to us as a kitchen vegetable.

HOREHOUND.

Marrubium vulgare. German, *Andorn;* French, *Marrube Blanc.*—A perennial hardy plant easily grown from seed sown in spring, or propagated by a division of the tufts. The plant is much used as a cough remedy, especially in the form of "horehound candy." Plant in drills one foot apart.

HORSE-RADISH.

Cochlearia (Nasturtium) Armoracia. German, *Meerettig;* French, *Raifort Sauvage;* Spanish, *Taramago.*—Horse-radish is hardly ever found in the home garden as a cultivated vegetable. It is allowed to propagate itself at will from pieces of root left in the ground where a plant had once been set out, or otherwise obtained a foothold, usually in the back-yard or some out-of-the-way place. From this source the family gets an abundant supply year after year, without ever bestowing care or attention to it.

For both the market and farm garden, however, horse-radish is a most important crop, and almost invariably a profitable one. It delights in deep, rich, moist soil; and requires but a minimum of cultivation, since it makes a very large amount of top, thus giving the weeds little chance, at the same time keeping the ground well-shaded, moist and mellow.

PLANTING AND CULTIVATION.—Horse-radish produces no seed, but is always grown from "sets" or pieces of the smaller roots, cut 4 to 8 inches in length, with upper end slanting and lower end square. For culture in the farm garden, the ground is well-manured, deeply plowed, and otherwise thoroughly worked; then marked out in rows from 2 to 3 feet apart. Here the root pieces or sets are planted 15 to 18 inches apart. This is done by making a hole with a long slim dibber or planting stick, or a small, light iron bar, and dropping the set, square-end down, into it, so that the top end is left slightly below the surface. The soil is then pressed firmly against the set. With cultivator (or wheel-hoe) and hand-hoe the ground is kept free from weeds, until the heavy top growth makes further working among the crop unnecessary.

The eastern market gardener adopts a somewhat different course. With him horse-radish is chiefly grown as a second crop, yet planted almost simultaneously with a first crop. It usually is made to follow early cabbages, cauliflower or early beets. Just as soon as the first crop is planted, the horse-radish sets are put out, in the manner described, in a row midways between each two rows of the first-crop vegetables, so to stand 2 or 2½ feet one way by 16 or 18 inches the other. The sets are put in deep enough so the upper or slanting end will be about 3 inches below the surface of the ground. This is done to give the first crop time to get out of the way before the horse-radish appears on the scene. In the cultivation of the former no notice is taken of the presence of the horse-radish underneath, except to clip off any sprout foolhardy enough to come to the surface prematurely. Horse-radish makes the most of its growth during the cooler and moister weather of early autumn. When the first crop is taken off, its opportunity has come, and it generally makes the most of it. It will need one thorough hoeing, and may then be left to take care of itself. The crop is dug late in the fall, or after all other crops are taken care of, freed from its small roots and large tops, and stored in root houses or pits, to be marketed during winter. A root when ready for market, appears as in annexed illustration. Being trimmed at both ends, it is Horse-radish. given a thorough washing, and a number of them are then tied together in a bunch, and thus put on the market. It is usually sold by weight, and one of the best paying late crops.

The small roots are used for sets. When removed from main root they are at once cut of the proper length and shape, tied in bundles, and buried in sand in the cellar or pitted in the open ground until wanted in spring.

An English Method.—I here also illustrate a so-called improved way of growing horse-radish, described some time ago, in the *Garden* (London). The discoverer of this method claims

A New Way of Growing Horse-radish.

that the roots, being so much nearer the influence of the sun, and in warmer soil than those planted perpendicularly (in the usual way) grow to a much larger size, and are harvested with much less labor than they would otherwise. The sets are planted only from 2 to 3 inches deep, almost horizontally, as indicated in illustration, and given the cultivation as described for those planted in the usual way.

HYSSOP.

Hyssopus officinalis. German, *Isop;* French, *Hyssope;* Spanish, *Hisopo.*—A low-growing, evergreen perennial, preferring warm, calcareous soil. In cold climates it is usually grown from seed sown in the open ground in April or May. The leaves and other parts of the plant have an aromatic odor, and pungent, bitter taste.

Hyssop.

KALE OR BORECOLE.

Brassica oleracea acephala. German, *Braunkohl, Grünkohl;* French, *Chou-vert;* Spanish, *Breton.*—This vegetable of the cabbage family is grown and used in various ways, most usually as "sprouts" for winter greens, similar to spinach or collards. Sow seed in early autumn, having drills one foot apart, and leaving the plants five or six inches apart in the row. South of New York City it is hardy enough to endure the winters without protection. In spring the plants are cut, dead leaves trimmed off, and put up in barrels for sale, or used for greens. The

Kale.

Germans usually plant kale as one would late cabbages. Seed is sown in spring, and the plants set out in June or July, in rows three feet apart, with two or three feet distance between the plants. Same cultivation is given as for cabbages. During early winter the leaves, which grow to a considerable size, are gathered frequently when frozen, or to be dug from under the snow, and used for greens. If properly prepared they are exceedingly palatable, especially as they come at a time when fresh green stuff is quite scarce. The young sprouts issuing in spring from the stumps are also utilized for greens; and when boiled and served with vinegar, make a very popular and palatable salad.

VARIETIES.

German Greens, Dwarf Curled, Sprouts, Green Curled, Canada, Labrador, with beautifully curled, dark green leaves, which usually rest on the ground, the plant being quite dwarf. Usually grown for market as "sprouts." Tender and of superior flavor, almost equaling Savoy cabbages.

Green Curled Scotch, Winter Greens.—Very hardy, two to three feet high, has many large and beautifully curled leaves, which, after exposure to frost, make excellent winter greens, and sprouts for spring salad. The plant is one of the hardiest of the whole tribe.

European seedsmen list a large number of varieties, little grown in America, among them the following:

Intermediate Moss Curled.

Tree Cabbage, or Jersey, which grows four to five feet high in the first year; for cattle.

Marrow Kale, a large, coarse sort, with thickened stem, for cattle.

Dwarf Purple Curled, with very dark, curled leaves, much used for winter greens.

KOHL-RABI.

Brassica Caulo-rapa. German, *Kohlrabi;* French, *Chou Rabe;* Spanish, *Col de Nabo.*—In this we have another vegetable much less cultivated in American gardens than it deserves. As easily grown as any member of the cabbage family, it yields in its

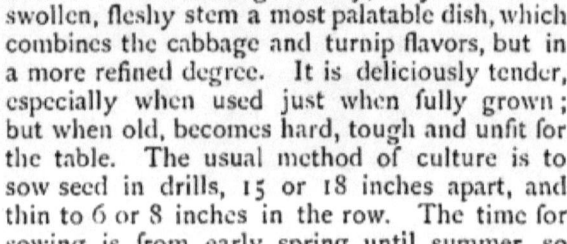

Kohl-Rabi.

swollen, fleshy stem a most palatable dish, which combines the cabbage and turnip flavors, but in a more refined degree. It is deliciously tender, especially when used just when fully grown; but when old, becomes hard, tough and unfit for the table. The usual method of culture is to sow seed in drills, 15 or 18 inches apart, and thin to 6 or 8 inches in the row. The time for sowing is from early spring until summer, so that a succession may be had from early summer until winter. Keep the ground loose and free from weeds. With careful handling, kohl-rabi can also be transplanted successfully.

VARIETIES.

Early Vienna, Improved Imperial.—This, unquestionably, is the best for forcing, late planting, and for general table use. The tops are very small and leaves short, with slim stalks; the balls (bulbs, heads or whatever we may call them) handsome, forming very early, and retaining their delicious tenderness for a long time. There is also a purplish variety of this in cultivation.

Large White.—The balls form much later in this than in the preceding and grow to a large size. The leaves also grow large, with stout leaf-stalks, so that it is easily distinguished from the Vienna by its much heavier top. Requires nearly the whole season to come to full development. For the kitchen garden it will be found a good companion to the Vienna. If both are planted at the same time, in early spring, the one will supply you with tender balls in the forepart, and the other in the latter part of the season.

LAVENDER.

Lavandula Spica. German, *Lavendel;* French, *Lavande;* Spanish, *Espliego.*—Lavender leaves are sometimes used for seasoning, but the chief value of the plant is in its flowers, which are used in the manufacture of the well-known perfumery. Grows in compact tufts with numerous stalks two feet high. Perennial, and generally propagated by division of the tufts, sometimes by cuttings, and in rarer cases from seed. Set the plants 15 or 18 inches apart, and keep free from weeds. They will last a number of years, succeeding best in light calcareous soil.

LEEK.

Allium Porrum. German, *Lauch;* French, *Poireau;* Spanish, *Puerro.*—Leek, although but rarely found in American home gardens, is quite extensively cultivated as a second crop, to follow early beets, cabbages, etc., in the market gardens near cities having a large foreign population. The ground should be rich from previous manurings, and receive an additional dressing besides.

CULTIVATION.—In April or early May sow seed in seed bed, having rows one foot apart, and cultivating same as onions from seed. In July, the young plants, then about as thick as a goose quill, are planted out on soil cleared from the earlier crop and well prepared, in rows one foot apart, with five inches distance between the plants. They should be set deeply (with a dibber) since their market value depends on the bleached condition of the root and stalk. For the same reason, the soil, in hoeing, is drawn up towards them. Leeks transplant very easily at any time while the soil is moist, but the loose roots and leaves should be trimmed back, and the roots dipped in water, previous to setting.

Giant Italian Leek.

The crop may be stored and wintered somewhat similar to celery, in trenches or root-houses, or marketed directly from the field in the fall. The decayed leaves are to be removed, roots and tops cut back, and the plants, after washing, tied in bunches of half a dozen or more, and marketed.

VARIETIES.

Long Flag, Large Flag, Broad Flag, London Flag.—Often ten inches long, and nearly two inches wide. A good early, productive sort, and popular with our market growers.

Scotch Flag, Musselburgh.—A form of the common long leek, somewhat hardier than the Large Flag, and with a stem sometimes 10 or 12 inches long, but only an inch in diameter.

New Giant Italian is introduced as a variety of very large size, hardy, and of mild flavor. Perhaps identical with the **Giant Carentan** introduced in England.

LETTUCE.

Lactuca Sativa. German, *Salat;* French, *Laitue;* Spanish, *Lechuga.*—The production of lettuce in hot-beds and hot-houses during winter, and in cold-frames and cold-houses in early spring, is one of the chief resources for money for a large number of market gardeners. The chapters on "Cold Frames" and "Cold Forcing Houses" deal more fully with this subject. As an early market garden crop for outdoor culture it is, perhaps, of still greater general importance.

GROWING FOR MARKET.—Plants are usually grown from seed sown in open ground in latter part of September, transplanted into cold-frames (allowing 4 to 5 square inches space to each) toward end of October or early November, and wintered over in same way as early cabbage plants. Just as soon as the ground is in working order in early spring, the plants are set out in warm, rich, well-manured and well-prepared soil, 12 by 10 to 12 inches apart, all by themselves, or in rows between early cabbages or cauliflowers. The latter plan is often adopted by good market gardeners for the sake of utilizing space. The lettuce crop comes off in time to give to the other crop the entire space, long before it is needed, and for this reason is almost clear gain. To a more limited extent lettuce is also grown for summer and fall market from seed sown in one foot drills in open ground; the drills one foot apart, and the plants thinned to about the same distance.

In favored localities in the middle states, and almost everywhere further south, lettuce sown or planted out in open ground in the autumn will usually winter all right, especially if protected (when thought necessary) by lightly covering with evergreen

Cultural Directions.—249

boughs, or coarse litter, and will give a crop much in advance of that planted out in spring. It should go without saying that the stimulus given to plant growth by free use of the hoes cannot be safely dispensed with in the lettuce patch.

GROWING FOR HOME USE.—People who know lettuce only as loose leaves (cut-lettuce, leaf-lettuce) grown in close rows or masses, as usually found in American kitchen gardens, have not yet learned to appreciate the possibilities of this vegetable as salad material, nor all its inherent virtues. My method of growing it for home use brings out all its best points.

At the earliest possible date in spring I sow seed of various varieties in drills 12 to 15 inches apart, and give clean and thorough cultivation from the start by means of the hand wheel-hoe, same as all the other closely planted vegetables in the patch.

Hanson.

Strict attention is given to early thinning, the most vigorous plants being left, so they stand about 3 or 4 inches apart in the drills. Rapid growth is forced by occasional light dressings of nitrate of soda (a little saltpetre will give similar results); and as soon as the heads have fairly begun to form, we commence using them for the table, thinning the plants as we go along, until they stand 10 or 12 inches apart in the rows. By this time they have developed into large heads, sometimes of mammoth size, and of the delicious crispness and tenderness which only rapid growth can give us. Thus we have always the very best quality of salad, the little partly-developed heads at first, and later the hard, solid, large ones. As we always have it in great abundance, the crisp inner hearts alone are used, and the large outer leaves go to the fowls. Thus grown, lettuce makes a most excellent salad, indeed, above all comparison with the stuff usually found in the markets, or in most people's kitchen garden. Repeated sowings should be made for succession.

For earliest use I often set a row of cold-frame-wintered (or hot-bed-grown) plants between two rows sown with early cabbages, which is merely a modification of the method of growing lettuce for early market in alternate rows with cabbages.

VARIETIES.

These are exceedingly numerous; and many new varieties, both for market and home use, are being introduced every year. Indeed we have so many really good sorts that the selection of a few is not without difficulty. Yet we can take any one out of dozens of them, and feel perfectly satisfied with our bargain.

Tennisball, Boston Market.—Well adapted for forcing under glass; very early, of medium size, and a reliable header.

Salamander.—A favorite with eastern market gardeners, and yet in the front rank as a market

Green Fringed Salamander.

Ohio Cabbage.

variety, as it makes large and firm heads, and endures the summer heat well, although in the latter respect it is now surpassed by many newer introductions.

Hanson.—An old favorite for market in the New England States. A good, reliable header, but perhaps surpassed in many characteristics by the recently introduced **Improved Hanson**.

Boston Curled and Green Fringed.—These form somewhat loose heads, and therefore not adapted for market purposes; but their curled or fringed masses of foliage make them attractive for the home garden.

Buttercup.—The most delicate appearing of any lettuce I am acquainted with. Only medium in size, but the heads are firm, and foliage of a most pleasing beautiful golden color, which would naturally suggest the name given it. It is one of the varieties that has come to stay in my garden.

Ohio Cabbage.—A beautiful summer lettuce, of very large size, firm head, tender and reliable. Also good for early.

California Butter.—A long-standing summer variety, making large, firm heads with dark foliage.

Marblehead Mammoth,

New York.—These two are newer sorts of remarkable thrift, giving us heads of the very largest size, but somewhat lacking in compactness. Beautiful and well worthy a place in the home garden.

Stubborn-Head, Stubborn-Seeder.—Introduced as a fine, firm-heading variety, able to endure the summer heat and drouth for a long time, and without running to seed.

Prize Head.—Forms a large, tender and crisp mass of leaves of superior flavor.

Passion.—A California variety that stands the heat remarkably well, and at the same time forms a very large solid head.

Philadelphia Butter.—Produces fine heads of large size; very certain to head.

Cos Varieties.—These are favorites in England, but little grown in our gardens. Leaves elongated, with a large thick mid-rib. The hearts are blanched by tying the tips of the leaves, which have an upright habit of growth.

MARJORAM (Sweet.)

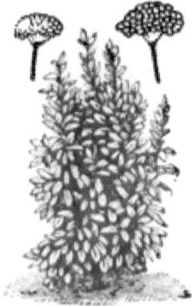

Origanum Majorana. German, *Majoran;* French, *Marjolaine;* Spanish, *Mejorana.*—The leaves and young shoots of this perennial sweet herb are highly esteemed by many people as a seasoning, and Mother's marjoram-flavored "veal pot-pie" will not easily fade out of my memory. The plant is cultivated as an annual, and of easy culture. Early in spring, sow seed in shallow drills, one foot apart, and keep free from weeds.

Sweet Marjoram.

MARTYNIA.

Martynia proboscidea. German, *Gemshörner;* French, *Martynia;* English, *Unicorn Plant.*—An annual of easiest culture;

Martynia.

plant large, strong-growing rather coarse, yet decidedly interesting. Flowers large and similar to catalpa in shape; fruit curved, and terminating in a long, hooked point. While young and tender it is frequently used for pickles. Sow seed where plant is to grow, giving each a space of 2 or 3 feet square. If seed is allowed to ripen on the plant, and to scatter upon the ground, plenty of plants may be expected to spring up the following season.

MELON—MUSK.

Cucumis Melo. German, *Melone;* French and Spanish, *Melon.*—Where climatic conditions in the northern states, and shipping and marketing facilities at the south are favorable to their culture, melons constitute a very important money crop of the farm garden. For the home garden they are almost indispensable everywhere. I believe there are few things, if any, that are a more general object of desire for the younger members of the family, or would be more painfully missed by them, than a good supply of fine melons; and I am sure no household that has once had its fill of the fruit, in all its freshness and lusciousness as it comes directly from the garden, will ever wish to forego the pleasures of the melon patch again, even for a single season.

SOIL AND CULTURE.—A rich, warm loam, more or less sandy, and plenty of good compost or fertilizers are required. New land —on the wide rotation system—is always preferable, in order to reduce the dangers from insect and disease attacks to a minimum, and nothing better could be found very easily than a young clover or old pasture lot. Plow deep, and otherwise prepare the ground well, then mark off rows from 4 to 6 feet apart each way, according to the strength of the soil, and vigor of variety to be planted. A shovelful or two of well-rotted compost is mixed with the soil at each intersection, and a large broad hill formed with the hoe.

Next drop a dozen or two of seeds scatteringly over the hill, and cover with half an inch of soil, pressing it firmly over the seed with the back of hoe. Only the three or four thriftiest plants are left in each hill; the rest must be pulled up at the first or second hoeing. Cultivate frequently with the horse wheel-hoe, and hoe afterwards, drawing fresh soil up to the plants. Guard against the attacks of the yellow-striped cucumber bug, the squash borer and other insects; and keep free from weeds. I usually pinch off the ends of leading shoots when they have grown several feet in length, for the purpose of forcing out the laterals, on which the fruit is always borne. In early September I also remove the later settings of fruit, which cannot be expected to come to maturity before frost. For shipping and marketing, melons must be picked when yet green, but fully matured, so that they will be in best condition for the table when they reach the consumer. In order to make the crop earlier, and at the same time protect the plants from bug attacks, they are frequently started on pieces of inverted sod, in hot-bed or cold-frame, in the same way as described for Lima beans. Care should be taken to make the transfer from frame to open ground on moist, cloudy days only; then cultivate same as directed for plants started in open ground.

Perfection.

VARIETIES.

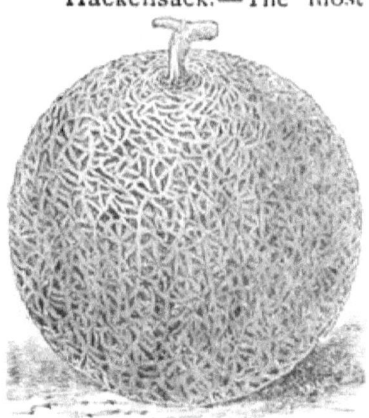

Superior.

Hackensack.—The most popular market sort among growers near New York City and in New Jersey. Large, round; depressed at the ends; deeply netted and productive.

Cassaba.—A large, long, green-fleshed melon of same excellent quality as Nutmeg. Can be recommended for market, as well as the home garden.

Nutmeg.—Green-fleshed, of delicious flavor. Size medium; round in shape; prolific; good for market and home use.

Early Christiania.—Very early, of fair size; productive, and valuable for early market.

Netted Gem.—Quite small, thick-meated, of fine flavor, and extremely early.

Perfection.—Nearly round, and of good size, frequently weighing 8 to 10 pounds. Of a dark green color outside, heavily netted, while inside they are of a rich orange color. Flesh very thick, there being scarcely room for the seed. Can be recommended alike for either home or market use.

Starn's Favorite.—This variety is nearly round, just a little oblong, thickly netted, with thick green flesh; rich and spicy and one of the best-flavored in cultivation. They are shy seeders; the cavity for seed in many of them is so small that if they were all seed inside the flesh, they could not contain many.

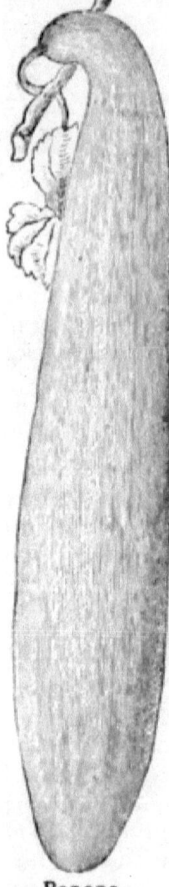

Banana.

Jenny Lind.—It is surprising that this, a most delicious small melon, is so little known outside of the State of New Jersey. There it is more largely grown than any other, and thousands upon thousands of baskets are annually shipped to the Philadelphia and New York markets. It is the earliest of all green-fleshed sorts.

Superior.—Ripens about the same time as the Jenny Lind, a strong and vigorous grower. So attractive in appearance that it is sure to command good prices.

Emerald Gem.—Plant and fruit small. The latter has a smooth, deep-green skin and salmon-colored flesh, unsurpassed for sweetness, richness, and lusciousness. Almost solid, containing but few seeds, and ripening thoroughly clear to the thin skin. When ripe it separates from the stem; but being of inconspicuous color, and inferior size, the "small boy" is apt to pass it by. This feature, combined with its unexcelled high quality and sweetness, renders it indispensable for the home garden. The markets also are just beginning to appreciate its fine qualities. It can be planted in hills only 3 or 4 feet apart each way, two or three plants to the hill.

Bay View.—A white-fleshed, oblong variety, with green, netted skin. Medium sized.

Montreal, Montreal Nutmeg.—A mammoth variety, much grown under glass at the northeast. I did not find it of much value for outdoor culture in New Jersey.

Osage.—A Western market sort; green fleshed, small, round, netted.

Banana.—Grows 18 inches and upward in length, and only 2 to 4 inches in thickness. Flesh thick, solid, reminding somewhat of bananas.

Hardy Ridge.

Algerian Canteloupe.—Flesh thick and juicy, sweet and having a delicate aroma. Fruit round, slightly elongated, with many roundish dark green warts or scabs, which change to an orange color when fruit is ripe.

Prescott, Hardy Ridge.—Thick fleshed, salmon colored; few seeds. This and the preceding are favorites with Paris (France) growers. Not grown to any extent in America, except as curiosity.

MELON—WATER.

Citrullus Vulgaris (*Cucumis Citrullus*). German, *Wassermelone;* French, *Melon d'eau;* Spanish, *Sandia.*—Culture of the water-melon is very similar to that of the musk varieties, except

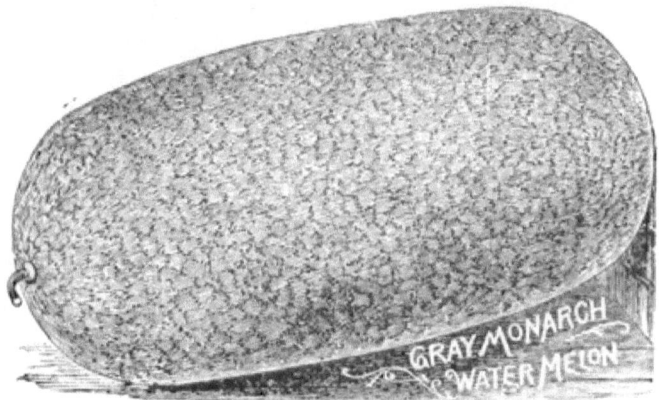

that the soil, if anything, should be warmer and richer, and the hills made from six to ten feet apart each way, according to vigor of variety and strength of soil.

The chief difficulty for the novice is to tell when the melons are fit for market or consumption, as they should not be picked too soon, nor left on the vines after the proper stage of maturity has been reached. The tendril or curl on the vine opposite the

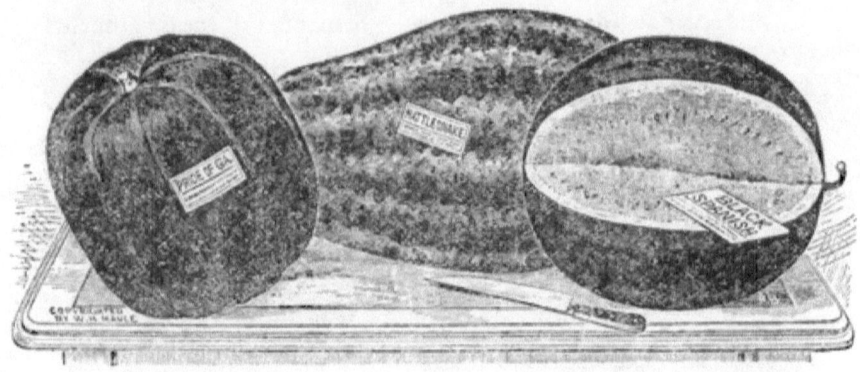

melon generally dries up and dies just about at the time when the melon ripens; but this is not always the case, and hence the sign is not infallible. A safer indication even than this is the turning of the whitish underside of the fruit (where it rests upon

the ground) to a sort of cream color. Experienced growers and dealers simply snap the melon with the middle finger, and tell the ripe from the immature melon by the difference of sound. The skin of the melon also becomes somewhat duller in color when

Cultural Directions.—257

approaching maturity, and somewhat firmer. The novice should compare ripe and green specimens, and try to note all these differences.

VARIETIES.

Vick's Early.

Mountain Sweet,
Mountain Sprout,
Black Spanish.—In these we have three old, but reliable sorts, still much grown for market. They are large, sweet and good.

Vick's Early.—A small, early, solid melon, valuable for the home garden.

Kolb's Gem.—Much grown for market on account of its earliness. Nearly round, flesh bright red.

Scaly Bark (Florida Favorite),
Seminole,
Georgia Rattlesnake,
Pride of Georgia,
Cuban Queen,
Gray Monarch,
Mammoth Ironclad.—All these are large melons, extensively grown at the south for northern market.

Colorado Preserving.

Hungarian.—Introduced a few years ago as a superior sort for the home garden. Medium size; skin dark green; flesh sweet, melting, brilliant red. Vine strong grower, productive.

Volga.—After two seasons' trial I am disposed to place this ahead even of the preceding as a reliable sort for the home gardener. Distinguished by the light color of its rind. A thrifty grower, enormously prolific, early, of medium size, and to my taste unsurpassed in quality. If I could plant but one variety in the home garden, this is the one I would unhesitatingly select.

Prize Jumbo.—This new melon is a cross between the Ironclad and Cuban Queen. In color dark-green, striped with lighter shades of the same color; flesh of a rich cardinal color,

Prize Jumbo.

free from strings. The rind, while unusually thin for so large a melon, is so tough it will bear transportation in first-class condition for very long distances.

Green and Gold.—Name comes from its rich green color outside, while the flesh is of a golden orange color, free from any tinge of white, even around the seeds. In productiveness it equals any of the red-flesh varieties; has a thin rind. It makes a desirable ornament for the table, if arranged in contrast with the red flesh of other varieties.

Christmas.—None surpasses this in vigor of vine. Fruit late, large, and of most remarkable keeping qualities. I had them last season in December, kept in a common cool room upstairs, and they were sound and palatable.

Colorado Preserving.—A productive sort for preserving and sauce. Flesh firm and solid; seeds few; vine thrifty.

MINT.

Mentha viridis. German, *Krauseminze;* French, *Menthe.*— A hardy perennial, often found in great masses along moist roadsides, near swamps and low places. Easily propagated by division of the creeping root-stock. In a small way it is forced under glass, for winter and spring market, and the growers find it very profitable. The leaves and young shoots are used for seasoning, mint sauce, and for flavoring liquors.

MUSHROOM.

Agaricus campestris. German, *Champignon;* French, *Champignon;* Spanish, *Seta.*—The very first and most important requirement for the successful production of mushrooms is a dark, damp place with an even temperature ranging from 50 to 70 degrees. This may be a common cellar, a cave, railroad or other tunnel, under the greenhouse benches, or in a building constructed or arranged for the purposes and heated with pipes. In proper situation mushrooms can be raised the year around, and it is done on a large scale in natural caves or abandoned tunnels in this and other countries. One of these mammoth mushroom factories is said to be in successful operation near Chicago, run by a stock company; and more chances equally good for starting an enterprise of this kind might be found in various parts of the country. It is reported to be a paying business.

Mushroom Spawn.

For culture in a common cellar or other place, on a limited scale, the best time for active operations is from the beginning of September until January. Take fresh horse droppings without long straw or litter, and mix it with one-third of its bulk of fresh loam, or finely cut-up sods from an old pasture, and put in a heap to heat. Turn frequently (perhaps once a day) until the first violent heat has nearly subsided. Then spread a layer of it, four feet wide and as long as desired, upon the place intended for the bed. This may be on the ground or on shelves. Beat the layer down firmly with a wooden mallet, or other convenient implement; spread another layer of the manure mixture upon the first, and beat down solidly once more, repeating this, if necessary, so the bed, when finished, will be about 8 or 10 inches in thickness.

Now insert a thermometer in the centre of the mass, and again allow the first violent heat to subside. When the temperature has been reduced to 85 or 90 degrees, the bed is ready for planting the spawn.

Break the bricks of spawn into pieces of the size of a small egg; then make holes 2 inches deep, and 10 or 12 inches apart each way, all over the bed, and drop a large piece, or two smaller ones, into each, afterwards filling the holes with the manure mixture, and again beat the beds down smoothly and evenly. Then cover the whole with two inches of fine loam firming it with the back of spade or shovel.

In a dark cellar and even temperature of from 55 to 60 degrees the mushrooms will appear in from 5 to 8 weeks. If the cellar is rather light, the bed had better be covered with 6 inches of hay or straw. In a reasonably damp cellar watering will not be necessary; but in a dry one warm water should occasionally be sprinkled over the bed with a fine rose sprinkler. A little nitrate of soda, or saltpetre, dissolved in the water will, I think, be found of great advantage in lengthening the bearing period of the bed. The spawn can be obtained of any large seed house.

A SUMMER MUSHROOM.—Recently a new species has been discovered and introduced, under the name *Agaricus subrufescens*. It seems to be of stronger growth and vitality than the ordinary fall meadow mushroom, flourishing in hot weather and moister soil and atmospheric conditions. The mycelium (root growth) will endure a soaking which would surely be death to that of *A. campestris*. I find this new mushroom of easy culture, of excellent quality, and so quick in growth when conditions are favorable, that the tiny maggot which during the hot season invariably ruins the ordinary slower-growing kinds, is not given an opportunity to do much harm to this if promptly gathered.

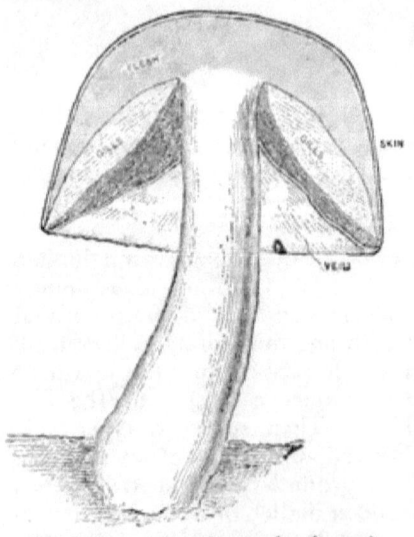

Mushroom (*Agaricus subrufescens*).

The illustration shows an average good specimen. The gills while under the veil are white, gradually turning to pinkish, then to light brown, and when old, finally to a blackish-brown. The top of the cap is sometimes clear white, more usually slightly colored a light pinkish or reddish brown.

The simplest way to grow it, especially for the amateur, is in hot-bed. Prepare fresh horse droppings, from well-fed horses, in same manner as directed for making ordinary mushroom beds. The proper time to do this is in spring, so that the hot-bed can be made up not later than in May. What we want is to have a solid layer of the mixture of horse droppings and loam, that will promptly come to a heat and retain a moderate degree of warmth for the longest practicable period. This layer may be made twelve to fifteen inches deep. Be sure to pack it down very firmly. Then when the temperature is right, say 90° Fahrenheit, insert the spawn and proceed in about the same way as required for the ordinary mushroom. A thin layer of sphagnum moss, marsh hay, leaves, or similar litter may be placed upon the loam covering of the bed, and then the sashes may be put on. The glass should be heavily shaded by means of a good coat of lime whitewash, and the sashes partially raised, especially during the hot weather later on, to provide some ventilation. If the work was done right, the mushrooms will appear in from four to five weeks, and should be gathered every day. Water may be applied quite freely during hot, dry weather.

MUSTARD. (White Mustard.)

Sinapis Alba. German, *Gelber Senf;* French, *Moutarde blanche;* Spanish, *Mostaza blanca.*—Annual of rapid growth and easiest culture. The leaves while young are used for salads and for garnishing, and are of pleasant pungency. Sow seed in drills one foot apart, and keep free from weeds. The ripe seed is variously used in the preparation of pickles, and when ground makes the chief ingredient in the well-known condiment on sale in groceries under the name "Mustard." The "curled mustard" seed, a sample of which years ago I received from a friend in the South for trial, has recently been introduced as "California peppergrass" or "Japanese mustard." It is thought to be of Chinese origin. This is one of the best plants for early spring "greens," as it grows very quickly, and makes a large, compact plant, and crisp and beautifully curled leaves, of pleasant pungent flavor.

Mustard.

NASTURTIUM. (Indian Cress) Dwarf.

Tropæolum Minus. German, *Kapuziner Kresse;* French, *Capucine petite;* Spanish, *Capuchina pequena.*—Annual of easy culture, and like the climbing form (*T. Majus*) more frequently found in the flower garden and border than in the kitchen garden. The flowers of both forms are sometimes used for garnishing, and the young seed pods, pickled in vinegar, for seasoning. Sow seed in border, or in rows one foot apart, thinning to 4 or 6 inches apart in the rows.

OKRA.

Hibiscus esculentus. French, *Gombaud;* Spanish, *Gombo* (*Quimbombo*).—The plant succeeds in almost any soil, being an annual of easy culture. Little grown in the north, but quite popular in the southern states, where the young and tender seed vessels are used as a table vegetable, in the form of soups and stews, to quite an extent. These pods are apt to grow somewhat tough at the North. Sow seed in rows 2½ to 3½ feet apart, and thin to 9 or 12 inches apart in the row. Cultivate same as corn.

Nasturtium.

Okra.

VARIETIES.

Dwarf Green, Improved Dwarf Green.—An early and productive sort of low growth.

Long Green.—Plant dwarf; pods long and ridged.

White Velvet.—Introduced as having very large, round smooth pods. Very productive.

ONION.

Allium Cepa. German, *Zwiebel;* French *Oignon;* Spanish, *Cipolla.*—Onion growing presents itself to our consideration in three materially-differing aspects, namely, culture in the market garden, culture in the farm garden, and culture in the kitchen garden. This vegetable, as a crop, is of value to the market gardener chiefly in the rôle of "bunch onions," *i. e.,* grown from sets, pulled and bunched in the green state when only partly developed, and thus put on the market. The sets, like mature onions for market, are chiefly grown by people who make it a specialty, and in farm gardens more remote from the larger market centers. Some of our market gardeners, however—probably induced by the high price which they are often compelled to pay for sets—, now grow not only enough to supply their own needs, but a surplus for market besides.

GROWING SETS.—The selection of soil is of greatest importance. It should be of a sandy nature, or even clear sand, free from weed seeds, rubbish and coarse gravel, and at least moderately fertile. A good top-dressing of some good fertilizer may be sufficient. Weedy manure must be scrupulously avoided. Such land needs thorough preparation. After plowing, the harrow and roller should not be spared, and the Meeker small disk harrow, or a steel rake, is needed to put on the finish. What we want is a perfect, smooth, mellow seed-bed. The seed is sown thickly in rows, either by hand or with the drill. The rows may either be made 9 to 12 inches apart, and sown in the usual way, only more thickly, or from 15 to 20 inches apart, and sown scatteringly in a strip 2 or 3 inches in width. I prefer the drills 12 inches apart, and to sow in a strip of about $1\frac{1}{2}$ inches in width, which allows of the convenient use of the wheel-hoe.

SOWING.—The easiest method of sowing onion seed for sets is with one of the common garden drills, and in doing so, I usually let the seed run moderately free, and go twice or even three times over the same row, thus sowing the required quantity, and at the same time spreading it over the desired width in each row. To give a full crop, the plants have to stand pretty thick. It is always an advantage to roll the ground after sowing.

For sowing by hand, the rows should be marked out with a marker having wide blunt teeth, in order to make wide marks, and allow the seed to be scattered over a wider space across the rows. The covering is done with both hands, the gardener moving along over the rows on his knees, and drawing the soil over the row from both sides, or with the feet in the way quite commonly practiced for covering the larger seeds.

The amount of seed needed ranges between 40 and 60 pounds per acre, according to distance between the rows, and width of sowing. The aim is to grow bulbs of less than $\frac{1}{2}$ inch in diameter, and the largest bulk without undue crowding. The varieties used for this purpose are Extra Early Red, Yellow Dutch, and Silver Skin.

CULTIVATION AND HARVESTING.—Cultivation is given in the usual way, with wheel-hoe; and weeds are pulled up by hand without thinning the crop.

When the tops begin to die down, in August, the bulbs are harvested, either by lifting out with the onion set attachment of the Planet Jr. wheel-hoe, or by raking in windrows, 5 or 6 rows together, care being taken, of course, to get the teeth well *under* the bulbs. They are left on the ground for 2 or 3 days to cure, and then taken under shelter, and spread out on a dry floor to be cleaned at leisure. This is done by rubbing the sets between the hands, to remove remnants of tops and roots, and adhering soil or sand, and by running through fanning mill afterwards. All bulbs that will not readily pass through a grain sieve with ¾-inch meshes are too large for sets and should be sold or used for pickling onions.

Another method of harvesting consists of running a large garden trowel lengthwise under the row, lifting up the bulbs, with soil adhering to them, and throwing into a small-meshed sieve to sift out the sand and soil.

STORING.—In storing for winter the bulbs (sometimes mixed with chaff) are piled up 4 or 5 inches deep in a dry loft, there allowed to freeze, and covered with a foot or so of straw or hay until spring. Or they may be stored in shallow open crates, and protected from alternate freezing and thawing.

GROWING BUNCH ONIONS—The ground should be put in best possible condition. Use 50 or more tons of good compost per acre, besides top-dressings of poultry manure, wood ashes, fertilizers, etc., not to forget of nitrate of soda. The same thorough preparation is required as for growing sets. Then mark out the ground in rows 9 to 12 inches apart, and plant the sets 2 or 3 inches apart in the rows. This is best done by picking up the set between thumb and forefinger, top up, and press firmly down into the soil. Thus they can be planted quite rapidly. Then cover still more soil over them with the feet, firming at the same time, and roll. Afterwards keep the ground loose and free from weeds by the frequent use of wheel and hand hoes, and at earliest date commence to bunch and market. While small, a dozen bulbs may be required for a bunch; later on 6 or 7 will be sufficient.

There is still another method of growing early bunch onions, and when successful, is more convenient, and often more profitable than the one described, as it requires less labor and expense, and gives an earlier crop. Seed is sown during August or September (perhaps later at the South), in drills one foot apart, and at the rate of 6 or 8 lbs. of good seed per acre. At the north this method is risky, and the whole crop may winter-kill; but even in an exposed situtation in Western New York, I have occasionally succeeded in carrying the crop through without any effort at protection, and without loss. Covering with evergreen boughs, or coarse litter may be a wise precaution. In the middle and southern states there is nothing, to my knowledge, that could hinder growing bunch onions on this plan with complete success.

GROWING THE BULB FOR MARKET.—This, as a business, sometimes pays, and sometimes it does not. The financial outcome depends on management, and on the season's prices. Onion growing in the farm garden can easily be overdone. Only last year thousands of barrels of as fine onions as were ever grown had to be left to spoil, or were fed to stock, for want of buyers at even 25 or 30 cents per barrel.

An *average* onion crop is not likely to ever yield big returns, but a *large* one (the result of plenty of manure and high culture generally) with a fair market price, always pays the grower reasonably well. The premium in this, as in all other undertakings, is invariably awarded to skillful management.

SOIL.—A good crop can be produced on soil of almost any composition (sand, sandy loam, clay loam, clay, muck), provided it contains a fair amount of decaying organic matter; but it should be free from weed seeds. Use the richest soil you have; thin soil if no other can be had; and sandy loam in preference to others. Muck lands sometimes produce enormous crops, but the bulbs are not as firm as those grown upland. Land in fine tilth, perhaps having been cropped with carrots, beets, cabbages, or other vegetable crops, is usually given the preference, and justly so; but a young, rich, clean clover sod, thoroughly worked, is seldom less profitable, and often more so, than old ground.

Manure and prepare the land as thoroughly as described for the production of bunch onions, being particularly careful to avoid manure which contains live weed seeds, for the greatest expense connected with onion growing is the destruction of weeds.

SOWING SEED.—The torrid heat and prolonged drought of August should find the crop ready for harvesting. Consequently it is absolutely necessary for best success to sow as early in spring as the ground can be got in working order, perhaps by the help of fall plowing and laying off in beds. In the middle and southern states fall sowing may be practicable, and should at least be tested in every locality there. Here we usually sow in April, seldom in March.

When the Meeker disk-harrow (or the steel-rake) has left the ground perfectly smooth and fine, good, plump, water-cleaned seed, that stands at least 75 per cent. germination test, is sown with the garden drill in rows 12 inches apart, at the rate of four or five pounds per acre. Most growers sow further apart, 16, 18, or even 20 inches; but I consider this a useless waste of space and opportunity, since the yield per row will be the same, whether the rows are 12 or 20 inches apart, and the narrower planting, with no greater outlay for manure and tillage (weeding excepted), increases the crop in exact proportion to the increased number of rows. The style of wheel-hoe to be used perhaps influences the question of width of row somewhat. A Ruhlman, going *between* the rows, works to best advantage when the rows are 14 or 16 inches apart; while the Planet Jr. (and any other row-straddler) can be profitably run among rows that are only 12 inches apart. The roller in the rear of the distributing tube and hopper, in our modern seed drills, firms the soil sufficiently to insure prompt germination of seed under common circumstances.

CULTIVATION.—Usually the young plants will begin to appear above ground inside of two weeks, and now an energetic and unceasing fight against weeds begins, which lasts all through the larger part of the growing season. Use the wheel-hoe early and often, and never attempt to do without one of these tools in the onion patch, as this would almost exclude any possibility of making it pay. The weeding has to be done on hands and knees, early and often enough to suppress all weed growth. One of the hand-weeders, a common table knife with blade sharpened on both sides and bent in a curve, or a common iron spoon, can be used to advantage in scraping away the soil from the growing plants, and with it all weeds just starting in the row. Never draw the soil up to the

onions, as they grow best on top of the ground. A second top-dressing of fertilizer, or of wood-ashes, at the time when the bulbs have made about half their growth, often has the happiest effects. Still I consider repeated applications of nitrate of soda, say at the rate of 100 pounds per acre each time, of more consequence than any other top-dressing I know of. Early attention should be directed to the proper thinning. At the second

Prizetaker.

weeding the plants must be left to stand not less than 2 inches apart in the rows. Remove the weaker—always leave the strongest plants. In subsequent weedings a narrow-bladed hoe may be used, thus allowing the work to be done in a standing position.

I cannot lay too much stress on the great importance of timely action in every stage of the proceeding. A few days' neglect in cultivating or weeding may increase the amount of labor required to such an extent as to double the cost of crop, at the same time greatly reducing the yield.

HARVESTING.—When the bulbs have reached their full size and maturity, as indicated by the dying down of the tops, the crop is ready to be harvested. Pull the onions by hand, or rake them out by means of a dull steel rake; taking great care to avoid cutting into them; then leave in windrows on the ground to cure. Afterwards twist or cut off the remnants of tops and roots, if there be such, and try to sell the crop immediately from the field. If this cannot be done, store in a rather thin layer on a dry floor or loft, until they can be disposed of. I would not advise the novice to attempt wintering even a part of the crop, as this is a task which involves risk even for the more experienced.

Wethersfield.

ONIONS IN THE KITCHEN GARDEN.—For home use we want variety at all times, consequently we should plant a few sets to give us an early supply of bunch onions. This we do in the way already described for market growing, setting them in a row or two among our regular patch of closely-planted vegetables. We also desire onions for late use, and so we must also sow seed of various varieties, a row or so of each. Here the general rules given for culture in the farm garden should be closely followed. The thinning can be done gradually, and the young plants thus pulled out of the rows will supply the kitchen with onion material and onion flavor during the larger part of summer, and until the bulbs mature. For convenience and uniformity's sake we allow the same space between rows as adopted for all the other small stuff, 15 inches being the usual and most convenient distance between the teeth of the hand marker designed for use in the home garden. Seed is usually sown by hand, but if a garden drill is handy, and seed is to be sown in larger quantities than single small packages, by all means use the drill.

Yellow Dutch.

THE NEW ONION CULTURE.—No recent innovation in horticultural practices has created such a stir among American gardeners as has been caused by the new method which I introduced under the name of "the new onion culture" in 1890-91. The idea of transplanting onions is not new; but it had never been systematically applied to practice in growing dry onions in America. The new method is of especial value in growing the large varieties of foreign origin, chief among them the Yellow Spanish or Prizetaker. Indeed it is so superior to the older method of growing the crop directly from seed, that I and many other growers now practice the former to the almost entire exclusion of the other, resorting to the latter only in the production of sets and pickling onions.

Extra Early Red.

By far the best variety for the "new onion culture," and almost the only one which I grow, is the Prizetaker, already mentioned. Seed is sown under glass, preferably in flats in the greenhouse, during February (perhaps earlier, even in the fall in more southern locations). An early hotbed will do here; a cold frame perhaps further south. Broadcast sowing gives the largest number of plants to a given space. By sowing $\frac{1}{16}$ to $\frac{1}{8}$ of an ounce of seed evenly over one square foot of space, we go about to the limit of allowable crowding. The tops will need to be sheared off once or oftener, to make the plants short and stocky. The transplanting should be done just as soon as the land can be gotten in best working order in spring. Earliness and promptness in this work largely determine the measure of success.

Make the land very rich. Have the surface very smooth. Then draw light straight marks one foot apart, and with the help of a dibber, or with the finger set the plants two to three inches apart in the rows. The professional gardener, used to such work, will do this quite rapidly, and perhaps be able to set 5000 and more plants in a day.

It should hardly be necessary to say much about the necessity of keeping the ground well cultivated and scrupulously clean from weeds. The Planet Jr. double wheel hoe, and a narrow-bladed hand hoe, are just the tools that will render material assistance in this task, and if they are used promptly, the weeds will have very little chance to become troublesome. One great advantage of the new method, indeed, is the small amount of hand labor required in caring for the crop after transplanting.

Thinning is entirely avoided, and the weeds are easily taken out from among the large plants standing at regular distances. I can grow an acre of Prizetakers by the new method with a saving of 20 or 25 per cent. of labor compared with the old way. But there are other, and no less important advantages of the former, among them:

(1). Earlier ripening of the crop. With six weeks to start in sowing, the crop will come to maturity several weeks earlier than it would otherwise. This gives a chance for marketing the bulbs much in advance of competitors who adhere to the old onion culture, as also in clearing the ground for succeeding crops, such as celery, turnips, fall spinach, etc.

White Globe.

(2). A decided improvement of the bulbs in respect to shape and uniformity. The bulbs standing at regular distances and having room enough for perfect development, grow to a much larger size, and as perfect as it is possible for onions to grow.

(3). A greatly increased yield, to the extent of even doubling or trebling that obtained by the ordinary method. A yield of 2000 bushels to the acre is within easy reach under the best conditions, and the crop can always be expected to exceed 1000 bushels to the acre where the conditions are only fairly favorable.

(4). Quicker sale and better prices, in consequence of marketing at a more favorable season, and of the finer appearance of the bulbs. I often get all my Prizetakers into the market when they bring a dollar and upwards per bushel, while the ordinary crops, later on, bring 50 cents or less.

(5). The elimination of almost all uncertainties from the business. Even failure, by blight or drouth, would often mean what average growers would call a "big crop." Nothing short of hail and flood could prevent a good profit in this new onion culture if managed with ordinary intelligence.

Readers who are especially interested in this new and profitable way of growing onions for market, will find all the minutest details explained in my "The New Onion Culture."

VARIETIES.

Our list of standard market sorts is not so very large, and often we have but little choice in this respect. On the other hand the strains and selections of the different kinds are numerous, and greatly differing in merit. Of the Danvers Yellow, for instance, we have strains of almost perfect globe shape, others more or less approaching it, and from this every grade to the flat shape of the Yellow Dutch. Some strains are so improved, by careful selection, that the scallion is a rare occurrence among them, while others

Rocca.

Top Sets.

Silver Skin.

give a large proportion of thick-necked bulbs. Our first concern, therefore, is not only to get *fresh* seed, but also the best strain of the best varieties. Repeated trials of the seeds offered under guarantee by leading seedsmen will give you the desired information about their worth.

Wethersfield, Wethersfield Red. — The leading red market variety, large, coarse, reliable and exceedingly prolific. Skin deep purplish-red; flesh white; flavor strong. Unsurpassed as a keeper.

Danvers Yellow, Yellow Globe Danvers.—Undoubtedly the most reliable market variety, and one of the most prolific. Early, good-sized, as round as a ball, and smooth as an apple, neck very small, flesh fine-grained. Cannot be praised too highly.

White Globe, Southport White Globe.—The most popular white market sort. Beautiful silvery-white in color, and of perfect globe shape. Large, prolific, reliable. Should be cured in the shade, otherwise it is apt to become discolored. Keeps well.

Red Globe, Southport Red Globe,
Yellow Globe, Southport Yellow Globe.—These resemble the White Globe in every way except color.

Yellow Dutch, Yellow Strassburg.—Prolific and of fine flavor. Shape rather flat. Largely grown for market, and almost exclusively for yellow sets.

Extra Early Red.—Desirable for early market. Hardy, reliable, growing quickly to fair size. A good keeper, and especially valuable for red sets.

Silver Skin, White Portugal, Philadelphia White.—Largely grown for pickling and for white sets. Of mild pleasant flavor, and decidedly handsome appearance.

Maule's Prizetaker.—This I consider the finest of all onions with which I am acquainted. I have grown almost every variety listed by seedsmen; but have never found one as large in size nor as handsome in shape and general appearance. This variety looks for all the world like the imported Spanish onion, which is sold in our fruit stores at five cents or more per pound.

White Barletta.—The earliest and smallest onion; excellent for pickles.

New Queen.—Another small, handsome early pickling onion, good keeper. White.

Silver King, Mammoth Silver King.—Introduced as the largest of all onions. Skin silvery-white, flesh remarkably sweet and tender.

Giant Rocca of Naples,
Giant Pompeii,
Mammoth Red Tripoli,
Giant White Tripoli, etc., etc.—All these are Italian varieties of quick growth, large size, remarkably mild flavor, but not long keepers.

Potato Onions.—These produce no seed, and are always grown from the bulbs, which when planted, increase in size, and also produce a cluster of bulbs around the one planted. I have had excellent success with it in New Jersey, and seen it do well in southern Pennsylvania and sections south of these localities. Profitable for market, and entirely reliable.

Egyptian Perennial Tree Onion.—This is probably grown more for its tops, to be used during winter for soups, etc., than for its bulbs. It is entirely hardy, and after once planted, can be had from the garden almost the entire year. I do not value it very highly.

PARSLEY.

Apium Petroselinum. German, *Petersilie;* French, *Persil;* Spanish, *Peryil.* Grown to a limited extent in market and home gardens. The leaves are used for seasoning soups, and for garnishing. Market gardeners sow for early supply in cold frame, or between rows of other vegetables. Seed is slow to germinate, and an early crop like radishes or lettuce can be taken off in time to give to the parsley the needed room. When large enough, the tops are repeatedly cut, and tied in little bunches for market, each containing about as much as can be encircled by thumb and forefinger. For later use, seed may be sown in open ground, in drills 12 inches apart. A little patch will go a great ways towards overstocking the market, and half a dozen plants, well fed, will be sufficient for a family garden. For winter use the leaves may be dried; or a few plants taken up and trenched in like celery. Or you may have a few plants growing in a box or keg in the kitchen or cellar, or under the greenhouse bench. To grow it in the latter way, the plants should be started from seed in the fall.

Double Curled.

VARIETIES.

Plain or Common.—Somewhat hardier than the curled sorts, and good enough for seasoning.

Double Curled, Extra Double Curled.—A beautiful variety with thick, curled foliage, and suitable both for flavoring and garnishing.

Fern-Leaved.—Foliage most beautifully serrated, excellent for garnishing.

PARSNIPS.

Pastinaca Sativa. German, *Pastinake;* French, *Panais;* Spanish, *Chirivia.*—Parsnip culture is very similar to that of the carrot, and the vegetable has about the same value as a garden and farm crop, and for stock feeding. Sow in April or May in rows 12 to 18 inches apart, being careful to use *new* seed only; and thin the young plants to 3 or 4 inches apart. The plants start slowly and feebly at first, somewhat like Parsley, but soon get strong and able to take care of themselves. Soil should be clean and moderately rich. Parsnips are perfectly hardy, and their flavor is improved by

Early Short Round.

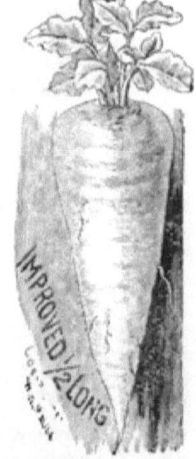

frost. That part of the crop which is wanted for use or market during the winter, should be dug before the ground freezes solid, and stored in root cellar. The balance is left in the ground, and will carry through the winter without loss. For stock in early spring it is very superior—equal to carrots—and the easy way of wintering gives to parsnips a great advantage over all other root crops.

VARIETIES.

Long Smooth.—The old standard variety, with very long roots. Large and reliable.

Hollow Crown, Student, Improved Half Long.—Roots handsome, and very clean-skinned; crown despressed or hollow. A superior half-long table variety.

Round, Early Short Round.—Very early; roots short and chunky, somewhat like a turnip in shape. Decidedly the best for very shallow soils.

PEANUT.

Long Smooth.

Arachia hypogœa. German, *Erdnuss;* French, *Arachide*, Spanish, *Chufa.*—The peanut is an important farm crop for Virginia and other southern states; and while interesting everywhere, it is very unreliable north of Philadelphia, as it requires a long season to bring it to maturity. In the northern home garden it will especially interest the young people, and the newly introduced "Spanish" or "Improved" nut should be tried just on this account where the common Virginia peanut cannot be expected to ripen. Select warm soil, if possible of a calcareous nature; mark out rows 3 feet apart, and drop the nuts about a foot apart in the

Improved "Ground Pea" or Peanut.

rows, one in a place, and cover with 2 inches of soil. It is not necessary to remove the hulls or shucks before planting. Cultivate and hoe freely, leaving but one plant in a place; and keep the soil well mellowed up around the plants when seeds (nuts) are forming. It is quite interesting to observe the flowers as they insert their ovaries into the mellow soil, where they complete their growth and form nuts. Before freezing weather the plants are dug, or pulled up. Hang under a shed to cure; then gather, clean and sort the nuts.

VARIETIES.

Common Virginia.—The common market sort of the south, and found in every fruit store in America. Prolific, nuts large and well scattered.

Spanish Improved.—Several weeks earlier than the preceding. Nuts all growing in a compact cluster near the main stalk, and can be harvested by simply pulling up by hand. Pods small but well filled. Worthy of trial at the north.

PEAS.

Pisum Sativum. German, *Erbse;* French, *Pois:* Spanish, *Guisante.*—In green peas we have an important crop for both the garden and the farm. The profits may not be so very large, but the product is always salable, and brings early money. Nor is it necessary that the soil be so very rich or heavily manured. I found no garden crop that I can grow with greater ease and certainty merely by a moderate application of some good complete fertilizer—say 500 or 600 pounds per acre. Peas seem to be partial to potash, and this in some form alone, or together with phosphate (in ashes) frequently give as good results as complete manure. Peas do best in the fore-part of the season, and should be planted early, as those planted late for "succession" hardly ever turn out very satisfactory. Sow in drills, 2 to 3 inches deep, and 2½ to 3½ feet apart, according to vigor of variety and strength of soil. When grown for market the first aim should be to get the crop ready for sale at the earliest possible date.

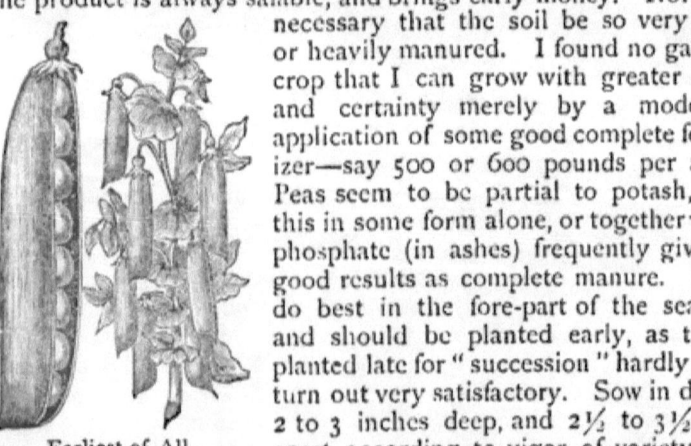
Earliest of All.

For the home garden I prefer to sow the best sorts—early, medium, late and latest—as early as I consider it safe, and often all at one time. This gives me a succession for 3 weeks or more,

Cultural Directions.—275

which is fully sufficient for my purposes. I also look with disfavor upon the practice of brushing; hence plant chiefly the more dwarf sorts which do not require support.

The sowing is usually done by hand in drills opened to the proper depth, and seed scattered pretty freely to insure a full stand.

VARIETIES.

Garden peas are classed in three great sections; namely, (1) the round or smooth peas; (2) the wrinkled peas; and (3) the edible-podded or sugar peas. The round or smooth sorts are hardier than the others and can therefore, be planted earlier. Although all peas are usually classed as perfectly hardy, it is nevertheless a fact that a large percentage of the seed annually planted rots in the ground, merely because the ground at the time of planting is not warm enough for germination.

The majority of farmers plant only the common smooth kinds, chiefly Black-Eyed Marrowfat, both for home use, and for market; and neither they, nor their village customers are aware of the real goodness, sweetness and tenderness of some of our newer wrinkled peas. I

confess I have no appetite for the Black-Eyed Marrowfats, and others of that class, and do not want it on my table, so long as I can just as well have wrinkled sorts, that are as much superior to them as cream is to skim-milk. Besides this the wrinkled sorts have larger and better-filled pods, and peas of very much larger size, while the plants perhaps are only 12 or 18 inches high. Our children, for instance, would pick three baskets of Stratagem, or Yorkshire Hero, etc., as quickly and easily as they could fill one of the Black-Eyed Marrowfats.

Earliest of All,

Maule's Improved Extra Early.—These two sorts are the only ones of the very early smooth kind, with which I have been entirely pleased. Pods are good-sized and well-filled, and the peas of very good quality. A few days earlier than Little Gem, and decidedly prolific. Good for both market and home use.

Alaska,

Daniel O'Rourke,

Philadelphia Extra Early,

First and Best.—In these we have other and very popular market

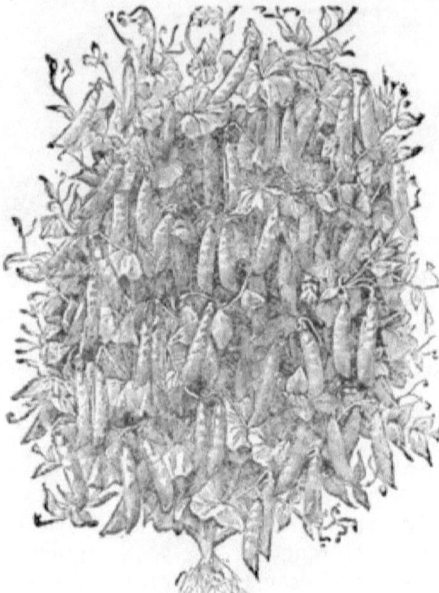

Bliss' Everbearing.

varieties of the first early smooth class. All of this kind are somewhat similar in general characteristics, and grow from 1½ to 2 feet high.

Black-Eyed Marrowfat.— Very popular with farmers for general use, and as a field variety. Good bearer; pods large and well-filled. A late, smooth variety.

Blue Peter, McLean's Blue Peter,

Blue Imperial, Dwarf Blue Imperial,

Blue Beauty.—These blue-seeded smooth varieties bear numerous and well-filled pods;

American Wonder.

and the peas are large and handsome, but not equal in flavor to the wrinkled kinds.

Little Gem, McLean's Little Gem.—A leading and reliable first-early wrinkled sort, with well-filled pods, and of fine quality.

Premium Gem.—Resembles the preceding, and is said to be an improvement on it.

American Wonder.—A very dwarf, very early wrinkled pea, of unsurpassed quality. Grows seldom more than 6 to 8 inches high; and should be planted only on very rich soil, where highest culture is given.

Abundance, Bliss' Abundance.—Half-dwarf, branching, exceedingly prolific. Pods large, well-filled, I might say overcrowded. Wrinkled and of fair quality. Late.

Bliss' Everbearing.—Similar in outward appearance to the preceding, but of vastly better quality. In this respect really one of the very best of all peas. Late.

Stratagem.—One of the finest peas in existence. Plant dwarfish, branching. Pods of very largest size, and crowded with peas which are of largest size and remarkably rich and sweet. Late.

Prince of Wales,
Yorkshire Hero,
Telephone.—These beautiful wrinkled sorts should be tested in every garden; pods and seeds large and the latter sweet and rich. Late.

Champion of England.—The old popular late wrinkled sort. Plant 4 or 5 feet high. Pods and peas of fair size and numerous. Peas of choicest quality.

New Perpetual.—A real summer pea, worthy its name. A strong grower, branching, and seemingly inexhaustible in productiveness. Late, and continues to produce its large and well-filled pods until fall. Peas very large and of fine quality, tender, rich and sweet.

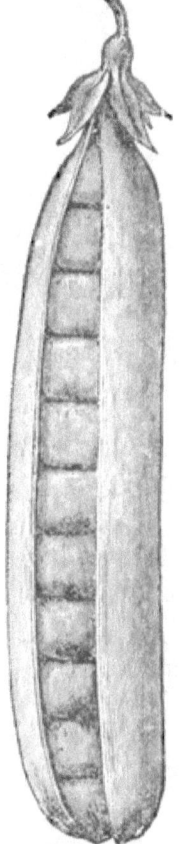

Stratagem.

Dwarf Sugar.—A low growing sort, bearing edible pods. None of this class are used to a very large extent in this country.

PEPPER (Chili Pepper.)

Capsicum Annuum.—German, *Piment Pfeffer;* French, *Piment;* Spanish, *Pimento.*—Easily grown in almost any rich soil, and almost any location of the United States. Plants should be started early in hot-bed or green-house, and treated similarly as tomato or egg-plants; but they do not require near as long a season as either of them to produce a crop. I usually sow seeds in boxes or flats, often rather crowded, and in early June transplant from there directly to open ground, 2 or 2½ feet apart, and plants 15 inches apart in the rows. Soil of a warm, sandy character is given the preference. I stimulate the plants to thrifty growth with liberal dressings of hen manure, and perhaps wood ashes, and thus have rows that for thrift and amount of fruit are beautiful to behold. I usually sell some of the peppers; a very few are utilized in the household, in preparing pickles and chowders, etc., and the rest are chopped up and mixed with other stuff to be prepared as a warm breakfast for the hens during fall and early winter.

Ruby King.

VARIETIES.

Ruby King.—Too much cannot be said in its praise both as a market and family variety. Fruit very large, brilliant red, well-shaped, always smooth, and of mild flavor. Prolific.

Large Bell, Bullnose, Sweet Mountain.—These are the principal older market sorts; early, bright red, mild, thick-fleshed and prolific.

Golden Dawn.—Resembles Bullnose, except in color, which is a beautiful yellow. Sweet and productive.

Red Cluster.

Golden Upright.—Fruit large, golden yellow, smooth, thick-fleshed, mild and always upright. Plants and foliage of remarkable thrift.

Golden Queen.—Resembles Ruby King, except in color which is a fine yellow.

Procopp's Giant.—Largest of all, being two or three times as long as widest diameter; pointed. Will need a few years more of careful selection for seed to make it more uniform and smooth, when it may become one of the grandest sorts in existence.

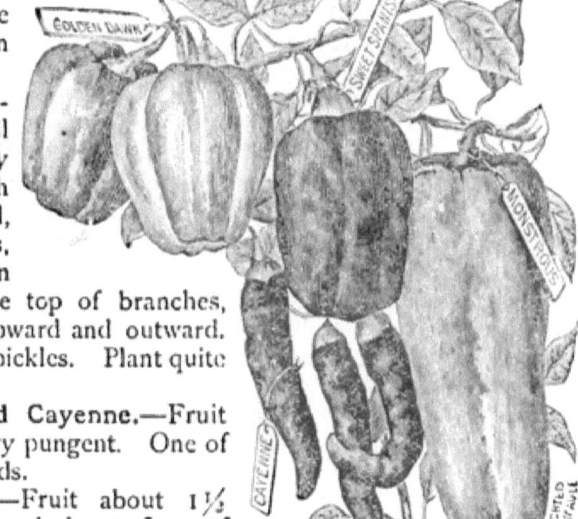

Red Cluster.—A small plant, perfectly covered with coral-red, small, thin peppers, all growing in bunches on the top of branches, and pointing upward and outward. Useful for hot pickles. Plant quite ornamental.

Long Red Cayenne.—Fruit small, long, very pungent. One of the old standards.

Celestial.—Fruit about 1½ inches long, conical, at first of beautiful waxy yellow, then changing to purplish scarlet. Plant a free grower and thrifty bearer, and at any stage of development, after fruit has begun to set, a most attractive thing, worthy to be cultivated as a pot plant in greenhouse or conservatory.

PENNYROYAL.

Mentha Pulegium. German, *Krausemünze;* French, *Menthe Pouliot.*—Perennial of the mint family, easily propagated by division of the creeping root-stock, often found growing wild in moist, clayey soils. Leaves have an agreeable odor, and are used for seasoning and for medical purposes.

PEPPERMINT.

Mentha Piperita. German, *Pfeffermünze;* French, *Menthe poirrée.*—Grows wild along the margins of swamps and streams, and other wet places. In a few localities it is largely cultivated and utilized in the manufacture of peppermint oil and essence. Propagated by division of root-stock or stem, and is easily grown. Plant pieces of root in rows 2 feet by 1, and give it a fair chance to grow, when it will soon take care of itself even on upland.

POTATOES (WHITE.)

Solanum Tuberosum. German, *Kartoffel;* French, *Pomme-de-terre;* Spanish, *Batatas.*—The invention of potato planters and diggers, and the adoption of simplified culture generally, with consequent greatly increased production and greatly diminished average prices, have rendered potato growing for fall and winter *market on a small scale* much less profitable than it was a few years ago, and are more and more taking the business out of the hands of the small grower, and concentrating it in the hands of a few who plant large areas. The extensive grower has immense advantages in the opportunities afforded him to make use of all the modern improved implements; and the small-scale operator can hope to stand up against this ruinous machine competition only by adopting a highly intensive system of cultivation. It is an unfortunate development, but seems to be the natural outgrowth of all our present industrial conditions, and in entire conformity with those in other branches of business. Potatoes may yet be grown on a similar plan as wheat growing is now carried on at the west by the Dalrymples; but while the yields on the large-scale plan may be a little above 100, and certainly less than 150 bushels per acre, the small grower, by careful selection of soil, varieties, manures, etc., should aim to bring his crop up to double the yields named, which together with the far smaller cost of getting the crop to market, must more than offset all large-scale advantages.

The production of late potatoes for market is a farm (not a garden) operation, but the cultivation of early varieties often fits nicely into market-garden rotation, and, of course, belongs to the family garden also.

SOIL AND MANURE.—Under proper treatment, the crop can be grown on soil of almost any composition, provided it has a good natural or artificial drainage. Sandy loam, however, is always considered best—best for the yield and best for quality of tuber. All soils for potatoes, however, should be generously provided with humus (decayed vegetable matter), the more the better; hence a young clover sod is always given the preference.

Where the humus supply in the soil is scant, nothing better in the way of manure could be applied than thoroughly-rotted compost. Raw stable manure is to be avoided unless it can be applied a year in advance, or on a preceding crop. As a general thing, it is much safer to depend on soil in good fertility rather than on manure applications; but on soils containing a sufficiency of vegetable matter I would use a good high-grade complete fertilizer, such as now made by most large fertilizer concerns especially for potatoes and other vegetables (a "special potato manure ") in preference to even the best of stable manure. It is pure nonsense and poor economy, however, to waste large quantities of such fertilizer on utterly run-down land, in the expectation of growing very large crops right away. I have often found out that this will not work. Accumulated fertility in the soil appears to be indispensable for a full measure of success. At the same time, it will be proper to state that these high-grade fertilizers, applied at the rate of from 800 to 1600 lbs. per acre, have sometimes given me an increase in the yield sufficient to pay two or three times the cost of manure, besides leaving the ground in better condition than before.

ROTATION.—To diminish the danger of attacks by potato beetles, flea beetles, and other insect foes, as well as by the diseases peculiar to the crop, its frequent change to a location as far as possible remote from any place where potatoes had been grown the year before, is to be heartily recommended as a safe and most practical means. This may not usually prevent the attacks entirely; but it will tend to render them far less serious and intense. Although perhaps not generally recognized, it is nevertheless a fact that few potato crops are now grown the foliage of which escapes considerable injury by beetles, blights, and poisonous applications, resulting in great reduction of the yield. Strictest adherence to the "wide rotation" principle, therefore, is a practice dictated by ordinary prudence.

AVERAGE YIELDS.—The average yield of the crop in the various states is ridiculously low. Some of the reasons for this fact have already been alluded to. Another is the yet common practice of planting in check rows, which, besides, are often needlessly wide apart. A change to drill planting, with not more than 3 feet space between the rows, and 12 to 18 inches between the seed pieces, frequently doubles the yield.

The size of seed pieces also has its decided influence upon the yield. Large seed pieces under average circumstances give the largest crops. Most growers use pieces too small for their own good. Let us make an examination of the potato fields a few weeks after planting time, in spring, and we see the great majority of the plantings come up slowly and weakly, with a single stalk growing from each hill, and many gaps in the rows. We may be sure the yield will be accordingly. Larger pieces, even whole tubers, have always given me the heaviest yields, and this to such an extent, that this extremely heavy seeding (sometimes over 30 bushels per acre) has turned out to be very profitable on good soil, and under average fair conditions.

The condition of seed is another factor in determining the yield. A full crop can only be grown from fresh, plump, seed-tubers that have not been weakened by the emission of spindling sprouts before planting. Southern growers were in the habit of planting "northern-grown" seed, and now northern planters call for "second-crop" southern seed.

EARLY CROPS.—The same methods suited for the production of early potatoes in the market garden may also be adopted for the family garden, and for small-scale operations generally.

The southern states supply the chief markets of the north with young potatoes long before the northern near-by grower can get his crop ready. It may be true that the southern potato grower takes the cream; but the milk that is left is yet very acceptable to the northern grower, who manages now to get his crop into market a little in advance of the rush, thus securing quite remunerative prices in spite of all southern competition. Earliness must be the foremost aim.

As means to this end we have (first), a judicious selection of soil, which should be well-drained, warm, somewhat sandy, and full of vegetable matter; (second), the selection of earliest good varieties, such, for instance, as Early Ohio and Early Sunrise; (third), the use of well-preserved seed tubers; (fourth), reasonably heavy seeding; (fifth), early planting, in a sheltered situation if possible; (sixth), stimulation of the plants by high feeding and high cultivation to induce rapid development; (seventh), digging and marketing just as soon as the tubers are in merchantable condition.

GARDEN CULTURE.—Early in spring the ground is thoroughly plowed and harrowed, and the furrows marked out with a one-horse plow, 2½ or 3 feet apart. Market gardeners, following their natural instincts and habits of close planting, usually have the rows 2½ feet apart. I find it more convenient for cultivation to make them for early sorts at same distance as for the late ones, 3 feet apart. If any fertilizer is applied in the bottom of the furrows—say a dressing of fine compost, wood ashes, hen manure, or "special potato manure," it is well mixed with the soil, and the latter at the same time nicely pulverized, by running a shovel-plow once or twice along in each furrow. On a small scale this may be accomplished by plying the hand hoe.

The seed pieces are then dropped 10 or 12 inches apart in the furrows, and covered about two inches deep with the hoe. Some good special potato fertilizer may now be scattered along the rows above the covered seed pieces, say at the rate of from 400 to 800 lbs. per acre; and if the land is not rich in accumulated plant food, a small dressing of nitrate of soda, broadcast, will assist in bringing out an early and thrifty growth of foliage. The cultivator (Planet Jr., or a similar narrow-bladed wheel-hoe) should be used very freely; and as the plants grow, the furrows are filled up level with the surface. Hilling is neither required nor beneficial. The old style of ridging by means of a winged shovel-plow is out of date; but the soil must be kept well stirred and mellow until the plants cover the ground. When the tops begin to die, or even sooner, the crop is ready for digging, and if the price is acceptable, should be marketed at once, since prices are usually declining very rapidly just at that time.

FIELD CULTURE.—The market gardener, on account of his larger yields and the better prices he receives, can well afford to take more pains with his crop; and so can the home grower, who will hardly miss the few hours he spends on his patch plying the hoe. In growing potatoes for main (late) crop, however, with the prospect of continued low prices for an average crop before us, we are forced to adopt a more economical system, especially in the employment of labor. The work must be done almost exclusively with horse and machine, and without calling on hand hoes and spading forks or potato hooks for assistance. Thus it is yet possible, even at the present low average prices, to make the crop one of the most profitable for the farm in favorable locations.

Early Sunrise.

A young, rich clover field, as already stated, is undoubtedly a superior selection for a site. In regard to the application of manures, I confess we are as yet quite ignorant. A number of ways are open to us, namely: (1) to apply the compost or fertilizers broadcast and plow it in; or, (2) to broadcast them after plowing and simply harrow them in; or, (3) to put the fertilizing material into the bottom of the furrows under the seed; or, (4) to scatter it over the lightly covered seed. Myself and other people have made various tests to find out which of these methods will give us the best results; but the outcome thus far has been of a rather negative character, and I believe the conclusion is justified that the mode of application is of far less influence upon the yield than the quantity of fertilizer. The indications, also, are that fertilizer applied above the seed usually gives slightly better returns than when applied in the bottom of the

Chas. Downing.

furrow before planting. My own practice—satisfactory to myself—is to spread the compost, if any is applied, evenly over the field before plowing; but to apply only half of the fertilizer broadcast, either before or after plowing, and to scatter the other half over the rows above the covered seed pieces.

I believe in planting early, say one or two weeks before the customary time for planting field corn. But it can also be done later in the season, and even up to July, provided that good seed is on hand. To preserve seed tubers until that time in best condition, they may be spread thinly upon the floor in a well-lighted room, or kept in cold storage until wanted for planting.

Size of seed pieces and distance of placing them in the drills depend somewhat on local conditions. Some growers report good results from planting single-eye pieces rather close. I have never been able to raise a full crop from single eyes, or small seed pieces generally; and in order to insure a chance for a good crop, always find myself obliged to resort to pretty heavy seeding. When planting time approaches, plow the ground 8 or 10 inches deep, or at least to the whole depth of the surface soil, if this be less. Fall plowing is seldom of much benefit except on heavier soils; neither is double or cross-plowing. Mellow the ground thoroughly by means of one of our modern deep-cutting harrows (Cutaway, disk, etc.)

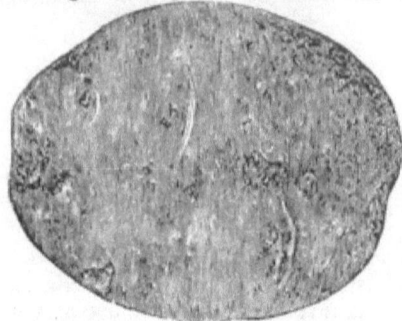

Clark's No. 1.

and drill in the seed by means of an Aspinwall, or other good potato planter, in rows 3 feet apart, and 12 to 18 inches apart in the rows. Of course, the potato planter is usually available only to large operators; and where the planting has to be done by hand, furrows must be laid out with a single-horse plow, 4 inches deep and 3 feet apart, and the seed, consisting of good-sized pieces, or whole small or medium-sized tubers, deposited at intervals of 12 to 18 inches in the bottom of the furrow.

In most cases, especially when the soil is not as mellow as it might be, the treatment of the furrows, which has recently become famous as the "Rural (New Yorker) trench system," will be found to give good results. It consists in mellowing up the soil in the bottom of these furrows very thoroughly, either by means of a common shovel-plow, going at least twice in each furrow, or by devices constructed for the purpose, such as I hope will be invented before long and put on sale in every hardware store. This is done in order to give to the roots of the vines, and to the tubers also, the best possible chance for development.

The seed is to be covered with about two inches of soil, and this should be firmed in same manner as other seed, best by setting the foot firmly and squarely upon each piece. The fertilizer is then scattered along in the half-filled trenches, and this finishes the planting.

Cultivation should be begun within a week. I have never found a method of cultivating the potato field during its earlier stages more effectual, cheaper and easier than by the early, thorough, and repeated use of a Thomas' smoothing harrow.

It gives us every advantage without a single drawback. The first harrowing, shortly after planting, had better be given in the direction of the rows; the next one four or five days after, across the rows; and one or two more, at intervals of four or five days each, in the same way. This treatment renders the surface smooth and even, mellows and pulverizes the soil thoroughly, and so utterly discourages the weeds, that they will not venture to show themselves for a long time. Now the young plants have probably grown several inches high; and the cultivator (Planet Jr., for instance) must take the place of the harrow. In the manipulation of the cultivator, we aim to crowd the row at the right-hand pretty closely, and going twice between the same two rows, stir the entire surface of the soil without leaving anything for the hand hoe to do. Cultivation is kept up until the vines cover the ground.

The Polaris.

DIGGING, HARVESTING AND STORING.—In clean, mellow soil our modern potato diggers do good service. Where none is available, a common one-horse plow (or a shovel-plow) often answers very well. Small patches may be dug with a potato hook, or a digging fork, or even a common hand hoe. If dug by machine or plow, the ground, after the crop is picked up, can be harrowed over with the smoothing harrow, thus bringing the few tubers, that had been covered up and hidden, into sight for gathering. The tubers may be left on the ground for a short time, and are then gathered in box-crates holding a bushel each, and thus drawn to market, cellar, root-house, or pit. The simplest, cheapest, and generally most satisfactory manner of storing for wintering over, next to that in root cellar, is in pits, provided the potatoes are covered up when cool, and protected sufficiently to keep them from contact with frost.

VARIETIES.

The most sensible way of classifying our hundreds of potato varieties, it seems to me, would be by bringing them under the head of types or families—Early Rose type, Burbank type, Beauty of Hebron type, Peerless type, etc.—The varieties are and will always be changing, new additions being made to the list, and old ones dropped. The following list includes the sorts now leading:

Early Ohio.—Yet the earliest good sort with which I am acquainted. Needs high culture, and is emphatically a garden potato; especially valuable for the market garden. Cooks dry and mealy even before fully ripe. Quality best. Keeps well, much better than its parent, the Early Rose.

Early Sunrise.—Another seedling of Early Rose, much resembling it, but considerably earlier. Good for home and market garden.

White Prize.—A very smooth, handsome potato and a great yielder. Flesh, white; and always cooks dry and mealy.

The Polaris.—A new extra early of considerable merit. It is of oblong shape, white skin; eyes few and shallow, always cooks dry and mealy. Matures a week ahead of either the Early Rose or Beauty of Hebron.

Early Rose.—The well-known early market variety. So many of its seedlings have been introduced in recent years, and are being marketed under the name of "Early Rose," that it may be difficult to procure the pure old variety under that name.

Beauty of Hebron.—Equals the Rose in popularity as an early market sort, and ripens at about the same season.

Clark's No. 1.—An early sort of the Rose type.

Peerless.—An old sort, formerly much grown for market, especially in sandy soils; very productive, and perhaps still good for the south.

White Elephant.—A large, late and immensely productive Beauty of Hebron; of fine quality, and still well thought of in some localities.

Burbank.—The old standard market sort. Of Rose-shape, and pure white color; prolific; a good keeper; but of good quality only when grown on light soils.

White Star.—Might be called an Improved Burbank, as it resembles that sort in general appearance, but seems to be superior to it in almost every respect. Now, next to the Rose, the leading market sort.

Empire State.—Superior in yield and quality.

Freeman.—A fairly early variety of the old Snowflake type. Tubers round, somewhat flattened; skin white, slightly russeted; flesh of snowy whiteness. The plant is of very strong growth, and liable to set a large number of potatoes which are unexcelled by any other for smoothness, handsome appearance, and high quality. Everyone who appreciates a really good potato, should grow the Freeman. It wants rich soil, high culture, and light seeding.

Irish Daisy.—Introduced in 1894; a seedling of Empire State; claimed to possess all the strong qualities of its parent. Eyes shallow; skin pure bright straw color. Ripens with Rural New Yorker No. 2 and White Star.

Rural New Yorker No. 2.—A mid-season variety which has quickly come to the front. It is a strong grower and heavy yielder of large, square, somewhat flattened tubers. Rather coarse, and desirable only where large yield is of more consideration than quality.

Carman No. 1.—Introduced in 1894. Resembles the preceding in growth, thrift, season, productiveness, and general appearance of tuber, but far surpasses it in quality. Probably destined to take the place of the former as a leading market variety.

POTATO (SWEET).

Convolvulus Batatas. German, *Batate;* French, *Patate Douce;* Spanish, *Batata*—In sweet potatoes we have a most important crop for the middle and southern states; but one which will hardly ever succeed in the short seasons north of New

York city, although by coddling a comparatively few plants, the tubers can be brought to some size. The crop, however, will not be a profitable one for market in such northern localities.

GROWING THE PLANTS.—To start the beds we need a good strong hot-bed, although not as early in the season as for eggplants or even tomatoes. The manure is but lightly covered with soil or sand, and the tubers are spread out in single layer, the larger ones split in halves, cut-side down, as closely as possible without overcrowding. The layer is then covered with 3 or 4 inches of sand. Water and ventilation have to be given as for egg plants or peppers. In five or six weeks the first plants will be large enough to sever from the seed tubers, which is accomplished by simply pulling them up. New plants continue to start, and may be pulled, and planted out as they grow large enough.

GROWING THE CROP.—Warm, well-drained soil of medium fertility is best. Rich soil is apt to produce too rank a growth of vines, and make it almost impossible to prevent them from rooting all over the ground, and thus wasting their energies in the formation of large numbers of tubers too small for use, instead of concentrating them on the development of the tubers in the hill.

Mark out light furrows 4 feet apart, and fill them rounding full with good manure, or scatter a liberal quantity (say 800 pounds or more per acre) of good special potato fertilizer in them. Next with a one-horse plow throw a furrow to the manure from each side of the row, forming a pretty good ridge, which is to be smoothed nicely with the hoe, and thus got ready for setting the plants. The proper time for doing this is when the ground has become thoroughly warm, say from May 15th to June 15th. Set the plants firmly on top of the ridge, about 24 inches apart, leaving them in the centre of a slight depression. I need hardly repeat that the roots of the plants, just previous to setting out, ought to be dipped in water. A half-pint of water should also be poured into the depression around each plant. Afterwards keep well cultivated and free from weeds, and occasionally lift up the vines to detach them from the ground, where they have begun to strike root between the hills and rows.

HARVESTING.—After the first light frost, the vines are to be cut off close above the ground, and the roots carefully lifted out by means of a spading fork. Great care is necessary in order to avoid bruising the tubers. The latter may be left out on the ground for a few hours to dry, and should then be stored in a dry and warm loft. To keep well, they should not be exposed to much change of temperature, or a lower temperature than 50 or 55 degrees Fahrenheit.

VARIETIES.

Yellow Nansemond.—The leading market sort in the middle states. A red sort is now gaining in popularity.

PUMPKIN.

Cucurbita. German, *Kürbiss;* French, *Potiron;* Spanish, *Calabaza.*—The cultivation of pumpkins is the same as described for squash, which see. Have the hills about 12 feet apart each way, with 2 or 3 good plants in a hill. Farmers generally plant pumpkin seeds in the hills with their corn, and often have a large crop, both for stock and for pies, in the corn-field.

VARIETIES.

The following are excellent for pies:

Japanese Pie.—This new pumpkin originated in Japan, and is said to surpass every other variety in flavor. Flesh is unusually fine grained, and when cooked is almost as dry and mealy as a sweet potato. They grow to a medium size; are very productive, and excellent keepers.

**Large Cheese,
Mammoth Etampes,
Potiron,
Yellow Sweet Potato, etc.**—All these are popular sorts.

RADISH.

Raphanus Sativus. German, *Radies* (*Rettig*); French, *Radis;* Spanish, *Rabanito.*—Radishes are one of the chief market garden crops for forcing under glass, and for early outdoor culture, and so easily grown that there is no need of giving lengthy directions. The whole crop can often be produced and disposed of within thirty-five or forty days from sowing seed, and, for this reason, it is often sown between the rows of other vegetables that occupy the ground for a longer period, but, starting slowly, give the radishes all the opportunity needed to come to full size. In outdoor culture broadcast sowing is not unfrequently practiced; but it is a method hardly worthy of consideration by good gardeners, and I neither practice nor recommend it. For culture under glass see the hints given in the chapters on cold-frames and forcing-houses. In open air culture, avoid new manure and old ground, *i. e.*, ground on

Early Deep Scarlet Olive.

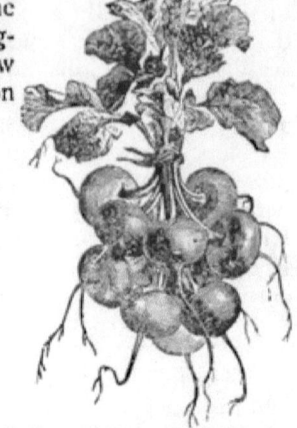

Earliest Deep Scarlet Turnip.

Mammoth Chinese.

which radishes, turnips, cabbages, and other plants of the same family have been grown the year before. Stimulate growth by light applications of nitrate of soda. In the market garden, to save space, the rows can be crowded very closely together, 6 inches between them being ample; in the home garden we usually plant twice that distance, or more, for convenience in cultivation. In either case, however, it is a good practice to utilize the space between widely planted crops—cabbages, beans, etc.—when first set out or sown, by growing a row or two of radishes between each two rows of the others. The great enemy of this crop is the maggot, which often entirely ruins whole patches. Rotation and avoidance of rank manure are our best weapons. Don't neglect early thinning to make the crop uniform.

VARIETIES.

These are divided in three classes, (1) early or forcing radishes, (2) summer and autumn radishes, (3) winter radishes.

EARLY OR FORCING SORTS.

Earliest Deep Scarlet Turnip.—One of the very earliest. I have had it fit for the table in less than twenty days after sowing. Round, handsome, of bright color, and fine quality.

Early Erfurt.—Another extra early sort, and one of the very best. Somewhat similar in general characteristics to the preceding.

Early White-Tipped Scarlet Turnip.—A handsome, early, round sort, bright carmine in color with white at tip end.

Early White Turnip.—Roundish or flattened, white, pungent.

White Box is sent out as an improved White Turnip.

Early Deep Scarlet Olive.—Considered one of the best and handsomest of the small or forcing varieties. Flesh tender and of mild flavor. Very early.

White Turnip.

French Breakfast.—Handsome and early, and quite popular as an early market sort. Remains in condition fit for table use but a few days after the bulbs or roots are fully formed, hence it cannot be recommended for the home garden.

All these early varieties are suitable to be planted for succession all through the season.

SUMMER AND AUTUMN VARIETIES.

Long Scarlet Short-Top.—A handsome second early, long-rooted variety, suitable both for forcing and out-door culture.

Long Vienna,

White Ladyfinger.—Two fine, long, white sorts, of tender flesh and superior flavor.

Large White Summer Turnip.—Grows to a large size, and remains in condition fit for the table longer than most other summer varieties.

Stuttgart Giant White Turnip.—Grows still larger than the preceding, and in flavor and otherwise has many of the characteristics of the winter varieties, and may be served in the same manner.

Yellow Summer.—A good, strong, long-standing summer variety with dark russety-yellow skin. Its flavor reminds of that of winter radishes.

Golden Summer is introduced as an improved Yellow Summer.

White Strassburg Summer.—One of the finest half-long varieties, very productive, growing to large size; skin and flesh pure white; of superior tenderness and quality.

1834.—Similar to the above, but of American origin.

Chartier.—One of the largest of this class, smooth, handsome, long roots; somewhat late, and of considerable pungency but crisp and tender when well-grown.

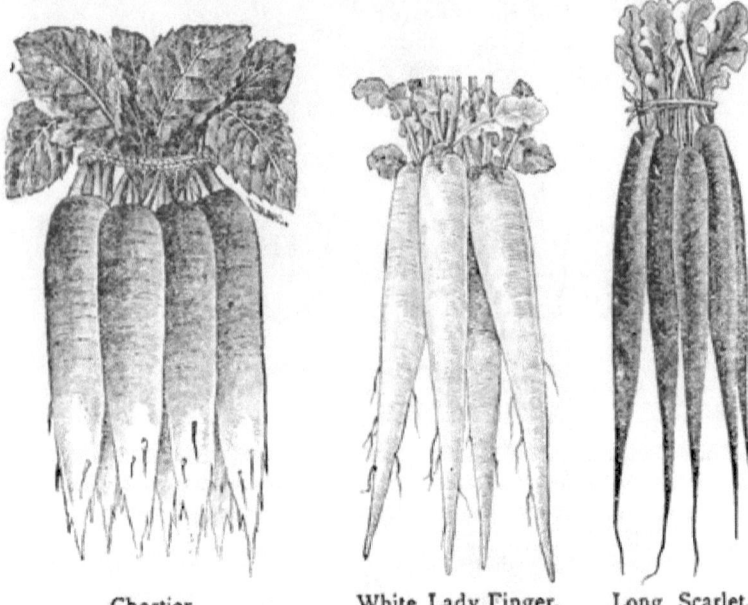

Chartier.   White Lady Finger.   Long Scarlet.

WINTER VARIETIES.

China Rose Winter.—Early, handsome, tender, of somewhat sweetish flavor. Quite popular.

Black Spanish Winter Long.—Very black, flesh white, firm, tender, pungent.

Large White Spanish Winter.—A quick grower, skin and flesh white. Firm and pungent. A good keeper.

Large White Russian.—A mammoth in size, but lacking in tenderness and crispness.

California Mammoth White Winter, Mammoth Chinese.—Of very rapid growth, large, tender, and of mild flavor. I prefer it to all other winter varieties.

RHUBARB.

Rheum Hybridum (*Rhaponticum*). German, *Rhabarber*; French, *Rhubarbe*; Spanish, *Ruibarbo*.—Rhubarb, or pie-plant, is largely grown for market near all larger cities, and found in almost every American home garden. It is usually propagated by division of the roots, each eye or bud with a piece of the fleshy root attached being capable of producing a large plant within a year's time. It also grows readily from the seed, at a year's delay in producing the crop. Plants grown from seed also vary very largely in habit of growth. Seed is sown in drills, 12 or 15 inches apart, and the plants thinned to a few inches in the drills. In fall or spring following they are to be set out in same way as pieces of roots from older plants.

Select warm, well-drained soil, plow deeply, if possible following with a subsoil plow, and mark out furrows four feet apart each way. A few shovelfuls of rich compost should be mixed with the soil at each intersection. Then set the plants carefully and firmly, and from this time on keep the ground cultivated and free from weeds. In spring following, the stalks may be pulled freely. A plantation will last many years, but the plants should be given a good dressing of rich compost every year or two. Home gardeners sometimes place boxes, or kegs with heads removed, over the hills in early spring, and by this means produce extra long and tender growth of stalk.

For winter and early spring use, Rhubarb is often forced in greenhouses and cold-frames, and usually with very fair profit. The roots are taken up in the autumn, crowded together in boxes or barrels with a little soil between them, and placed in any convenient place in the greenhouse (under the benches, for instance), where they soon start into growth. For cold-frame culture the roots are planted closely together in a deep frame in the autumn, and covered with a heavy layer of dry forest leaves. In February or March the leaves are removed, and the sashes put on. Forced Rhubarb is usually more tender and succulent than that from open ground.

VARIETIES.

Victoria, Wyatt's Victoria.—Stalks red, and very thick. Leaves broad. Productive. Late.

Linnæus, Wyatt's Linnæus.—Stalks deep green, early.

ROSEMARY.

Rosmarinus Officinalis. German, *Rosmarin*; French, *Romarin*; Spanish, *Romero*.—A shrub-like perennial, the leaves of which are used for seasoning. Propagated from seed, or more generally from division of the root-stock. A tuft or two of it planted in any convenient, well-drained spot, will furnish all a family may possibly want, without requiring further attention.

RUE.

Ruta Graveolens. German, *Raute;* French, *Rue.*—The leaves of this little perennial shrub, although bitter and very pungent, are nevertheless sometimes used for seasoning. Plants are easily grown from seed, or from division of the tufts. Set the plants 20 or 24 inches apart each way in well-drained but rather moist soil. Little or no further attention is required.

SAGE.

Sage.

Salvia Officinalis. German, *Salbei;* French, *Sauge;* Spanish, *Salvia.*—A perennial shrub of easiest culture, the leaves of which are largely used for seasoning sausages, meat, etc. Readily propagated from seed as well as by layering. Sow seed in early spring in drills, in well-drained soil. The plants will last for many years without requiring much attention. It is largely grown for market as a second crop. The Broad Leaved is an improved variety.

SALSIFY, OR OYSTER PLANT.

Tragopogon Porrifolium. German, *Haferwurzel;* French, *Salsifis;* Spanish, *Salsifi.*—It is only recently that people have begun to like salsify, and to cultivate it more generally. It is becoming so important as a market crop that some market gardeners near the large cities of the east now grow acres of it.

CULTURE.—Seed is sown in spring in drills 12 inches apart, and the plants thinned to 3 or 4 inches apart in the rows. The soil should be rich and well prepared, and kept well cultivated and hoed during the growing season. The crop may be dug late in the fall, and stored away like other root crops for use during the winter. Frost improves its flavor. That part of the crop which is intended for spring use, may safely be left in the ground over winter, and only at the extreme north it may be necessary to draw a little soil over the rows for winter protection.

VARIETIES.

Until recently only one variety was catalogued, sometimes under the name of **White French**. Some years ago a much larger sort was introduced as **Mammoth Sandwich Island**. This is so much more productive, and generally so superior to the old sort, that we have no further use for the latter.

SAVORY (SUMMER).

Satureia Hortensis. German, *Bohnenkraut;* French, *Sarriette (annuelle);* Spanish, *Ajedrea.*—The leaves of this bushy annual are frequently used for seasoning. Sow seed in spring in good, warm soil, and keep free from weeds. Sometimes grown for market as a second crop.

SAVORY (WINTER).

Satureia Montana. German, *Winter Bohnenkraut;* French, *Sarrietta* (vivace); Spanish, *Hisopillo.*—A small perennial shrub, the leaves of which are used in same manner as those of the summer savory. Seed may be sown in spring in any convenient, well-drained spot where the plants are to remain. They need very little attention.

Savory.

SCORZONERA.

Scorzonera Hispanica. German, *Schwarzwurzel;* French, *Scorsonere;* Spanish, *Escorzonera.*—A perennial, cultivated either as annual or biennial, exactly like Salsify, with this difference that the roots, if left in the ground, will continue to grow in size and to remain fit for use. Used like salsify, but grown in America only to a very limited extent.

SEA-KALE.

Sea-Kale.

Crambe Maritima. German, *Meerkohl;* French, *Crambe;* Spanish, *Soldanella; Maritima.*—Sea-Kale is found in very few American gardens. When well-grown, it makes such an excellent dish that it is well worth the trouble required to raise it. Propagated both from seed and root cuttings. Make the soil very rich and mellow. Then plant a few seeds, or a four-inch piece of root, in hills, three feet apart each way, and keep well cultivated and free from weeds. If more than one plant grows from the seed, all but the strongest are pulled up as soon as the one remaining has attained sufficient size. At the extreme north the crowns must be protected during winter by a covering of leaves or litter. The second season from root cuttings, or the third season from seed, the plants are strong enough to yield a supply. To make sea-kale fit for use, it has to be blanched. For this purpose the crowns must be covered in early spring with sand or muck, to the depth of at least twelve inches; or an inverted flower pot, with hole in bottom entirely stopped up, be placed over each crown, and further covered with leaves or dry soil. The bed will last quite a number of years, but should be manured with good compost every fall or spring.

SHALLOT.

Shallot.

Allium Ascalonicum. German, *Schalotte;* French, *Echalote;* Spanish, *Chalote.*—Used to some extent as a substitute for green onions in early spring. The bulbs are usually divided and planted in early autumn, in rows one foot apart, and five or six inches apart in the row. Perfectly hardy, and coming earlier than onions, they are often quite a profitable crop for market.

SORREL (BROAD-LEAVED).

Rumex Acetosa. German, *Sauerampfer;* French, *Oseille.*—Used to a limited extent for soups and salads. Usually grown from seed, which is sown in early spring in good soil, having rows one foot apart. Thin the plants to stand five or six inches apart in the rows. The leaves are the part used. Cut out the seed-stalk, as soon as it appears.

Sorrel.

SPINACH.

Spinacea Oleracea. German, *Spinat;* French, *Epinard;* Spanish, *Espinaca.*—In spinach we have a most important market garden crop, valuable alike for open-air culture and for forcing under glass. There is hardly a time during the entire year that spinach could not be produced, or find ready sale in the city markets. Southern truck farmers grow it quite extensively as an early spring crop for shipping to the north. Within reasonable distance from New York city and Philadelphia spinach is largely grown in cold-frames and forcing houses, and usually affords the grower very fair returns. For fuller information on this point see the respective chapters.

As early in spring as we can get the ground in working order, we begin outdoor culture by sowing seed in drills in the usual way, and in very rich and well-prepared soil. Nitrate of soda, applied in small and repeated doses, tends to produce large foliage. Use the hand wheel-hoe freely, and keep the ground free from weeds. When ready for gathering, run a sharp scuffle or push hoe along the rows under the plants, thus cutting them off close to the ground. They are then picked up, freed from dead and decaying leaves, and washed clean, when they are ready for use or market. For longer distances, spinach is usually packed in barrels, having openings in bottom and sides. In many market gardens spinach is sown as a secondary or auxiliary crop between rows of early cabbages, etc. It comes off in time to give the cabbages the needed space. For fall market, seed is sown in August, for winter and earliest spring crops, in September and early October. Make the land very rich, using the best of compost freely. Top dressings of poultry manure and nitrate of soda seldom fail to increase the yield largely, and sometimes immensely.

Spinach.

Plant in drills one foot apart, using seed very freely (twelve or fifteen pounds to the acre), and firming it very thoroughly. At this time of the year it is often so hot and dry, that seeds refuse to germinate, unless extra precaution is taken in sowing. Keep the ground well cultivated and free from weeds. Should the plants come very thick, they may be thinned late in October or in November, and the thinnings used or sold. The main crop usually winters over without loss, but in exposed situations should be lightly covered with coarse litter or leaves. The crop is cut and marketed in early spring.

VARIETIES.

Round-Leaf.—Very popular with market gardeners on account of its great hardiness.

Long-Standing Summer.—Closely resembles the Round-Leaf, but runs to seed a week or more later. For this reason it is decidedly preferable, especially also for the home garden.

Thick-Leaved.—An old market sort, both for spring and fall sowing.

Viroflay is said to be a more productive strain of this.

Savoy-Leaved.—Leaf somewhat curly, reminding of the Savoy Cabbages. I do not see in it any merits above those of other sorts.

Prickly.—So named from the prickly character of its seeds.

Substitutes.—Various plants are now used as substitutes for spinach, among them the following:

New Zealand Spinach, *Tetragonia expansa.*—An annual with spreading stem, and thick, heavy leaves. Seeds large and prickly. Stands the summer heat remarkably well, and is therefore frequently used in place of spinach during June, July and August, or in very hot and dry locations.

Orache, *Atriplex Hortensis.*—Annual with broad, arrow-shaped leaves; stands the heat remarkably well, but succeeds best in rich, moist soil. Otherwise treated like spinach.

Sprouts.—Much grown at the south for home and northern markets. See Kale.

Strawberry Blite, *Blitum Capitatum.*—An annual weed, extremely hardy, and sometimes recommended as a substitute for winter spinach at the extreme north. When loaded with its bright-red, berry-like fruit in spring, it is quite ornamental.

SQUASH.

Cucurbita. German, *Speise Kürbiss;* French, *Courge, Potiron;* Spanish, *Calabaza.*—Their rank growth and demands for space exclude squashes from the market garden, but they can usually be made a profitable crop for the truck farm. All squashes thrive best in a warm, highly-enriched soil and in a warm location. An old pasture or clover field is one of the best selections. Apply good compost liberally, plow and harrow well, and plant after the weather has become thoroughly settled and the ground warm.

Summer Crookneck.

Striped bugs are usually so destructive to the young plants, that it is frequently considered the only safe way to start plants on inverted sods under glass in April or May, in same manner as described for Lima beans, and afterwards plant out in the open field. Mark out rows four feet apart each way for the bush or summer sorts, and eight to twelve feet each way for the running or winter varieties, and mix three or four shovelfuls of rich compost with the soil at each intersection; then plant a dozen seeds, or set a sod with plants in slightly raised hills. Afterwards cultivate and hoe frequently, always drawing some fresh soil up to the plants. Pull up all but two or three of the most vigorous plants, and continue fighting the cucumber beetle and squash bug. Also guard against the attacks of the squash borer. Covering the first one or two joints, after the vines have begun to run, should never be neglected. The summer varieties are gathered and marketed while young and yet tender. The winter sorts must be harvested before frost, and marketed in bulk or in barrels. If carefully handled and stored in a dry room, like sweet potatoes, they may be kept until spring. Winter squashes thus kept can generally be marketed during winter or spring at prices that make the crop a very profitable one.

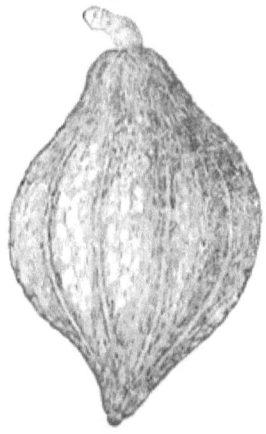

Hubbard.

SUMMER VARIETIES (*C. Pepo*).

White Scallop, White Bush,
Yellow Scallop, Yellow Bush.—These are leading sorts for market, differing only in color of the skin.

Summer Crookneck.—Quite popular, especially for the home garden.

Brazilian Sugar.—A running variety, fine for late summer and fall. Prolific and of superior quality.

WINTER VARIETIES (*C. Maxima*).

Hubbard.—The leading market variety. Fruit dark green, sometimes marked with red. Unexcelled for quality, and as a keeper.

Marblehead.—Similar to Hubbard, except in color, which is ashy-gray.

Boston Marrow.—Much grown for market, and highly prized for quality.

Prolific Marrow has been introduced as an improvement on Boston Marrow. Both are fine autumn sorts.

Sibley, Pike's Peak.—A new introduction, highly recommended.

Bay State.—Another new sort of great promise.

Olive.—Fruit of medium size, elongated. Vine remarkably vigorous.

Essex Hybrid.—Fruit thick, almost cylindrical; of salmon pink color.

Red China.—A beautiful fruit of recent introduction. Its bright color makes it especially attractive, and desirable for the home garden.

Chestnut,
Perfect Gem,
Cocoanut.—Three vigorous growing varieties with small but numerous fruits. Quality good. Vines seem to be as hardy as those of the bush sorts. Worthy a place in the home garden.

No. 1, White Bush.
No. 2, Boston Marrow.
No. 3, Marblehead.
No. 4, Cocoanut.

Yokohama.—A variety of *Cucurbita moschata*, from Japan, of most rampant growth, and fully as hardy as the summer sorts; also apparently less subject to injury from bug attacks. Fruit flattened, of very dark green color, deeply lobed or ribbed. Quality good.

THYME.

Thymus Vulgaris. German, *Thymian;* French, *Thym;* Spanish, *Tomillo.*—A small perennial shrub, the leaves and young shoots of which are often used for seasoning. Generally raised from seed sown in April in permanent bed and border, or to be transplanted to the permanent patch. For market, near large cities, it is grown as a second crop, planted out in June or July, in rows one foot apart.

Thyme.

Broad-leaved is the only variety in profitable cultivation.

TOMATO.

Solanum Lycopersicum. German, *Liebesapfel;* French and Spanish, *Tomate.*—In many sections of this country, tomatoes are a leading farm crop, and grown almost more extensively than potatoes. The market garden has little use for them, except as an early or a forcing crop; for this vegetable, to do its best, requires more space than high feeding and high cultivation. With good plants to start with, tomatoes are one of the easiest crops to grow where the climate is warm enough to bring the fruit to maturity.

GROWING THE PLANTS.—It is of especial importance to start the plants early (not later than in March) in hot-bed or greenhouse, in order to get an early crop. Give the plants all the space they need for full development, during every stage of growth, in order to make them stocky; then harden them off thoroughly before their transfer to the open ground.

CULTURE.—To give the best results, tomatoes require the soil in a fair state of fertility; but the richer it is, the wider should the plants be set, 4 feet square usually being the very

Dwarf Champion.

Turner Hybrid.

Trophy.

least distance, except perhaps for some of the very dwarf sorts. Keep the crop cultivated and hoed, same as a good farmer would his corn.

WINTER FORCING.—For forcing the crop in greenhouse, plants may be obtained by rooting cuttings of old plants in the fall, then planting out in beds in greenhouse, or in large pots or boxes, giving each plant a space of about 2 feet each way. All laterals are removed and the main stalks tied to stakes, or wires, or strings. During the time of fruit-setting the atmosphere inside of the building has to be kept dry. In order to secure the proper fertilization (pollination), good growers now gather tomato flowers from the field in the fall when pollen is produced most freely, dry them and keep them in a box or jar until wanted. The pollen dust is then applied to each flower as soon as it opens.

ENEMIES, MARKETING, ETC.—The potato stalk-borer sometimes attacks the tomato vines, and the green tomato-worm the foliage. Both enemies, when appearing, should be hunted up and destroyed. Tomato rot and blight appears very destructive in some localities, and the proper precautions, of which "wide" rotation is safest, must be taken. The farmer and market gardener can hardly afford to stake or train his thousands of plants; neither is this of any special benefit. It is different in the home garden, where a few plants, nicely trained, can easily be made an interesting and attractive feature of the vegetable patch. A simple way of training the plants is by single stake. Set the stake at time of setting the plant, and keep the latter tied up from the very beginning. In packing for distant market, be sure to send only nice, smooth specimens, and sort out all the rough and otherwise faulty ones.

Strawberry Tomato.

VARIETIES.

Our list now includes a large amount of most excellent sorts, and if I were restricted to a single one, I would hardly know which to choose. Leaving a few early dwarfish sorts out of consideration, there is but little difference between all our really good varieties so far as earliness and productiveness are concerned. They vary greatly in color, size, shape, as well as habit of growth, and character of foliage. Scores of new varieties have been introduced during the past few years.

Dwarf Champion.—Fruit of purplish color, fair size, solid, smooth and uniform. Vine of remarkably stiff and compact growth; foliage heavy, of dark bluish-green. Can be planted as close as 3 feet each way, and if staked when first set out, will be apt to remain in an upright position right through.

Early Ruby.—This for a number of years has been our principal early market variety. It has its faults. It is not always regular in shape; its size might be a little larger; and the plant is lacking in thrift, size and vigor. High cultivation remedies these faults to some extent. We have grown it because it has been by far the best of its season, far better than *Early King*, *Earliest Advance*, *Atlantic Prize*, etc., and it has given us ripe fruit weeks in advance of the ordinary standard sorts. Other, smoother sorts, I hope will soon take its place.

Maule's Earliest.—This comes highly recommended as a first early and very productive sort.

Matchless.—This newer tomato is certainly matchless in form, regularity of growth, and desirable shipping qualities.

Fruit free from core; in color, a rich cardinal red, and less liable to crack in wet weather than any other large tomato. It is good every way.

Trophy.—An old favorite on account of superior solidity and quality of fruit, which, however, is not always smooth.

Acme.—A popular sort for early market. Of purplish color; round, smooth, solid and productive.

Beauty seems to be an improvement on it.

Paragon,
Perfection,
Favorite,
Mayflower,
Cardinal.—All these are excellent for market and canning factory use, varying but slightly in their leading characteristics. Fruit large-sized, red, smooth, solid.

Turner Hybrid, Mikado.—Mammoth in plant, foliage, fruit, and productiveness, but fruit not always smooth.

Potato Leaf Tomato.

Potato-Leaf.—Similar in habit of growth and foliage to the preceding; fruit of good size, purple color, and uniformly smooth. One of the best for home use or early market.

Essex Hybrid,
Volunteer,
Optimus, and many others might be named that prove to be good and reliable sorts for all purposes.

Golden Queen.—One of the best of the yellow sorts.

Peach.—Quite distinct. Foliage much serrated and delicate. Fruit small, fine color and shape, growing in clusters. More interesting than practically useful, however.

Lorillard.—Superior for forcing, but also does well in open air. Fruit early, large, smooth and solid.

Strawberry Tomato (Alkekengi), *Physalis.*—Fruits yellow, of size of cherry, growing enclosed in a husk; of sweetish, fruity flavor. Sometimes grown for preserves. The plant, when once grown, is apt to reproduce itself year after year from self-sown seed.

TURNIPS.

Brassica napa (campestris). German, *Steckrübe, Kohlrübe;* French, *Navet;* Spanish, *Nabo*.—The market gardener has but little use and room for turnips, except to a limited extent for the early flat varieties, which are grown and marketed in the same manner as early beets. The ground is made very rich by applications of thoroughly-rotted compost, supplemented, if convenient, with some good, plain superphosphate strewn in the drills, and seed sown as early in spring as the soil can be got in readiness, in drills 15 inches apart, using seed at the rate of two pounds per acre, and firming the soil in the often recommended manner.

CULTIVATION, ETC.—Use the wheel-hoe as needed, and thin the plants, when danger from flea beetle injury is past, to 2 or 3 inches. When the roots are about 2 inches in diameter, pull, trim, wash and bunch for market.

TURNIPS AS FARM CROP.—These turnips are of still greater importance as a fall crop for the farm. Sometimes they find ready sale at very acceptable prices for table use, during late autumn and winter, but usually the swedes or rutabagas,

Improved Purple Top Swede.

Extra Early Milan.

with their richer flavor, are grown for this purpose in preference to the quicker-growing flat turnips.

As a crop for stock feeding this vegetable is not yet appreciated to its full value by the average farmer. I have not yet seen the farm where suitable pieces of land are not annually available for turnip growing in the latter part of the season, and after the main crop is removed. An early potato field, an old strawberry patch, a pasture lot, etc., after the crop is harvested in July or August, may yet produce many hundreds of bushels of flat turnips (or of rutabagas either, if early enough) per acre the same season, with very little labor and trouble. Being easily wintered, they will materially aid in carrying stock through the winter in good condition, and with a saving of grain.

Cultural Directions.—305

But even if such land should not be available, the farmer can at least provide for a superior lot of fall feed, just when pastures are short, by scattering the seed of the flat turnips all

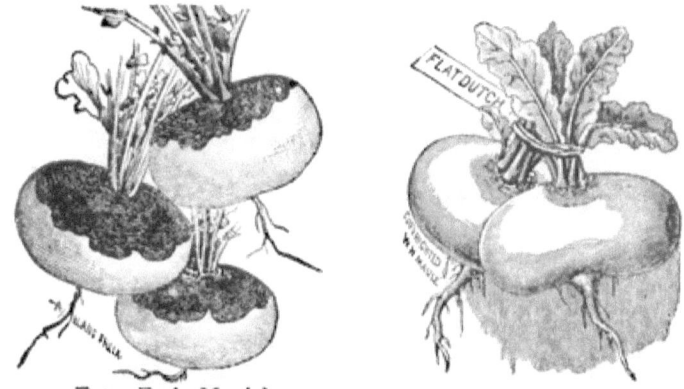

Extra Early Munich.

over his corn fields immediately after the last working. The turnip crop will make its best growth after the corn is cut, and entirely cover the ground with foliage and crisp roots—alike acceptable to cattle, sheep, and hogs. Here the simple expense for a few pounds of seed, without any other trouble besides the little effort it takes to scatter it, will greatly add to the aggregate income of the farm.

RUTABAGAS.—The rutabagas or Swede turnips are quite an important crop for the farm garden; but while the flat varieties

in the latitude of Philadelphia will give a crop even if sown as late as the middle or end of August, the rutabagas must go into the ground 4 or 6 weeks earlier. The drills should not be less than 18 inches apart, and the plants be thinned to 6 or 8 inches. The same cultivation and attention to weeds is required as for other crops of similar character. Gather before settled cold weather; trim off the tops, and ship in barrels, or store as directed for other root crops.

VARIETIES—FLAT EARLY SORTS.

Extra Early Milan.—Earliest of all, and just the variety for early bunching. In general appearance like Red-Top Strap-Leaf, only smaller and earlier.

Extra Early Munich resembles this very closely, perhaps a few days later and less reliable than the Extra Early Milan.

White Rock.

Red-Top Strap-Leaf.—The old reliable fall turnip, flat, white with red or purplish top. Red-Top White Globe is introduced as a round, consequently more productive sort of this type.

Early Flat Dutch.—A fine white garden turnip, resembling Red-Top in shape.

White Egg.—Of egg shape and quite handsome and productive.

Large White Norfolk.—Valuable for stock.

Among other sorts worthy of planting, we have
Cow Horn,
Large Yellow Globe,
Yellow Aberdeen,
Jersey Lily, etc.

VARIETIES OF RUTABAGAS OR SWEDES.

Improved Purple Top Swede.—Of fine quality, prolific, reliable.

Maule's Heavy Cropping.—An extra good sort.
Sutton's Champion.—Very productive.
White Rock.
Hardy Imperial.
Large White French, and others.

CHAPTER XXIX.

STRAWBERRY CULTURE.

IN THE HOME AND MARKET GARDEN.

"And it was called the Queen of Fruits."

NO work on vegetable and market gardening could justly be called complete if it had refused to take notice of the strawberry and its culture, not only because this is the most luscious, the most desired and desirable, indeed the queen, of all fruits, and indispensable in any well-regulated home garden—coveted alike by young and old, a most enjoyable luxury, and a most potent medicine at the same time—but also because it often fits so admirably in the crop rotation of the market garden. The skilled market gardener, who retails his own garden stuff to local or near-by customers, always finds it a most useful crop, which adds many dollars to the cash receipts during a period of two or three weeks annually, without requiring extra time to dispose of it. A single crate of berries, occupying but a few square feet of room on the wagon, and adding comparatively little weight to the load, will sell quickly along with the other products, and increase the day's sales by $3 or $4. This, however, is true also of raspberries, blackberries, and all other small fruits. Indeed, I think the grower for local market can generally combine vegetable gardening and small fruit growing to the best advantage.

During the entire strawberry season we usually find the city markets abundantly supplied with this fruit—such as it is—poor, coated with dust, jammed, ill-looking, and anything but inviting to people who are used to getting them fresh from the garden, in all their prime and glory. I have never been tempted to buy the average fruit as I saw it on the market stands of the cities. It averages poor, and so, usually and deservedly, does the price, which the grower realizes for them.

On the other hand, really first-class fruit—large, even, fresh, packed neatly in attractive and clean packages—is rare, and always in good demand at paying prices. The premium here is on superiority. There is no overproduction of fine berries, and I do not think there ever will be. Large, well-colored, perfect berries have always been scarce, always commanded good prices, and consequently always proved profitable to the producer, and to the dealer as well. Like the onion among vegetables, so the strawberry among fruits is the great money crop for the skillful grower, but a source of annoyance, disappointment, and even loss to the shiftless manager.

The chief aim of the grower must be directed towards growing fine berries, picking them when just right, and bringing them to market in best possible shape. Mr. John Burdett who lives seventeen miles from Buffalo, and is known to fruit growers as the originator of the "Long John" strawberry, a particularly prolific sort, equaling the Wilson in its best characteristics, picks his berries very early in the morning (from 3 to 7 A. M.), grades and arranges them, all of uniform size and appearance in each package, upon fancy plates or in fancy baskets; takes his morning's product to Buffalo, on train at 8 A. M., and delivers this fancy article at fancy fruit stores an hour later—only a few hours after they came from the patch—and always receives 25 or 30 cents a quart for them. As he is the only one furnishing this class of goods, and only in limited quantities at that, he virtually controls the market, and gets his own price for his fancy article.

Soil.—In the selection of soil for strawberries I would give a deep, well-drained clay loam the preference, although a good crop can be grown on any soil adapted for the production of a good crop of corn. The lay and composition of the land has a great influence upon the season of ripening. Among the chief factors favoring earliness of crop are sandy composition of soil, porous subsoil, south-eastern exposure, and selection of early varieties; while the following conditions, viz., muck or clay soil, clay subsoil, north or north-western exposure, heavy mulch left on until late in spring, and selection of late varieties, tend to make the crop a very late one. The market gardener who has a variety of soils and situations may make such selections and combinations which suit his particular purpose. By proper selection of conditions, the berry season can be greatly lengthened, or the bulk of crop ripened in just such season as the market may be expected to be most favorable.

Old sod should be avoided, as it is usually infested with white grubs (the larvæ of the May beetle), and with other insect enemies. Nothing will fit a piece of ground so nicely for planting to strawberries, as cropping for a year or two with onions, beets, carrots, or other close-planted vegetables, which need high manuring and thorough cultivation, and leave the land in a high state of fertility, and reasonably free from weeds.

Manuring.—Really fine strawberries can only be grown on fertile soil, and poor ones are hardly worth growing. Too much manure cannot well be applied, although an overdose is not necessary. Well decomposed stable manure is always a reliable fertilizer, provided it is free from weed seeds, and if we only have enough of such, we have no reason to look for anything else. Under no circumstances use manure liable to befoul the land with weeds, as the latter are the great curse of the strawberry grower. I believe it is easier to grow a good crop of onions on weedy land (although not an enjoyable task) than to keep a strawberry patch clean when once well stocked with weeds. The latter invariably interfere very seriously with the strawberry crop.

On fairly good soil I have had most excellent success with concentrated commercial fertilizers. They have the advantage of being free from weed seeds, and may be used alone, or in combination with smaller quantities of stable compost. They also lessen the dangers from fungus diseases, and make a firmer and better berry than the stable manure alone.

Potash fertilizers are of especial benefit to all fruit crops, and I would recommend, as a good, safe ration for strawberries on most soils, 400 pounds of muriate of potash and from 600 to 1000 pounds of bone-meal per acre. Wood ashes, especially if unleached, are also a most excellent manure for strawberries, being rich in the mineral plant foods, particularly in potash—the one substance most urgently needed.

PREPARATION OF THE SOIL.—The roots of strawberries go down deeply into the ground without spreading a great deal. Consequently the soil must be loosened up deeply. Stable manure, if applied, is to be plowed in. The use of a good subsoil plow, after the common plow, is always advisable, and time spent in cross-plowing and in thorough harrowing is always well employed. If ashes and concentrated fertilizers are used, they should be put on the surface after plowing, and then thoroughly mixed with the soil by means of a Disk harrow, cultivator, or hoe. If soil is lumpy, roller or Meeker harrow may be brought into use. In short, no means should be neglected by which the desired mellowness and smooth surface of the soil can be secured. The next thing is to mark out furrows four feet apart, either with a corn-marker or a one-horse plow, taking particular pains to run them straight and even.

QUALITY OF PLANTS.—Early fall, or even summer, is the time usually selected for planting strawberries in the southern states. At the north we oftener prefer to plant in spring, unless we have a chance to get good plants—the first runners made after the fruiting season—not later than August. If these plants are "pot grown," or taken up with a clump of soil, they may be expected to do all the better.

The quality of the plants influences the result, both immediate and permanent, very materially. I believe in "pedigree" with strawberry plants as well as with vegetable seeds, or with live-stock. If the first, most vigorous runners from young vigorous plants that have not yet been weakened by fruiting, are used, and this method of propagation is continued for some time, the strain will be improved, and stock of such strain is likely to give better results than the later, and less vigorous runners taken from old plants, debilitated by years of fruit production. The grower also has to take in consideration that there are sorts with perfect flowers, and others with imperfect flowers. The former possess both male and female organs of reproduction, and are called hermaphrodite or bi-sexual, sometimes (although erroneously) staminate sorts, and will produce fruit, even if a single plant or variety is standing all by itself. The imperfect or pistillate varieties have a perfect pistil (female organ), but no stamens, or these but imperfectly developed. Consequently they cannot be depended upon to produce fruit, at least not in profusion and perfection, unless planted in proximity to varieties that have perfect stamens (male organs) and can furnish pollen (the principle of fecundation) to the pollenless pistillate sorts. Purely staminate plants— those having no pistils and always barren— are more rarely met with. In buying and setting plants these facts must be kept in mind, and whenever imperfect varieties, which usually are the most fruitful, when pollen is furnished by others, are planted, a row or two of some suitable and perfect sort should always be alternated with every four or five rows of the pistillates. I might make this statement still stronger by saying that lack of proper pollen is the chief cause of barrenness, or of improper development of seed or fruit, in many plants. Putting many varieties in close proximity usually seems to prove beneficial to all, with strawberries as well as with many other bush and tree fruits.

Pot-Grown Plant.

Perfect Strawberry Blossom.

Pistillate Blossom.

SELECTION OF VARIETIES.—No "best" variety can be named. One that is doing elegantly in one locality often turns out to be an utter failure when transferred to another location. Each sort seems to have a combination of soil, climate and treatment that suits its nature best, or special requirements of its own. The grower must try to learn what sort or sorts are best adapted to his surroundings. Those giving the best results in one's nearest neighborhood are usually the ones to plant and experiment with. The highly-lauded, expensive novelties had better be touched very lightly, and in a cautious, experimental way only.

PLANTING.—Where, in accordance with these suggestions, really good plants are procured from a grower near-by, success will be rendered much more certain from the very start, than where one has to depend on plants purchased from a distance. Reliable nurserymen send out a pretty fair lot, such for instance as shown in annexed illustration; and if these are well packed, and suffer no unusual delay in transportation, they will do well enough. Often such plants, when received by express, are not exactly what we would wish them to be. Immediately after arrival place them in a damp, cool place, (cellar or the like), and keep their roots covered with moist sand until wanted for setting out. When this time has come,

Bunch of Strawberry Plants.

and the field is all in readiness, trim off about one-third of the roots with a slanting cut, using a sharp knife, and remove all partly-decayed leaves; next dip the roots in water, and let a boy scatter the plants along the rows, one plant to every twelve or fifteen inches, and follow (or let your man follow) on hands and knees, taking up each plant in its turn, spreading the roots carefully, and plant it in the bottom of the furrow, on a little mound of soil, filling in mellow earth around it, so the crown will be the veriest trifle below the surface of the ground, but not covered. This is done because the crown-growth has an upward tendency, and the plants gradually rise higher out of the ground as the seasons go by. The annexed illustration shows a fine sample plant, well planted. As always in setting plants or other growths, the most important point, and the one making success reasonably sure in any case, is the thorough firming of the soil around the roots,

A Good Plant Well Planted.

not merely around the crown. It need hardly be said, that the soil, when moist, but yet crumbly, is in exactly the right condition for the operation of setting plants. Where only shallow marks, no deep furrows are made to indicate the rows, the planting may be facilitated by the use of a gardener's trowel, or one of the improved dibbers illustrated on page 43.

TREATMENT AFTER PLANTING.—Now comes the tug-of-war. Weed growth must be prevented all through the season, and to do this the cultivator should be started soon after planting, and used at short intervals pretty much during the entire season. Weeds appearing in the rows are to be pulled up by hand, or cut out with the hoe.

Spring-set plants should not be allowed to fruit, as this would be a great strain on them so soon after the check received by the rough treatment of transplanting. The little labor required in picking off every fruit-stalk as soon as noticed, and the exercise of a little patience on the part of the grower, will always be well repaid in increase of crop the year following. The whole vital force of the plant is thus thrown into vigorous growth of the plant itself, and the production of runners.

The amateur frequently, and the market grower rarely, practices what is known as the "stool" or hill method, which consists in growing large individual plants or "stools," and preventing the full development and rooting of runners by their early and careful removal. This method requires much attention, but gives fine plants, and very large and perfect fruit, but not so much of it as can be produced by the so-called matted-row system. This is the one commonly practiced by market growers, and the more popular everywhere. The runners are allowed to strike root on a strip from one to two feet wide. As the season advances the cultivator has to be gradually narrowed down until, at last, we have a strip of cultivated ground only about two feet in width. The cultivator should also be run in one and the same direction, not back and forth between each two rows, so that the runners will not be disturbed or torn out more than necessary.

This frequent stirring of the soil by means of hoe and cultivator serves another good purpose, and performs a most important office. The strawberry succeeds best when the soil is moist. In rare cases only can irrigation be made use of. Usually we have to depend on moisture already stored up in the soil, and supplied by rains. The underground-reservoir is always well filled during winter, and all we have to do during the growing season is to prevent waste by over-rapid evaporation. Of the means at our command to retard this evaporation, mulching with a few inches of mellow soil is probably the simplest and most inexpensive, and, I believe, also the most efficient. We might accomplish this same object by mulching with litter—straw, hay, saw-dust, tan-bark, etc.—but it always involves more expense and is usually less convenient. It also affords undesirable hiding places for vermin, prevents the needed airing of the soil, and favors the propagation of fungi. Altogether, the loose soil mulch, which is the result of good tillage, is usually the most satisfactory. A clean straw or hay mulch, however, comes very acceptable during the picking season. It then protects the berries from contact with the soil, and keeps them bright and clean.

WINTER PROTECTION.—Strawberry plants are quite hardy, yet liable to heave out by the freezes and thaws of winter, and for this reason should be given a winter overcoat. Without protection of some kind, say by a mulch of litter or snow, best results ought not to be expected, as great loss of plants, and damage to fruit buds and roots will be unavoidable. If you have a nice strawberry bed, whatever you may do with it, don't neglect to provide a winter mulch. It is not enough to apply fine compost to the patch in the fall. Coarse, strawy manure will do very well, and should be put on all over the ground (not only over the rows) as soon as the ground is frozen hard enough to hold a wagon. Evergreen boughs are often quite serviceable; but nothing in the shape of winter mulch can be superior to salt or marsh hay. This is to be had quite cheaply in many localities. Evenly spread over the ground it will afford a perfect protection, and the grower may feel at ease concerning his strawberry bed when thus covered, in the most trying kind of winter weather.

GATHERING THE FRUIT.—At the approach of spring the winter mulch should be removed, or rolled aside until the patch can be given a thorough stirring up with cultivator and hoe. Whatever weeds start up, are pulled up by hand or killed with the hoe. Afterwards the clean mulch may be put carefully around the plants on each side of the rows to keep the fruit clean.

The berries, when ripe, are picked in clean quart baskets, level full, and if for market, only nice, clean, sound, good-sized and well-colored berries are wanted in the baskets. Leave the imperfect fruit on the vines, or throw them away. Neither is there any place in the baskets for leaves and rubbish. Strawberries are perishable, and do not improve in any respect after being taken off the vines. The sooner they are used or disposed of, the better.

STRAWBERRIES IN HOME GARDEN.—Farmers and townspeople who grow only their own home supply, usually plant a little patch in their garden, and here the plants are set quite close, perhaps fifteen inches each way, and all tended with the hand hoe. Here the ground is almost always very rich, and a large crop can be grown on a small area. In all other ways the plants should be treated as already directed for general culture. This plan, although well enough suited to the narrow limits of the average village garden, is not the one which I would advise the farmer to adopt. The size of his kitchen garden is (or should be) in correspondence with the greater opportunities in regard to area, manure supply, and available labor which the farm affords, and with the greater demands of the farmer's large household for vegetables and fruits. One acre—rather more than less—is just about the proper area, and it should be arranged somewhat similar as shown in the diagrams on pages 20 and 22. This will give him the largest possible results with the least possible demands for hand labor. By all means let the farmer plant his strawberries, and his other small fruits in same plot also, in long rows, as advised for the market grower, and cultivate by horse power, early, often, and thoroughly, to save hand labor.

ROTATION.—Many growers, especially market gardeners, take off only a single crop, plow up the patch after the fruiting season, and plant it to potatoes, turnips, celery, or other crops. But if to be kept for another year, the matted rows after fruiting should be narrowed down again, using a one-horse plow, a sharp-cutting cultivator, or wheel-hoe, and left not over 6 inches in width. New runners are now allowed to occupy the whole space of the original matted row, thus renewing the plantation. Guard against weeds. I do not believe in fruiting a patch more than two years, or three at most, and new beds should be planted every other year to take the place of the old ones.

INSECTS AND DISEASES.—The larvæ of the sawfly is sometimes and in some sections very destructive to the foliage. For a remedy try a solution of hellebore, one ounce to two gallons of water, and sprinkle or spray it on the plants.

The strawberry leaf-roller is another destructive foe, the larvæ of a moth which is two-brooded. The presence of this worm is easily detected by the rolled-up leaves. The simplest remedy is to mow the field after fruiting, and when the stuff is dry enough, set fire to it.

For the crown-borer, troublesome in the west and far north, and the strawberry root-borer, a small caterpillar, I know no remedy except plowing up the whole patch and starting a new plantation elsewhere.

The white grub has been already mentioned. The larvæ of the goldsmith beetle resembles it in appearance and life habits, and should be managed in the same way.

The tarnished plant-bug, and the dusky plant-bug are very unwelcome visitors to many strawberry plantations, and little can be done to keep them off. Spraying with the kerosene emulsion, or solution of buhach may do some good.

These and all other insect foes can most easily be kept in check by a frequent renewal of the plantations (wide crop rotation), and by mowing and burning the foliage after fruiting. This treatment will also tend to prevent the strawberry diseases, such as scald, rust, etc.

ANOTHER METHOD OF PLANTING.—For loamy soils that are free from stones, I prefer setting the plants with a spade. I think it is by far the most convenient and most expeditious method. Let one person take a common sharp spade, and another (a boy will do) take a bundle of plants made ready for going into the ground. The field has been marked out four feet apart, or the plants are set by line. Thrust the spade into the ground where you want the first plant, and slightly turn or pull the handle toward you, thus making an opening two or three inches wide on top at the back of the spade. The boy takes a plant, spreads the roots with a quick, jerky motion, and inserts them, as deeply as needed, into the opening. At the same time withdraw the spade and press the soil against the newly-set plant with the foot. Then repeat the operation where you want the next plant. One man and boy can plant an acre in a day in this manner with ease.

FORCING STRAWBERRIES.—Sometimes this crop can be grown under glass with profit. In July young thrifty plants are started in pots for next winter's crop. Fill three-inch pots with good soil, and sink them to the rim along the rows of the stock plants. The earlier this is done after the layers start the better. The layers will need directing to the pots, and can be kept in place by means of a peg, stone or clod of earth. By keeping the plants well watered they will be rooted in about three weeks. Then place them in the shade until the pots are full of roots, and after that shift into six-inch pots. Pot rather firmly into good fibrous earth, standing the pots in an open, airy place, preferably in coal ashes, and giving them all the water they need. Before freezing weather, plunge the pots into cold frames and water sparingly. Any time after this, according to the exact time that you want the ripe fruit, the plants may be started up. Place them in the greenhouse, beginning with a temperature of 45 degrees Fahrenheit, gradually increasing until it reaches 60 degrees. Also increase the water supply gradually as the season advances. Plants for later use must be protected from severe freezing. Don't allow the plants to set too much fruit, else the berries will be small. A moderate number of good-sized berries will be more satisfactory than a large number of small ones. When enough have set, clip off the remaining flowers, and later on pick off the smallest berries also. Syringe freely to keep down red spider. Water moderately at the roots. Give liquid manure at times until the fruit shows indications of ripening, when it should be withheld, and the fruit exposed to heat and light as much as possible. In the mean time, of course, plants may have been started up for successional crops.

VARIETIES.

The following is a list of the leading sorts:

1. PERFECT FLOWERING.

Beder Wood.
Captain Jack.
Chas. Downing.
Cumberland Triumph.
Kentucky.
May King.
Michel's Early (Mitchel's).
Miner's (Prolific).
Neunan's (Prolific).
Old Ironclad (or Phelp's Seedling).
Parry.
Sharpless.
Wilson (Albany).

2. IMPERFECT FLOWERING.

Must have one or more of the preceding list planted with them.

Bubach (No. 5).
Champion (or Windsor Chief)
Crescent.
Gandy.
Greenville.
Haverland.
Manchester.
Warfield.

The most popular and most reliable of the list are the following:

May King.
Haverland.
Neunan's Prolific. (For the South).
Beder Wood.
Greenville.
Sharpless.
Wilson.
Bubach.
Crescent.
Manchester.
Warfield.

APPENDIX.

ELECTRO-HORTICULTURE.

INFLUENCE OF SOIL ELECTRIFICATION AND OF ELECTRIC LIGHT UPON PLANT-GROWTH.

"Light is Life."

ECENT development of electrical science has wrought wonderful changes in all our industrial and social conditions, changes so wonderful in number and character, indeed, that we now are constantly in expectation of the discovery of new manifestations and new uses of this wonderful natural force. It was a very natural idea to direct electrical energies upon the soil and plant growth in the hope of finding marked influences.

DIRECT ELECTRIFICATION.—At the agricultural college at Amherst, Mass., and at several places in Europe, wires have been stretched across fields and gardens and passed through the soil, and then charged with electricity. In many cases certain crops were largely increased by these influences; while other crops seemed to be injured rather than benefited. That a powerful influence of the artificial use of electricity, either in the air or in the soil, about plants, does exist, seems hardly open to dispute. Yet it is my conviction that this discovery will remain of little practical value to the average soil tiller. At any rate, it is not of practical use now, and before it could possibly become so, a great deal more of accurate knowledge about this yet mysterious force will have to be developed.

ELECTRIC LIGHT INFLUENCE.—More marked upon plant growth perhaps than the effects of this direct electrification, have been those of the electric light. Yet there is no telling, at present, to what extent the new factor will ever be employed in vegetable growing. The home gardener will scarcely feel justified in incurring much expense for electric lights when these are wanted solely for the purpose of stimulating plant growth in his small garden or greenhouse; and he cannot be expected to receive any benefit whatever from the stimulative effect of electric light except in the rare instance, when his garden or greenhouse happens to be placed where an electric street lamp of the town or city sheds its light directly upon his plants.

The results of experiments conducted recently by Prof. L. H. Bailey, at the Cornell Experiment Station, seem to endorse those of the earlier experiments by C. W. Siemens, in England, and P. P. Dehérain, in France, and show beyond doubt, that periods of darkness (or rest) are not necessary to the growth and development of plants, and that the electric light can be profitably used in forcing the growth or maturity of at least certain kinds of plants. The injurious influences upon plants near the naked light can be prevented by the interposition of a transparent glass (opal globe) between light and plants.

Different kinds of plants seem to be differently affected by the electric light. While some crops are markedly benefited,

Bench of Lettuce in Ordinary Greenhouse.

others seem to be injured, and still others show no effects either way. The best results have been observed on lettuce, and next to it, on radishes. Indeed, I believe that the electric light as a promoter of plant growth will be of practical value chiefly or only to the extensive grower of greenhouse lettuce and greenhouse radishes.

The material difference in the rate of growth made by lettuce plants in an ordinary and a lighted greenhouse, may be seen plainly in the annexed illustrations, which represent parts of the houses at the Cornell Experiment Station (from photographs taken in 1891; reduced from station bulletin). Prof. Bailey's report was as follows:

"Three weeks after transplanting both varieties in the light house were fully 50 per cent. in advance of those in the dark house in size, and the color and other characters of the plants were fully as good. The plants had received at this time $70\frac{1}{2}$

hours of electric light. Just a month later the first heads were sold from the light house, but it was six weeks later when the first heads were sold from the dark house. In other words, the electric light plants were two weeks ahead of the others. This gain had been purchased by 1613¾ hours of electric light, worth at current prices of street lighting about $7; this will give an idea as to economic values. The electric light plants were in every way as good in quality as those grown in the dark house; in fact, the two could not be told apart except for their different sizes. The illustrations show representative portions of the crops as they appeared five weeks after being transplanted to permanent quarters. The electric light plants were upon the benches 44 days before the first heads were sold. During this time there were 20 nights in which the light did not run, and there had been but 84 hours of electric light, worth about $3.50. The lamp exerted this influence throughout a house 20x30, and

Bench of Lettuce in House with Electric Light.

the results were as well marked in the most remote part as they were near the lamp. If the same results can be obtained by hanging the lamp over the house, instead of inside of it, by that means several houses might be lighted at once."

Mr. W. W. Rawson, the famous market gardener of Arlington, near Boston, Mass., was probably the first to use the electric light for commercial lettuce forcing. The street lamps which hung near his houses, and their beneficial effects, pointed the way to the successful employment of electric light for this purpose. He estimates the gain of time in the production of a lettuce crop at about 10 per cent, over the time required for the production of an equal crop in a dark house, and says that the gain produced upon one crop pays for running the lamps for the entire winter. The plants seem to head up better under the light and the quality to be superior. The effect of the light is marked at a distance of 100 feet from the lamp.

www.ingramcontent.com/pod-product-compliance
Lightning Source LLC
Chambersburg PA
CBHW030803230426
43667CB00008B/1036